Alert America!

D1797352

ALSO BY OR EDITED BY MICHAEL SCHEIBACH
AND FROM MCFARLAND

Protecting the Home Front:
Women in Civil Defense in the Early Cold War (2017)

Atomics in the Classroom:
Teaching the Bomb in the Early Postwar Era (2015)

"In Case Atom Bombs Fall":
An Anthology of Governmental Explanations, Instructions
and Warnings from the 1940s to the 1960s (edited, 2009)

Atomic Narratives and American Youth:
Coming of Age with the Atom, 1945–1955 (2003)

Alert America!

The Atomic Bomb and
"The Show That May Save Your Life"

MICHAEL SCHEIBACH

McFarland & Company, Inc., Publishers
Jefferson, North Carolina

LIBRARY OF CONGRESS CATALOGUING-IN-PUBLICATION DATA

Names: Scheibach, Michael, 1949– author.
Title: Alert America! : the atomic bomb and "the show that may save
    your life" / Michael Scheibach.
Description: Jefferson, North Carolina : McFarland & Company, Inc.,
    Publishers, 2019 | Includes bibliographical references and index.
Identifiers: LCCN 2019009037 | ISBN 9781476678047
    (paperback. : acid free paper) ∞
Subjects: LCSH: Alert America! (Television program) |
    Civil defense—United States—History—20th century. |
    Atomic bomb—Social aspects—United States—History—
    20th century. | Nuclear warfare—United States—Safety measures. |
    Nuclear warfare—United States—History—20th century. |
    Cold War—Social aspects—United States. | Cold War in mass media.
Classification: LCC UA927 .S335 2019 | DDC 363.350973/09045—dc23
LC record available at https://lccn.loc.gov/2019009037

BRITISH LIBRARY CATALOGUING DATA ARE AVAILABLE

ISBN (print) 978-1-4766-7804-7
ISBN (ebook) 978-1-4766-3659-7

© 2019 Michael Scheibach. All rights reserved

*No part of this book may be reproduced or transmitted in any form
or by any means, electronic or mechanical, including photocopying
or recording, or by any information storage and retrieval system,
without permission in writing from the publisher.*

The front cover image is of African-American children at Alert America
exhibit (Office of Civil and Defense Mobilization Region 1, 1958–1961,
National Archives at Boston); *background* Alert America's convoy,
consisting of ten 32-foot semi-trailers January 7, 1952 (National Archives)

Printed in the United States of America

McFarland & Company, Inc., Publishers
    Box 611, Jefferson, North Carolina 28640
    www.mcfarlandpub.com

For Jamie

Table of Contents

Alert America Pledge

You can count on me to be an alert American because I want to help protect our freedoms and construct an enduring peace.

I WILL ...   volunteer for one of the local Civil Defense services

I WILL ...   train myself and my family now in Civil Defense self-protection

I WILL ...   prepare a family shelter area and equip it with first-aid supplies

I WILL ...   prepare my home against fire and atomic attack

I WILL ...   take an active part in Civil Defense where I work

I WILL ...   take First Aid training

I WILL ...   donate my blood for our war wounded

I WILL ...   pass along the Civil Defense lessons I learned to my friends and neighbors

Official *Alert America!* Booklet

Preface

"The worst of all wars in human history is ending. The people of the world now have the choice of two paths to the future. They can take the way of peace … or they can take the way of war, to which science will be prepared in due time to contribute weapons more hellish even than the new atomic bomb."[1]

Newspaper columnist Lowell Mellett wrote those words on August 14, 1945, V-J Day—a day of celebration marking victory over Japan and the end of World War II. For most Americans today, it is difficult to grasp the magnitude of a war that spanned eight-plus years, involved practically every nation on Earth, and resulted in the deaths of 50 to 75 million people. Nor is it easy to fully comprehend the impact—sudden and world-changing—of the atomic bombings of Hiroshima and Nagasaki on American society, as the United States, in the short span of four years, went from being the world's most powerful nation at the end of the war, to one locked in an atomic stand-off with a communist adversary bent on world domination.

President Harry Truman formally announced Japan's surrender at 7 p.m. Eastern War Time on August 14. He then walked onto the White House lawn to lead the thousands who had gathered outside in victory cheers.[2] Only a few weeks earlier, while attending a meeting with Great Britain's Winston Churchill and the Soviet Union's Joseph Stalin in Potsdam, Germany, Truman had given his final approval to unleash a new weapon on the Japanese. And on August 6, at 8:15 a.m., a specially equipped B-29 dropped a single atomic bomb on the unsuspecting city of Hiroshima, instantly killing between 70,000 and 100,000 people. Three days later, a second B-29 dropped another atomic bomb on Nagasaki, killing between 40,000 and 80,000. Five days later, Japan surrendered and the war came to an end at last.

Truman had assumed the presidency on April 12, 1945, the day President Franklin Delano Roosevelt's death stunned the world. For twelve years—from his first inauguration on March 4, 1933, until his death—Roosevelt had held the hopes of Americans in his hands. And he did not disappoint. Roosevelt

1

led the nation through the Great Depression, although he had been challenged by the economic downturn in 1937–1938. During these difficult times, Roosevelt introduced and enacted a wide range of legislation that helped the nation recover and, in the process, reshaped society, including the Wagner Act, protecting labor unions; the Social Security Act, providing financial aid to senior citizens; the Fair Labor Standards Act, establishing a national minimum wage; and the Glass-Steagall Act, creating the Federal Deposit Insurance Corporation to protect Americans' bank deposits, to name just a few. With the coming of war, he again rose to the occasion, orchestrating the fight against the Axis countries of Germany, Italy, and Japan. He demonstrated his leadership by working closing with Churchill and other allies, appointing General Dwight Eisenhower as supreme allied commander of the Allied Expeditionary Force, and approving the Manhattan Project to develop an atomic bomb.

Although in poor health, Roosevelt had been reelected in 1944 to an unprecedented fourth term as president. As 1945 unfolded, he followed the progress of Allied troops as they moved closer to victory in Europe. Then, less than a month before V-E Day, he passed away at his retreat in Warm Springs, Georgia. John McCormack, majority leader of the House of Representatives, called Roosevelt "the savior of democracy throughout the world." Supreme Court Justice Hugo Black said, "He seems to have been the man for the times at every recurring emergency."[3] The *Chicago Daily Times* wrote, "The hosts of righteousness throughout the world have lost the one man they needed most to carry on."[4] Upon hearing the news of Roosevelt's death, wartime colleague and friend Winston Churchill immediately sent a message to Eleanor Roosevelt, Franklin's widow, calling her loss "also the loss of the British nation and of the cause of freedom in every land…. I trust you may find consolation in the glory of his name and the magnitude of his work."[5]

In addition to his many accomplishments, Roosevelt gave Americans reassurance through his words, such as his first inaugural address, declaring that "the only thing we have to fear is fear itself"; and his declaration of war, proclaiming December 7, 1941, the day Japan attacked Pearl Harbor, as a "date which will live in infamy." He also held more than thirty "fireside chats," informal talks delivered over radio stations nationwide. On May 26, 1940, for example, with war raging in Europe and concerns at home that the war might entangle the United States, Roosevelt once again allayed Americans' fears, telling those listening intently to his words: "It is whispered by some that only by abandoning our freedom, our ideals, our way of life, can we build our defenses adequately, can we match the strength of the aggressors…. I do not share these fears."

Although he did not have an opportunity to deliver a speech scheduled for the following day, April 13, on the occasion of Thomas Jefferson's birthday, he did leave a draft of what he planned to say. Written before the atomic bombings in August, Roosevelt's speech anticipates their impact: "Today, science has brought all the different quarters of the globe so close together that it is impossible to isolate them one from another," he wrote. "Today, we are faced with the preeminent fact that, if civilization is to survive, we must cultivate the science of human relationships—the ability of all peoples, of all kinds, to live together and work together, in the same world, at peace."[6]

Roosevelt would have smiled with satisfaction and a great sense of relief as he watched Americans celebrate on V-J Day, a day long in coming, and, at least for the moment, a day where everyone looked ahead with optimism, strength, and faith. Yet as he seemed to predict, the world had changed dramatically on the day a B-29 named *Enola Gay* pulled away after dropping its bomb on Hiroshima, Japan. That day marked a sea change, blasting the world from one era into a more precarious and uncertain one: the atomic age.

Lowell Mellett was by no means alone in his view of the future. A few days before his column appeared, a newspaper editorial warned that the atomic bomb had brought destructiveness to a new level. "Above all," it read, "the atom bomb intensifies the power to destroy. It forewarns us of the nature of future wars. It challenges man the world over to find a way to permanent peace."[7] Another editorial said the atomic bomb's "destructive possibilities would indicate that civilization could soon destroy itself, and even the planet on which we live, unless the new power is curbed.... [M]ankind must find the road to peace or witness the destruction of civilization."[8] Jack Ramey, another newspaper columnist, wrote, "It needs no supreme intelligence to picture the next war, the all-destructive war.... So we know Japan's defeat settles nothing. That the final test will be mankind's. We know the United States never again can relax, must always be ready for anything."[9]

Ramey cautioned that someday another Hitler would appear. "And if he is not spotted early ... he will cause more trouble than Hitler." Arguably not the next Hitler, Stalin, the strong-armed ruler of the Soviet Union, represented the nation's and the free world's primary adversary. An ally during the war, the Soviet Union soon reassumed its historic role as archenemy to Western democracies. Stalin's quest for postwar power had resulted in an "iron curtain" being drawn across Eastern Europe in the late 1940s. Then his quest for power became magnified on August 29, 1949, with the Soviet Union's successful test of an atomic bomb. The Cold War, which had slowly coalesced after World War II, hardened as the new decade began.

In December 1950, President Truman issued Proclamation 2914—Proclaiming the Existence of a National Emergency, in which he announced to the nation that the Soviet Union presented a real threat—an atomic threat—that warranted immediate action. "The increasing menace of the forces of communist aggression," said Truman, "requires that the national defense of the United States be strengthened as speedily as possible." He then called upon all citizens to unite to ensure that the nation "may be readied for the dangers which threaten us."[10] From celebrating victory to proclaiming the existence of a national emergency took less than six years.

In the draft of the speech he never gave, Roosevelt wrote, "The only limit to our realization of tomorrow will be our doubts of today. Let us move forward with strong and active faith."[11] For Americans who had won a world war fought on foreign soil and the high seas, their faith had been shaken at the realization that an atomic bomb capable of inflicting death and destruction on their own home front—on their own community—was now a frightening reality. For some, the best way of dealing with this unprecedented threat was to remain indifferent or apathetic. After all, how can a person survive an atomic war? For others, the best approach was to learn how to protect one's family and how to contribute to the nation's defense.

This was the state of the nation when Truman signed the Federal Civil Defense Act of 1950 in January 1951, which formally established the Federal Civil Defense Administration (FCDA) as the primary federal agency responsible for preparing Americans for what many believed was an inevitable atomic attack by the Soviet Union. The act provided the basic framework for minimizing the effects of such an attack on the civilian population through advance civil defense training, as well as for dealing with the emergency conditions of the post-attack devastation.

The FCDA wasted little time in launching a national civil defense program, with one of its most ambitious efforts being the creation of Alert America, a traveling exhibit designed to make Americans more aware of the atomic threat and the importance of civil defense. Alert America opened in the nation's capital in January 1952 before beginning a cross-country tour. The same month, Truman again issued a warning to Americans that the nation was in "a national emergency as grave as any we have ever faced." His message still resonates today: "If war comes to America, we may well win or lose as the result of how ready we are when the first attack comes.... I cannot tell you when or where the attack will come or that it will come at all. I can only remind you that we must be ready if it does come."[12] This was Alert America's mission: to ensure that America's civilian population was, indeed, ready.

Even with today's mounting international tensions and ongoing threats of terrorism and nuclear proliferation, it is difficult to envision the federal government undertaking a national traveling exhibit designed to educate Americans about potential dangers and to provide guidance on how to safeguard themselves, their families, and their communities—even though such an exhibit might be warranted. Although Alert America has been largely dismissed or overlooked by historians of the early Cold War, nothing like it had taken place before, and nothing like it has taken place since. For this reason, the time seems appropriate to take a closer look at what was appropriately billed as "The Show That May Save Your Life" and its impact on Americans living during another—and perhaps even more—tenuous time of uncertainty and unpredictability.

Introduction:
Victory, Apathy
and Alert America

With the monstrous weapons man already has, humanity is in danger of being trapped in this world by its moral adolescence. Our knowledge of science has clearly outstripped our international capacity to control it. —General Omar Bradley, Chairman, Joint Chiefs of Staff, 1952[1]

A father sits at the breakfast table with his wife and two children, 12-year-old and 7-year-old girls. The father, reading the morning newspaper, exclaims, "Well, I see they've exploded the hydrogen bomb." The 12-year-old asks, "What's a hydrogen bomb?" The father responds after some hesitation, "I don't really know what a hydrogen bomb is. But I know it's a lot more powerful than an atom bomb." He then proceeds to describe the various tests in the Pacific Ocean, telling the girls that the hydrogen bomb blew an island "clean away." "Will it kill everybody?" asks the 7-year-old. The father thinks for a moment about what the bomb might do to a city if it completely annihilated an island. By then, the 7-year-old has finished her breakfast and gets ready to leave for the school bus. But as she gets up from the table, she looks back at her father and says matter-of-factly, "You and your hydrogen bomb. The old atom bomb was strong enough for me."[2]

Nuclear weapons are a fact of life in today's world. This is the reality. And it has been a reality for more than 70 years. Americans live with the knowledge that nuclear weapons are capable of mass death and destruction. Americans also know that no nuclear bomb has been used in warfare since August 9, 1945. To some extent, they take solace in this fact. Such was not the case when newspaper columnist Arthur Edson shared the above story in November 1952, the same month the United States successfully tested its first hydrogen bomb. It also was the same year the government's traveling Alert America exhibit warned Americans that they needed to learn self-preservation skills in case of atomic attack.

The United States had persevered through the Great Depression with its unprecedented economic downturn, devastating unemployment rates (estimated as high as 20–25 percent), homelessness, and a destructive and demoralizing Dust Bowl that caused some three million people to leave their homes in the nation's heartland in search of a better life, primarily going westward toward California. Americans had put their faith in President Franklin Roosevelt, who had to combat not only the economic crash and the resulting social upheaval; he also had to confront the likes of Catholic priest and radio commentator Father Charles Coughlin and avowed populist Senator Huey Long of Louisiana who were outspoken critics of his policies. Moreover, as he launched his New Deal programs designed to restore the nation's well-being and protect the very foundation of democracy, Adolf Hitler and his Nazi Party seized power in Germany and threatened all of Europe, Fascist Benito Mussolini militarized Italy and aligned himself with Nazi Germany, and the Japanese pillaged Manchuria and set up the puppet state of Manchukuo under its rule. Then, on December 7, 1941, the Japanese attacked the U.S. naval base at Pearl Harbor in Hawaii, and the following day the nation found itself at war—a world war.

Americans returned to peacetime following Japan's surrender on August 14, 1945, with renewed optimism for a better future. Over the next year, millions of men came home from the war, as millions of women in the workforce either quit or lost their jobs and returned to more traditional gender roles. Young families soon gave birth to the Baby Boom Generation and moved into Levittown and other expanding suburban developments. Some 40 percent of the nation's Gross Domestic Production (GDP) had been devoted to war production in the early 1940s, but manufacturers retooled quickly to meet the growing demand for consumer goods, with Americans finally having the opportunity—after fifteen years of depression and war—to buy into the "American dream."

America celebrated what historian Tom Engelhardt has labeled "victory culture"—a culture built on being the victor in a long and horrific war and emerging as the most powerful nation in the world, but also a culture that started dissolving almost as soon as it began as the nation confronted the aftershock of the atomic bombings of Hiroshima and Nagasaki. "The atomic bomb that leveled Hiroshima," Engelhardt writes, "also blasted openings into a netherworld of consciousness where victory and defeat, enemy and self, threatened to merge."[3] On August 7, in fact, the day after Hiroshima, Hanson Baldwin, military editor of the *New York Times*, wrote, "Yesterday man unleashed the atom to destroy man, and another chapter in human history opened, a chapter in which the weird, the strange, the horrible becomes the trite and the obvious. Yesterday we clinched victory in the Pacific, but we sowed the whirlwind."[4]

Historian William Graebner adds to Baldwin's point by suggesting that although some people may have experienced the late 1940s with "unqualified optimism," the sense of optimism was "tempered and tainted with ambiguity, cynicism, and doubt" about the new atomic age.[5] In his seminal book on this period, *By the Bomb's Early Light*, Paul Boyer also argues that soon after achieving final victory in the war, the nation experienced a cultural crisis "when the American people confronted a new and threatening reality of almost unfathomable proportions."[6] Expanding on Boyer's observation, Engelhardt writes, "Shadowed by the bomb, victory became conceivable only under the most limited of conditions, and an enemy too diffuse to be comfortably located beyond national borders had to be confronted in an un–American spirit of doubt."[7]

The United States had achieved victory but had been thrust into an atomic age beyond its control and beyond the scope of most people's understanding. "The immediate, the greatest threat to us," President Harry Truman told the American people in October 1945, "is the threat of disillusionment, the danger of an insidious skepticism—a loss of faith in the effectiveness of international cooperation. Such a loss of faith would be dangerous at any time. In an atomic age, it would be nothing short of disastrous."[8] At a Chicago meeting of representatives of seven industrial associations in January 1947, General of the Army Dwight Eisenhower issued his own warning, saying, "We cannot permit complacency or an atomic bomb mentality—a possible modern counterpart of the Maginot Line mentality [of World War I]—to lull us into another postwar apathy."[9]

Eisenhower's comments came at a time when the Soviet Union had pulled an "iron curtain" across Eastern Europe, tightening Communist control and closing off relations with the West. With Turkey and Greece threatened by this expansion, Truman had gone before Congress in March 1947 to request aid in what became known as the Truman Doctrine. He made clear that the United States would not allow free nations to be overtaken by the Soviet Union. "At the present moment in world history," the president told Congress, "nearly every nation must choose between alternative ways of life. The choice is too often not a free one." He continued:

> One way of life is based upon the will of the majority, and is distinguished by free institutions, representative government, free elections, guarantees of individual liberty, freedom of speech and religion, and freedom from political oppression. The second way of life is based upon the will of a minority forcibly imposed upon the majority. It relies upon terror and oppression, a controlled press and radio; fixed elections, and the suppression of personal freedoms. I believe that it must be the policy

of the United States to support free peoples who are resisting attempted subjugation by armed minorities or by outside pressures. I believe that we must assist free peoples to work out their own destinies in their own way.[10]

The following year Truman acted again, this time with the European Recovery Program, or Marshall Plan. With Eastern Europe being absorbed into the Communist sphere and Western Europe still reeling from the war, Truman proposed providing financial aid to help rebuild England, France, West Germany, and other former allies. From 1948 to the early 1950s, the United States gave these countries more than $13 billion in economic assistance, strengthening their resolve against the Soviet Union. Just three months after launching the Marshall Plan, however, the Soviet Union attempted to tighten its iron curtain by blocking land, rail, and water corridors to West Berlin, located 100 miles inside East Germany. As part of the final peace treaty in World War II, England, France, and the United States had gained control of West Berlin, while the Soviet Union controlled East Berlin. In an attempt to force the Western allies out, Stalin, whose official title was general secretary of the Central Committee, refused to allow any goods to be delivered, but the allies did not back down. From June 24, 1948, until May 12, 1949, the allies flew more than 200,000 flights to West Berlin and delivered some 9,000 tons of supplies every day. In a related action designed to demonstrate allied strength, 29 North American and European countries formed the North Atlantic Treaty Organization (NATO) on April 4, 1949, a month before Stalin ended the boycott. Under NATO, members agreed to come to the defense of any member nation attacked by an external party. To lead NATO, first headquartered in London, members named Eisenhower as its supreme commander.[11]

Even with the intensification of international tensions between East and West, Americans at home continued to display a general indifference toward the political and military situation. Apathy, moreover, became part of the social lexicon to describe people's general indifference. The *Hartford* (Connecticut) *Courant* even humanized "Apathy" in its attack of President Truman during the 1948 presidential campaign. "Unwanted and unasked," the newspaper wrote, "Apathy is President Truman's fellow traveler on this transcontinental jaunt. He has clung closer to the president than a burr to a donkey's tail."[12] Writing in a 1949 issue of *Collier's Weekly*, General Omar Bradley, U.S. chief of staff, warned about postwar apathy and what he termed "delinquent citizenship" at home, in school, at church, and in community. "At a time when peoples thruout [sic] the world are being courted by an aggressive stateism that would have them abdicate their personal share in government and entrust their welfare to rule by clique," he wrote, "the American people must put their faith in not less—but more—personal responsibility in the affairs of their community and nation. A democracy such as ours cannot be defeated in their struggle; it can only lose by default."[13] Michael Straight, editor of *The New Republic*, wrote in 1950 that many people were marking time until war comes, becoming apathetic "because of the conviction … that domestic and world trends have moved beyond their control." He argued that this apathy was as destructive as fear and harder to overcome. "Fear can be met by resolution," he wrote, "but apathy can be overcome only by restoring to ordinary men the sense of participation in a clear and inspiring cause."[14]

Straight's belief that apathy could be overcome by restoring a sense of participation failed to materialize in the 1950s. This is borne out by President Truman's announcement in 1950 that the Atomic Energy Commission was proceeding with work on a hydrogen or super bomb. Despite a Gallup poll finding that 69 percent of Americans favored the development of the H-bomb, *Life* magazine reported that most Americans did not want to think much about it. In fact, wrote *Life*, "People wanted to talk about anything else but."[15] The new decade experienced resurgent consumerism, the expansion of suburbia, and the increasing Baby Boom bubble. Television exerted its presence, reaching most households by 1960 and contributing to the crystallization of "mass society." As many historians have chronicled, the 1950s also saw the solidification of teen culture, men joining "the organization," and women becoming "contained" within the home.[16] Yet as the decade began, the Soviet Union had become an atomic-armed adversary and American troops had again gone to war, this time in a little known Asian country called South Korea, which had been attacked by North Korean forces supported by communist China and the Soviet Union.

Victory culture arguably ended on December 16, 1950, with Truman's Proclamation 2914—Proclaiming the Existence of a National Emergency, issued six months after the outbreak of hostilities in Korea and a little more than a year after the Soviet Union's entrance into the atomic age. Truman called for a stronger national defense program to combat the "increasing menace of the forces of communist aggression." This required the nation's military, naval, air, and civilian defenses to be strengthened as fast as possible in order "to repel any and all threats against our national security."[17] In the event of an atomic attack, the country could lose the war in a few days because of its inadequate civil defense. "Let me warn you again," he said, "that there is no such thing as bargain basement preparedness or escape from the hard realities of the time. There are no shortcuts to civil defense preparedness. It is a tough, unpleasant but grimly necessary job." He continued:

> Regardless of the wishful talk you may hear to the contrary, you and I are now in a national emergency as grave as any we have ever faced. We have not won the war against time. We have no right to feel safe militarily or on the home front. We must do it [organize civil defense] before it is too late. If war comes to America, we may well win or lose as the result of how ready we are when the first attack comes. Civil

defense readiness throughout the nation is not something that can be done tomorrow. It must be done today—or it may be too late.[18]

Two weeks before Proclamation 2914, Truman signed Executive Order 10186.[19] This order, issued December 1, 1950, created the Federal Civil Defense Administration in the Office for Emergency Management, which formally began operations on January 12, 1951, with Truman's signing of the Civil Defense Act of 1950.[20] From 1951 until 1958, when the Office of Civil and Defense Mobilization (OCDM) superseded it, the FCDA represented the primary federal government agency for civil defense matters. This included the authority to oversee the development of and standards for civil defense measures and equipment; to disseminate civil defense information; and to conduct or arrange for civil defense training. Under the Civil Defense Act, the federal government also provided matching grants to states for building air-raid shelters, procured and stockpiled medical and other disaster supplies, and established a national warning system. The FCDA, in short, had the daunting task of preparing the American people for the possibility of an atomic attack.[21]

Truman named Millard Caldwell, former governor of Florida, as the FCDA's administrator, a position he held until November 1952. Caldwell traveled the nation promoting civil defense, as well as wrote a series of articles based on the agency's booklet, *This Is Civil Defense*. Acknowledging the paucity of federal funding for the agency, Caldwell stressed the importance of the individual taking responsibility for his or her safety and the safety of the family. "A soldier is trained to take care of himself and to keep on fighting," he wrote. "As a defender of your home front, you must learn to protect yourself and keep on working. Despite every precaution, a soldier might be killed. So might you. But the more you know, and the better trained you are, the better your chances for survival."[22]

From its very beginning, the FCDA focused on its mission to alert Americans to the atomic threat. Within a few months after its formation, it had introduced duck and cover drills in American schools; promoted statewide and local air-raid drills; created training classes; sponsored meetings and conferences; sent speakers throughout the nation to address the urgency of civil defense; published pamphlets, booklets, posters, and other materials about civil defense; and formed a National Advisory Council to help guide its efforts to prompt the American public to take a proactive role in the nation's defense. By the end of its first year, the FCDA had worked in some capacity with thousands of national organizations, representing approximately 100 million members, to enlist their support. From the Parent-Teacher Association and Veterans of Foreign Wars, to women's and religious organizations, to the Boy Scouts and Girl Scouts, and many more, the FCDA promoted the importance—the necessity—of preparedness. The dissemination of civil defense materials constituted a significant component in the agency's efforts, and here it cooperated with a range of organizations. The American Legion, as an example, printed and distributed materials to its 17,400 posts, as did the Veterans of Foreign Wars. The Boy Scouts of America printed and distributed a series of five pamphlets on civil defense. The American Hotel Association even became involved, placing "Alert Cards" in the rooms of its 6,700 member hotels.[23]

In response to these efforts, many Americans became active participants in civil defense programs at the state and local levels, with some four million people volunteering for civil defense by the end of 1952. Volunteers served in the FCDA's various service areas, including warden, police, nursing, fire, rescue, transportation, welfare, staff, and communications. Although not necessarily active volunteers, millions of other Americans learned about civil defense and the atomic threat by reading government-prepared materials, magazines, and newspapers; listening to radio programs or watching television; attending meetings and special events; and taking courses on such topics as home nursing, first aid, shelter building, and mass feeding techniques.

The Alert America exhibit represented a major component in the FCDA's overall strategy. Billed as "The Show That May Save Your Life," Alert America resulted from a June 1951 proposal by the agency's National Advisory Council. The council declared that Americans lacked a true understanding of the atomic bomb; therefore, they needed to be educated about the repercussions of an atomic attack by the Soviet Union, as well as the necessity of learning civil defense in order to have any opportunity of surviving such an attack. The council's proposed national campaign to "alert America" to the dangers of the atomic bomb was only six years removed from the nation's victory in World War II. It also came less than two years after the Soviet Union's detonation of an atomic bomb—a monumental and history-changing occurrence that altered the nation's military strategy and approach to home-front protection. As the National Advisory Council concluded: "Civil defense must be ready at all times to meet any need which might arise. Once the bombs hit, it will be too late."[24]

In October 1951, the FCDA worked in cooperation with the patriotic, non-profit Freedoms Foundation at Valley Forge, established in 1949, to create the Valley Forge Foundation to manage the exhibit.[25] Kenneth Wells, president of the Freedoms Foundation, agreed to become president of the new organization in addition to his current position. With the organizational structure in place, Alert America began to come together, with trial exhibits held in Richmond and Norfolk, Virginia, before its debut in the nation's capital in January 1952, a month after the original plan. From there, three convoys, each carrying an identical exhibit, embarked on their 36,000-mile cross-country schedule encompassing 82 so-called target cities—cities most likely

The Federal Civil Defense Administration, in cooperation with the newly formed Valley Forge Foundation, distributed the official *Alert America!* booklet to the cities on the exhibit's tour. The booklet contained guidelines for promoting Alert America to local media, as well as recommendations for obtaining the support of private industry, civic leaders, local organizations, women, and youth.

to be bombed. Alert America spanned the length of a basketball court and featured graphic displays, movies, and audio recordings explaining the potential of atomic energy and the threat of the atomic bomb. Most cities on the tour expanded the exhibit with local and military displays. Alert America presented the positive and destructive sides of atomic energy, as well as threats from biological, chemical, psychological, sabotage, and incendiary warfare. A syndicated article from the Associated Press read, "The Alert America show to be put on the road … may hit your town soon, but don't look for anything too bloodcurdling. Atomic horrors are fairly well toned down in spite of some upper level men in FCDA who think efforts to awaken the nation to the dangers of atomic attack are too tame."[26] Costing more than $1 million to create, and with widespread support from private industry and national associations, Alert America had but one major challenge: overcoming Americans' apathy and indifference, resulting from a belief that they would not survive an atomic attack, which they could not prevent because the world situation had gone beyond their control.[27]

To allay Americans' fears and resulting apathy, Wells and Caldwell traveled extensively during the year, visiting scheduled cities and often speaking before multiple organizations at each stop. With limited government funds available, Wells secured financial contributions and equipment from private companies, individuals, and organizations. Among the companies were General Motors, General Electric, Motorola, RCA Victor, Shell Oil Company, Chrysler Corporation, DuPont, Ford Motor Company, and International Harvester. The Alert America exhibit, said Wells, was based primarily on the fact that the Soviet Union was the enemy of the United States, it now had atomic weapons, and it was determined to rule the world. He hoped Americans would overcome their apathy and actively participate in the nation's civil defense program. "It is urgent that every American rise above all partisanship and, realizing the common danger, prove his citizenship by actively and personally backing Civil Defense," he wrote in the official *Alert America!* booklet. "For here in our time, the destiny of the world is being decided."[28]

A survey of newspaper articles published in the early 1950s confirms Wells' concerns about the widespread apathy to the nation's civil defense program, and documents the attempts by federal, state, and local officials as well as military personnel, civic leaders, and the media to overcome it. Articles addressing the nation's apathy, in fact, began just a year after the Soviet Union's successful test of an atomic bomb in August 1949. Colonel Ben Stafford, director of civil defense for Jackson County, Oregon, told a gathering in August 1950 that public apathy was the greatest enemy of an effective civil defense program. Moreover, people had to realize their lives will be affected by an atomic attack in one way or another.[29]

At a meeting in New Brunswick, New Jersey, the same month, the Civil

Defense Council blamed the public's indifference for the number of volunteers being well short of the city's needs, adding that it was difficult to arouse their interest.[30] That October, in Raritan Township, New Jersey (population 2,800), the chairman of the local Civil Defense Council distributed a film about the atomic bombings of Hiroshima and Nagasaki to area organizations as a way of encouraging persons to volunteer.[31] Writing for the *Minneapolis Tribune*, Nat Finney, an authority on atomic energy and a staff correspondent, addressed both panic and apathy, which he linked together. "The word panic keeps cropping up in statements about civil defense.... The other side of panic is apathy. Apathy may become as much a problem as panic if tension drags on and on and nothing happens," he wrote. "The America that ultimately awaits atomic attack on its civilian vitals may well be an angry nation, frightened at its inability to adequately defend its homes, and more bitter in hatred of its enemy than ever before in its history."[32]

Representative William P. Bolton, a Democrat from Maryland's Second District, addressed Americans' apathy before the U.S. House of Representatives in February 1951. Bolton said his purpose in speaking out was to awaken people to the real danger of atomic attack. "Responsibility rests on the leaders of our society in local communities to impress upon their people the necessity of establishing at once a civil defense program in order to minimize as far as possible a sudden devastating attack against the United States," Bolton told his House colleagues. "The apathy of our people is interfering with this program in most of our communities."[33] In Valparaiso, Indiana, Joseph Alinsky of the local civil defense organization told a meeting in early 1951 that apathy had made it increasingly difficult to adopt a civil defense plan of operation. "But let that emergency arise," he said, "and we will doubtless have a deluge of hysterical citizens looking for help. Someone always has to get hurt before there is an awakening."[34]

The issue of apathy continually arose at FCDA-sponsored conferences, such as a two-day Conference of National Organizations held in May 1951. Speaking to the more than 1,000 leaders from 286 organizations, Caldwell placed people into one of two groups: those who were apathetic about the atomic bomb because of their lack of confidence in controlling their survival, their future; and those who suffered from fear of atomic destruction with little if any hope for survival. The problem, he said, was helping those people to understand that they can survive an atomic attack by taking certain simple precautions. "We must persuade them to stop defying the first law of nature—that of survival," Caldwell told attendees.[35]

In June 1951, Governor Thomas Dewey of New York placed the blame for the public's apathy on the state's inability to set up effective civil defense programs. He, as many other public officials around the country, believed apathy stemmed in large part from a lack of civil defense leadership. He based his opinion on a report by Colonel Lawrence Wilkinson, chairman of the New York Civil Defense Commission and a member of the Defense Council. If local officials created civil defense organizations with "sound, capable" staffs, the report stated, "there is reason to believe that evidence of real accomplishment … will in itself serve to arouse public interest and participation in the civil defense organization." To emphasize the urgency and seriousness of the situation, Dewey declared that any community failing to establish a civil defense organization within sixty days would be "publicly enumerated."[36]

The following month, Edward Gillette, director of civil defense for Nebraska, acknowledged the rampant apathy but remained hopeful that through education the public would respond.[37] Brigadier General R. L. Tilton, director of civil defense for Virginia, also expressed cautious optimism at a meeting in Newport News. Although he blamed the poor response to the state's civil defense program squarely on the public's apathy and lack of interest, he remained "confident that the people of this community will go all out if necessary."[38] In San Francisco, Lieutenant General Albert Wedemeyer, director of the Western States Civil Defense, placed blame for the widespread apathy on Congress, which repeatedly refused to meet President Truman's request for funding—appropriating only a small percentage of his proposals.[39]

An editorial published in the *Winona* (Minnesota) *Republican-Herald* in June 1951 also placed some of the blame for the public's apathy on the actions of Congress for approving just $74.9 million for civil defense when Truman had requested $535 million. Yet it went on to question why any American would be apathetic toward civil defense when Russian planes could fly the transpolar route and drop atomic bombs on most major American cities. "Some persons, no doubt, take the ostrich-like view, 'It's can't happen here,'" the editorial read. "They are clearly wrong. Another global war inevitably would be an atomic war. And no conceivable defense could prevent some bombing planes reaching the United States."[40] A similar message appeared in *The Tampa* (Florida) *Times* on the sixth anniversary of V-J Day, calling public apathy "the greatest danger we face." It continued: "Victory in Europe and Asia was not fought for and won so we could throw our sacrifices on an altar of apathy."[41]

That December, a New York City department store had its Santa Claus wear a civil defense armband and helmet, rather than his traditional red cap, on the same day as a citywide air-raid test in the hope of stimulating people to take an interest in civil defense. Unfortunately, the attempt failed as everyone continued shopping after the ten-minute air-raid test ended. This prompted Colonel Evan Seaman, with the Lehigh County civil defense control center, to comment, "I wish everybody looking at his Christmas tree … would think for a moment about the horrible mess we would have next Christmas if this area is hit by an air raid." A newspaper article summed it up this way: "Not even Santa Claus, the merry old soul himself, can dent the armor of apathy surrounding civil defense, it seems."[42]

In his July 4, 1951, radio address to the nation, Truman had expressed his concerns about public interest in national defense possibly waning when the Korean War ended, without regard to mounting tensions with the Soviet Union. "We cannot ignore the danger of military outbreaks in other parts of the world," he said. "The greatest threat to world peace, the tremendous armed power of the Soviet Union, will still remain, even if the Korean fighting stops. The threat of Soviet aggression still hangs heavy over many a country—including our own."[43] Six months later, on January 9, 1952, he presented the same message to Congress in his annual State of the Union address, stressing that the next twelve months would be critical for defending the free world. Truman had entered what became his last year in office. In March, he announced his decision not to seek re-election—no doubt prompted in part by Dwight Eisenhower's decision to run for president on the Republican ticket.

Less than seven years after victorious celebrations marked the end of World War II, the nation faced a communist nemesis in the Soviet Union bent on world domination with the capability of launching an atomic attack, or so many believed. The world situation had become perilous, the president warned, and the nation must take action. "If we falter," said Truman, "we can lose all the gains we have made. If we drive ahead, with courage and vigor and determination, we can by the end of 1952 be in a position of much greater security. The way will be dangerous for the years ahead, but if we put forth our best efforts this year—and next year—we can be 'over the hump' in our effort to build strong defenses."[44]

Two days after his State of the Union address, Truman visited Alert America on display in the nation's capital. As a demonstration of his support for the exhibit, he signed a "Count on me" card, which indicated his willingness to learn the skills necessary to protect his family in case of atomic attack. He also had "dog tags" made for his wife, Bess, his daughter, Margaret, and himself. The tags, replicating military metal tags, included personal information to help identify the dead or injured after an atomic attack.[45] After his visit, Truman voiced his confidence in the American people, saying that just a year after the formation of the FCDA, the nation had become "more alert and better prepared against enemy attack than it has ever been in our peacetime history—but we are far from being fully prepared."[46]

Even as the Alert America convoys began their national tour in January 1952, newspapers chronicled concerns about the public's apathy and indifference toward civil defense, as well as the lack of federal and state funding for civil defense programs. The same month, an editorial in the *Petaluma*

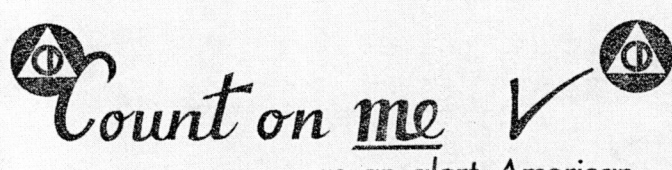

Count on me ✓
...as an alert American

To help protect our homes and our Country in Peace and War, I WILL:

(CHECK ACTIONS YOU WILL TAKE NOW!)

- [ ] Volunteer for one of the 10 local Civil Defense services
- [ ] Train myself and my family now in Civil Defense self-protection
- [ ] Prepare a family shelter area and equip it with first-aid supplies
- [ ] Prepare my home against fire and atomic attack
- [ ] Take an active part in Civil Defense where I work
- [ ] Take First Aid training
- [ ] Donate my blood for our war wounded
- [ ] I will pass along the Civil Defense lessons I have learned to my friends and neighbors

NAME _____
(Please print)

STREET ADDRESS _____

CITY & STATE _____

PHONE NUMBER _____

GPO : 1952 O - 982084

Before leaving the exhibit, everyone was given a "Count on me" card to encourage them to participate in some form of civil defense activity, such as volunteering for a local civil defense organization, preparing a family shelter area, or taking a first-aid training class. President Harry Truman completed the card on his visit to Alert America on January 11, 1952.

Visitors at Alert America could purchase identification "dog tags" for 25 cents. President Harry Truman acquired them for his family at the exhibit in Washington, D.C. Here, John Maloney's cartoon, published in the now defunct *Los Angeles Herald-Examiner* in 1952, promotes the ID tags at the Los Angeles exhibit, held in May.

Argus-Courier in Petaluma, California, a small town 40 miles north of San Francisco, lamented that despite an area civil defense organization being formed, apathy still existed. "We realize that it is difficult to keep the people stirred up about the need for Civil Defense," the editorial read. "They prefer not to think about a war, they hold the hope that there will never be another war, or at least that it will be in the distant future. But Civil Defense is like insurance, something we hope we will never need, but if we do need it, then it will come in very helpful. It may, indeed, tip the scales toward victory." It concluded by urging readers to get over their apathy and sign up as a civil defense volunteer.[47] R. P. Harman, director of South Dakota's civil defense program, expressed concern about apathy, which he contended handicapped the state's goal of 8,000 volunteers for its civil defense program. His comments came after traveling 25,000 miles the previous year, as well as holding 91 meetings and speaking before state conventions, service clubs, women's clubs, civic groups, veterans organizations, and church groups.[48]

Historian Andrew D. Grossman has written that Alert America represented sophisticated propaganda in the form of "performance art." Its aim, he argues, was to convince the public that their participation in civil defense, the nation's defense, had become critical in an era in which enemy planes could drop atomic bombs on American cities. Moreover, through Americans' role in civil defense, they could survive such an attack.[49] In this respect, he is correct that the FCDA wanted people to take an active role in civil defense, or at least to acknowledge its importance, and to convince them that survival was possible. The real issue is whether this objective should be considered propaganda, which carries with it a negative connotation of manipulation and deceit. Historian Dee Garrison offers a more positive view, writing that Alert America "provided ideological and moral guidance, along with information designed to calm public fears while teaching the value of civil defense."[50]

In 1952, the FCDA and the Valley Forge Foundation set their goal to change the public's attitude toward civil defense and the threat of atomic war. The objective of this study is to examine this goal and Alert America's effect on the American public. Chapter One provides an overview of America in 1952, a presidential election year—the year in which the nation exploded its first hydrogen bomb, greatly escalating the stakes in the Cold War; and the year that saw the nation's civil defense program take direct aim at public apathy.

Chapter Two takes a close-up view of Alert America, from its origin in June 1951 at a meeting of the FCDA's National Advisory Council, to its development into a full-scale exhibit, and, finally, to its unveiling in the nation's capital.

Chapter Three travels with one of the three convoys as it leaves Washington,

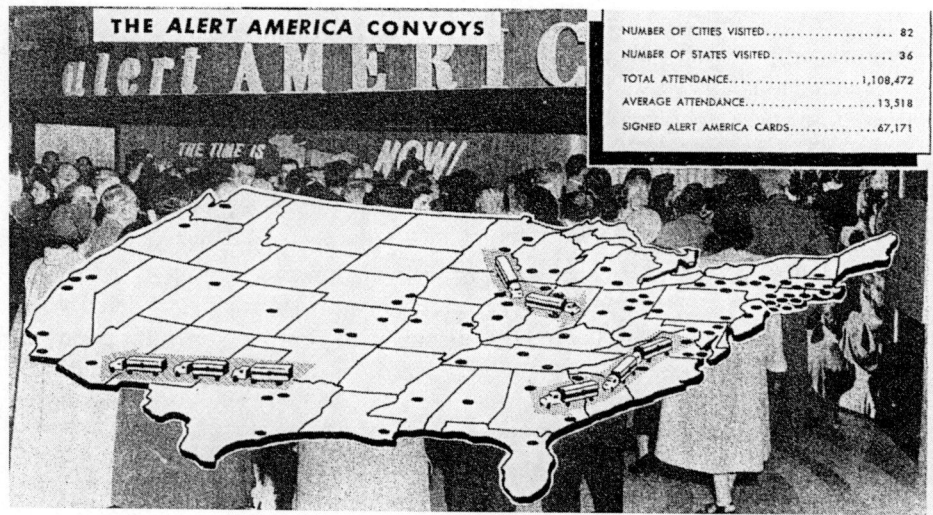

NUMBER OF CITIES VISITED	82
NUMBER OF STATES VISITED	36
TOTAL ATTENDANCE	1,108,472
AVERAGE ATTENDANCE	13,518
SIGNED ALERT AMERICA CARDS	67,171

This illustration, published in the FCDA's *1952 Annual Report*, shows a map of the three convoys carrying the Alert America exhibit and a summary of its success: visiting 82 cities and attracting 1.1 million visitors.

D.C., and opens in Wilmington, Delaware, an important stop that set the model for other target cities on the tour schedule.

Opening-day parades and other festivities comprised a significant component in this model, and Chapter Four describes some of these grand spectacles—from military demonstrations and flyovers, to elaborate floats and marching bands, to scores of official cars and emergency equipment, to coinciding air-raid tests.

Chapter Five travels cross-country with the Alert America convoys to describe how the various stops prepared for and hosted the exhibit.

Chapter Six examines the role of women and children in Alert America. The FCDA, which had identified women as essential from its very beginning, encouraged local civil defense groups to appoint women's committees and work with women's organizations to enhance attendance and to enlist volunteer guides and hosts for the exhibit. The involvement of elementary and high school students, who constituted as much as 30–40 percent of visitors in some cities, is also explored, as well as the support of local officials and school districts to ensure that children had an opportunity to see the exhibit.

Chapter Seven then looks at the extensive newspaper coverage received by Alert America—before, during, and after the exhibit. Kenneth Wells and Millard Caldwell placed a major emphasis on advance publicity, and newspapers clearly responded.

The Conclusion chronicles the impact of Alert America after it ended its national tour in September 1952, including its impact on public apathy and subsequent civil defense programs. It also looks at the repackaging of Alert America as a Canadian exhibit, "On Guard, Canada." In addition, several documents are included to provide additional details about Alert America: the campaign's October 1951 progress report, an excerpt from the official brochure, a promotional pamphlet, and a fact sheet.

Finally, the 12-part series written by FCDA Administrator Millard Caldwell, titled "U.S. Needs Civil Defense," is included to gain a better insight into the government's efforts to convince Americans to support civil defense. Installments appear at the end of chapters.

President Truman had endorsed Alert America as the government's best opportunity to reach Americans throughout the nation. What Grossman calls "performance art" featured educational displays and graphic demonstrations of both the positive and the destructive aspects of atomic energy. Unfortunately, with the exception of Grossman and Garrison, most historians writing about civil defense in the 1950s give Alert America only a cursory mention, if any mention at all. Yet upon closer examination, Alert America becomes one of the more significant government-backed public awareness campaigns ever conducted. Although public apathy remained an issue throughout the early postwar years, Alert America prompted millions of Americans to volunteer for civil defense programs at the state and local levels. At the conclusion of its nine-month tour, Alert America had been visited by 1.1 million people, while some 67 million people—the combined population of the cities visited—had been made aware of the exhibit. With a national population of 157 million at the time, the Alert America convoys had a direct impact on approximately 43 percent of the population.

Grossman makes the point that Alert America promoted the concept of the "responsible Cold War citizen" with each person becoming a citizen soldier.[51] For Wells and Caldwell, and the thousands of people who worked diligently toward Alert America's success, this observation is absolutely correct … in a positive sense. Wells hoped the exhibit would "awaken all Americans to the urgent need for strong civil defense and to encourage each to enlist for such specialized training as may be possible."[52] Speaking at the American Legion's National Convention in October 1951, Caldwell told attendees, "We know today there are thousands of lives that will be saved because many people in our target cities have learned a few of the simple facts of survival. The healthy nucleus of a civil defense system is here."[53]

America's victory culture had been replaced by a tumultuous time in which the government became increasingly concerned about the ability of the civilian population—the nation's "citizen soldiers"—to survive an atomic attack. As 1952 began, the Alert America convoys set out to educate, inculcate, and, to some extent, frighten Americans into participating in the nation's defense.

ONE

America 1952

Life like that we knew before 1929 will never return.... The Soviet Union is committed to the conquest of the world. It cannot be satisfied with anything less than global dominion. The Soviet intentions resemble those of Naziism with one difference—the Nazis couldn't wait, but the Soviets can.— Arthur Schlesinger, Jr., American historian, 1952[1]

Imagine a man—a World War II veteran, husband, and father of two—waiting to enter "The Show That May Safe Your Life," being staged at the city armory in the year 1952. Born in the 1920s and coming of age during the Great Depression, he enlisted in the Marines shortly after the Japanese attacked Pearl Harbor on December 7, 1941. He had survived more than three years of hard fighting in the Pacific Theater, moving from island to island—Tarawa, Guam, Peleliu, Iwo Jima. After helping take Okinawa in one of the deadliest battles of the war, he had joined thousands of American troops preparing for a final assault on the Japanese homeland as part of Operation Downfall.

Then, on August 6, 1945, a B-29 "Superfortress" dropped a single weapon of mass destruction, an atomic bomb, on Hiroshima. Another was dropped on Nagasaki three days later, effectively ending the war. Our Alert America visitor had celebrated V-J Day along with millions of others, and soon returned home to begin a new life. America had been victorious and solidified its position as the most powerful nation in the world—and the only one with "The Bomb." But that status ended just four years later with the Soviet Union's successful testing of its own atomic bomb.

Prior to arriving at the city armory, our visitor read articles in the local newspaper emphasizing the importance of attending the Alert America exhibit to learn how to prepare for an atomic attack by the Soviet Union—an attack predicted to result in some 40,000 Americans dead and 110,000 casualties from each bomb blast, according to government and military officials. The mayor had issued a proclamation for this to be "Civil Defense Week" and requested all citizens to attend the exhibit. Posters on buildings and signs in the front windows of retailers across town made sure he knew the dates and the location. A Boy Scout had wedged a promotional brochure in the screen door of his house. Local radio and television stations had presented programs about the exhibit. A parade of semi-trailers with the words "Alert America" painted on the sides in large, boldfaced letters, along with scores of cars carrying dignitaries, assorted military vehicles, marching bands, and patriotic floats had passed by his office the day before, as people watched from building windows and crowded streets. Six Air Force F-51 Mustang jets even swept over the parade, exciting the crowd with the thunderous sound of their 1700-horsepower engines. His children were slated to tour the exhibit as part of a citywide plan for schools, although those under twelve were cautioned about seeing its more graphic displays. His wife, a member of a local women's group, had volunteered to be an exhibit guide.

Upon entering the Alert America exhibit, free to the public, he first encounters a panel with photographs of how atomic energy is being used both for peacetime applications, such as medicine and science, and for mass destruction. John Paxton, the Alert America field manager for the Valley Forge Foundation, which managed the exhibit, described this first display to one newspaper as demonstrating how "man's capacity for good and evil is growing as the world shrinks."[2] Continuing on, he views a model of an atomic pile, depicting atomic power in a world of peace. Next, he enters a circular chamber labeled "Or Will It Be This?" The answer is given through a series of displays: biological, sabotage, psychological, chemical, and atomic warfare. Flashing lights in the sabotage display create an illusion of an exploding factory. A man dressed in a trench coat prepares to empty a vial of germs onto wheat for the biological warfare display; an image of a man choking alerts him to the dangers of chemical warfare; and simulated flames consuming a building demonstrate an incendiary bomb. For atomic warfare, the exhibit presents a continuous loop of black-and-white movies showing the Berlin and London air raids during World War II, and a diorama depicting the atomic destruction of "City X," narrated by radio personality Arthur Godfrey. *The Baltimore Sun* described the sequence of events:

> The corridor ends in a room known as "City X," where a graphic demonstration is shown of an atomic air raid. Built into one wall is a case depicting a cardboard outline of City X's skyscrapers. A sound film comes on. There is an announcement of "condition red": the wall of sirens; the gurgling cry of a baby; then the roar of approaching bombers. The room is darkened and on the screen behind the mythical city anti-aircraft bursts flash, followed by a long shrill whistle and then the "mushroom" cloud of an atomic explosion. The center of the city automatically sinks below the table, leaving only the glow of burning debris.[3]

As visitors entered the Alert America exhibit, they passed several poster displays of the various forms of warfare, including chemical, sabotage, psychological, and biological (National Archives).

Commenting on the destruction, Tom Curtin, director of the Alert America convoy, said, "When they come into this part of the show everybody is chattering away. When they leave, there's no conversation."

As our visitor leaves behind City X, he reflects on his role as protector of his family and is awed by the destructive demonstration he has just witnessed. Although he understands the power of the atomic bomb, he has not really thought about the threat of atomic warfare. Continuing on, he turns left into another corridor and passes a chart of how many deaths and casualties will occur within a three-mile radius of the blast. Then it is on to the "transition room" with a life-sized figure of a defiant mother carrying her child away from the atomic ruins, next to a sign asking, "Can This Menace Be Beaten?" Here, an audio recording by news commentator Edward R. Murrow reassures visitors that "we needn't take it lying down," emphasizing that the potential fatalities from an atomic attack can be reduced by half through an effective civil defense program.

Next is the "pay-off" room with panels describing the various opportunities in civil defense at the national, state, and local level. Included in the display are posters showing civil defense organizational charts; various services and operations; and instructions on the protective steps each person can take to minimize the deaths and injuries from an atomic attack. Finally, at the end of the exhibit, our visitor is reminded through photomurals that he enjoys the American way of life, with its political and economic rights derived from religious faith and constitutional government. Before leaving, he is handed a "Count on me" checklist and asked what he plans to do for civil defense, such as preparing a home shelter, volunteering, and learning first aid. He leaves with more knowledge about atomic power and the role of civil defense, but he is not sure about getting involved just yet.

Our visitor represents how most Americans in 1952 likely approached the Alert America exhibit. Although they understood the seriousness of the atomic bomb—a topic continuously covered by the media—civil defense was still a relatively new concept. It must be remembered that the United States had ended the war in August 1945 with the devastating destruction of Hiroshima and Nagasaki, Japan, by two atomic bombs, which it alone possessed. In the late 1940s, Americans reclaimed their lives in a world finally at peace, even as they followed the development of more powerful atomic bombs through news reports of military tests on the Bikini Atoll in the Pacific Ocean.

Over this same timespan, however, the United States watched the Soviet Union transition from a war ally to a peacetime archrival in an ever-intensifying Cold War. Exactly four years later to the month of the destruction of Hiroshima and Nagasaki, on August 29, 1949, the Soviet Union successfully detonated its first atomic bomb, realigning the balance of international power.

The most dramatic display was a diorama of "City X." As visitors watched, enemy planes approach and drop an atomic bomb, destroying what "could be your city" (National Archives).

Seven months later, Senator Joseph McCarthy of Wisconsin decided to correct this realignment by launching his own war. In February 1950, he made a bold assertion that members of the Communist Party had infiltrated the State Department, thus spawning what came to be called McCarthyism to describe a national wave of anti-communist hysteria for the next four years.[4] This wave gained strength on June 25 when North Korea, with the backing of the Soviet Union and China, invaded democratic South Korea, launching the Korean War. Although early military efforts by the United Nations—consisting overwhelmingly of U.S. troops—were successful, the tide turned in October 1950 after Chinese troops crossed the Yalu River, marking the Chinese border, and pushed back the U.N. forces through the first half of 1951. North Korea launched another offensive in the spring of 1952 along the 155-mile battlefront.[5]

Addressing the American people about Korea on July 19, 1950, President Truman told the television and radio audience, "This attack has made it clear, beyond all doubt, that the international communist movement is willing to use armed invasion to conquer independent nations. An act of aggression such as this creates a very real danger to the security of all free nations." He then called for increasing defense production "not just for the immediate future but for the next several years." He also set the tone for the role of all Americans in the new world of communist aggression by putting the onus on ordinary citizens. "Our military needs are large," Truman said, "and to meet them will require hard work and steady effort. I know that we can produce what we need if each of us does his part—each man, each woman, each soldier, each civilian. This is a time for all of us to pitch in and work together."[6] In view of the escalating conflict in Korea and the closing off of Eastern Europe to Communist control, Senator Pat McCarren (D–Nevada), a leading member of the Senate Internal Security Committee, exacerbated Americans' fear and trepidations in August 1951 by asserting that the country "is faced with the inevitable—all-out war" with the Soviet Union.[7]

As if McCarthy's rhetoric, Truman's warning, and McCarren's declaration of all-out war were not enough to create fear and uneasiness among Americans, the Federal Civil Defense Administration, created in January 1951 by President Truman to oversee the nation's civil defense program, asked Congress for $2.1 million to purchase what were described as "olive-drab plastic sheets" to bury the dead in the aftermath of an atomic blast. It claimed wooden caskets would be too cumbersome and could not be provided fast enough to handle the projected fatalities. As one newspaper summarized: "The dead would have to be disposed of within a limited time—48 hours … in most climates. Where it is very dry or very cold, the period could be longer. In any case, experts say, embalming would be entirely unfeasible. The skilled technicians available could hardly make a start at the task." Moreover, according to the FCDA, the average city did not have the mortuary facilities needed for such a catastrophic event. The most urgent need would be to get the bodies out of sight. "If this weren't done, the psychological effect on survivors—relatives, friends, and all other persons—would be bad. On their morale and efficiency, the continued existence of the city and nation would depend."[8]

The Reverend Joseph Connolly of South River, New Jersey, joined other religious leaders around the country pledging to provide their facilities to the local civil defense organizations for this use in such an emergency situation. Msgr. Paul Tanner, assistant general secretary of the National Catholic Welfare Conference, urged the training of more people in church sacraments, while cautioning that sacraments would take too long to administer after an atomic attack. He warned that 200,000 to 300,00 people might be dead within a few hours. As an alternative, Tanner recommended the preparation of cards containing simple prayers to help bombing victims in "finding spiritual comfort and in reaching the proper spiritual state for the final moment."[9]

As 1952 got under way, President Truman faced myriad issues on the domestic and international fronts, including deciding whether to run for re-election. Republicans, faced with the prospect of having either Senator Robert Taft or Senator Thomas Dewey as their presidential candidate, actively pursued General Dwight Eisenhower to enter the race. Then, after months of speculation, Eisenhower, stationed in Paris as supreme commander of the North Atlantic Treaty Organization responsible for holding the Soviet Union in check, finally announced on January 7 that if drafted, he would accept the Republican nomination for president of the United States. In simple terms, he would run if he "got a clear cut call to political duty."[10]

Eisenhower had served as supreme commander of the Allied Expeditionary Forces in Europe during World War II, becoming an American hero by directing the final victory over Germany in May 1945. Although he acknowledged his ambition to become president of the United States, he also made clear that he would not actively campaign for the nomination in order to fulfill his current responsibilities, stating, "I shall continue to devote my full attention and energies to the performance of the vital task to which I am assigned."[11] His announcement made newspaper headlines from coast to coast, and pushed Taft and Dewey onto the back pages. The *Lincoln* (Nebraska) *Journal Star* reflected how newspapers reported the story, with a bold headline stretched across the front page that read, "Ike Will 'Accept' Nomination." The *Tallahassee* (Florida) *Democrat* blazoned its front page with "General Eisenhower Will Run." In Redlands, California, the local newspaper used bold type in all caps to announce "EISENHOWER, REPUBLICAN, WILL RUN." *The New York Times* and *Chicago Sun-Times* "enthusiastically" gave Eisenhower their support in the upcoming presidential race.[12]

On the same day in Paris that Eisenhower announced his decision, a coalition of Communists, de Gaullists, and Socialists voted Premier Rene Pleven's government, proponent of French rearmament and strong supporter of NATO, out of power. Pleven and his cabinet, which had been in power only five months, resigned after losing a vote of confidence. Paul Ward, Washington Bureau reporter for *The Baltimore Sun*, wrote that members of the coalition "for different reasons, oppose either the North Atlantic defense alliance or domestic economies essential to fulfillment of commitments to that alliance."[13] In the Far East, attempts to negotiate a peace agreement in the Korean conflict fell apart, with Vice Admiral C. Turner Joy, head of the United Nations truce delegation, flying to Tokyo to meet with Supreme U.N. Commander General Matthew Ridgway. "With each passing day," Joy said, "there is less and less reason to think the Communists want a stable armistice."[14]

The rash of disturbing news did not deter President Truman, however, who was meeting in the White House with 77-year-old British Prime Minister

Winston Churchill. Churchill, who had begun his second tenure at prime minister only two months earlier, had arrived over the weekend, along with Sir Oliver Franks, the British ambassador; British Foreign Secretary Anthony Eden; and a diplomatic and military entourage. After a weekend of general talks, Truman and Churchill, no doubt chomping on his usual cigar, got down to the business at hand on Monday, January 7, to finalize a strategy for countering international communism despite the bad news from Paris and Korea. This was no easy task, as the agenda covered the situation in the Far East, both China and Korea; policies toward the Soviet Union, now an atomic-armed power; military command problems; international control of atomic energy; defense of Europe, including West Germany's rearmament; and Britain's request for more steel from the United States.[15] Two days later, on January 9, the two leaders issued a 1,200-word joint statement in which they shared "the hope and the determination that war, with all its modern weapons, shall not again be visited on mankind." Promising to monitor developments that might threaten world peace, they continued: "We do not believe that war is inevitable. This is the basis of our policies. We are willing at any time to explore all reasonable means of resolving the issues which now threaten the peace of the world."[16]

For Churchill, despite his cautious optimism in the joint statement, the prospect of resolving the problems with the Soviet Union still appeared dim. Less than a year after final victory in World War II, on March 5, 1946, he had delivered his "iron curtain" speech at small Westminster College in Fulton, Missouri—a speech that, in essence, formed the opening salvo in the Cold War between the West and the Soviet Union. He said that an "iron curtain" had been drawn across Eastern Europe, and the countries behind this curtain had become "subject in one form or another, not only to Soviet influence but to a very high and increasing measure of control from Moscow."[17] Then, in June 1948, the Soviet Union flexed its muscle and launched a blockade of railway, road, and waterway access to West Berlin, controlled by the French, British, and Americans. Only after the Western allies carried out some 200,000 flights for nearly a year, with nine thousand tons of supplies delivered each day, did the Soviet Union lift the blockade in May 1949. The same year, the United States, Great Britain, and its allies formed the North Atlantic Treaty Organization (NATO); China fell to Mao Zedong and the Communist Party; and the Soviet Union successfully tested an atomic bomb, thus escalating international tension.[18]

Despite the joint statement with Churchill about war not visiting mankind again, Truman believed the government had a responsibility not only to have a strong military to counter the Soviet Union and the Communist threat but to prepare the nation's citizenry to survive a potential atomic war. An important first step in this responsibility was passage of the National

Security Act in 1947, which established the postwar agencies responsible for protecting the nation: the National Security Council, the Central Intelligence Agency, the Department of Defense, and the National Securities Resources Board. Five years later, in his 1952 State of the Union, President Truman told Congress and the American people that the nation could not relax but rather had to continue building its defenses until the Soviet Union "accepts a sound disarmament proposal, and joins in peaceful settlements." The military, he said, had added more than a million men and women in the past year, bringing the total to nearly three and a half million. More significant, the nation had made "rapid progress" in the development of atomic weapons. He continued:

> The way seems long and hard. The goal seems far distant. Some people get discouraged. That is only natural. But if there are any among us who think we ought to ease up in the fight for peace, I want to remind them of three things—just three things.
>
> First: The threat of world war is still very real. We had one Pearl Harbor. Let's not get caught off guard again. If you don't think the threat of Communist armies is real, talk to some of our men back from Korea.
>
> Second: If the United States had to try to stand alone against a Soviet-dominated world, it would destroy the life we know and the ideals we hold dear. Our allies are essential to us, just as we are essential to them. The more shoulders there are to bear the burden the lighter that burden will be.
>
> Third: The things we believe in most deeply are under relentless attack. We have the great responsibility of saving the basic moral and spiritual values of our civilization. We have started out well—with a program for peace that is unparalleled in history. If we believe in ourselves and the faith we profess, we will stick to that job until it is victoriously finished.
>
> This is a time for courage, not for grumbling and mumbling.[19]

Truman's call for courage underscored the world situation in 1952. Looking back at this period, the first impulse is to focus on the burgeoning economy; the sprawling suburbs; the rapid expansion and impact of television; Detroit's new generation of powerful and chrome-ladened automobiles; rock 'n' roll and teen culture. This was, after all, the "Fabulous Fifties." Yet the 1950s also experienced McCarthyism and the implementation of blacklists banning suspected Communists from pursuing their professions; the Korean War and military policies of "containment" and "mutually assured destruction"; and, underlying all of this, the knowledge that an atomic war was a very real possibility. A Gallup Poll conducted in August 1951, in fact, found 58 percent of respondents predicting an atomic war with the Soviet Union in five years, the highest mark in the four years of taking the poll; with 26 percent thinking war would come in one year.[20]

Early in 1952, the FCDA released its projections that the Soviet Union had enough atomic bombs to launch simultaneous attacks against twenty to thirty cities, with that number increasing to almost seventy cities the following year.[21] A few months later, Secretary of the Air Force Nathan Twining, in a report to the Senate, said the Soviet Union not only had enough planes to launch an initial atomic attack; it also has "a reserve for succeeding tries if the first [attack] should fail." Twining's report indicated an all-out atomic war with the Soviet Union would last a few weeks or few months—not years.

Making this even more alarming, intelligence reports revealed that the Russians had at least twice as many first-rate combat planes as the United States: 20,000 Russian aircraft organized into 250 wings (or units), compared to 10,000 U.S. aircraft, which would reach 143 organized wings by 1955. Plus, the Soviet Union had approximately 20,000 planes in reserve. The U.S. had none.[22] Secretary of the Army Frank Pace added to the discussion by saying, "We are doing our best to take no chances either now or in the future. What we are earnestly trying to do is to guard ourselves to the utmost with present-day weapons while at the same time developing an atomic army that can meet any threat in the future."[23]

The day before the Truman-Churchill meetings in January, the Atomic Energy Commission (AEC) delivered its eleventh semi-annual report to Congress. The 211-page report detailed plans to spend as much as $6 billion over the next five years on the expansion of its atomic weapons. Also noted was the completion of two projects aimed at increasing the production of bomb materials: a $300 million addition to the atomic explosives plant in Hanford, Washington; and a $222 million addition to the uranium 235 gaseous diffusion plant at Oak Ridge, Tennessee. In addition, the AEC announced plans to construct two new plants that would effectively double the production of materials for nuclear bombs: a $1.25 billion plant near Aiken, South Carolina; and a $500 million plant in Paducah, Kentucky.[24] These various plants would benefit from the addition of South Africa, Australia, and Canada as resources for the critical uranium ore.[25] Commenting on the Aiken program, AEC Chairman Gordon Dean told Congress that the cost had almost doubled, from $600 million to $1.25 billion, because the reactors to be used for building the hydrogen bomb cost more due to their advanced design.[26]

This became vital on November 1, 1952, just three days before the presidential election, when the U.S. successfully detonated a hydrogen bomb at Eniwetok in the Marshall Islands, something that had been anticipated and reported on for more than a year. The H-bomb, or what many commentators termed the "super bomb," reportedly had a thousand times more destructive power than the atomic bombs exploded at Hiroshima and Nagasaki. Typical headlines included such pronouncements as "Whole Cities Can Be Wiped Off Map With Single Blast," "Successful Test of World's First H-Bomb Is Warning to Russians," and "H-Bomb Joins U.S. Arsenal of Atomic-Age Weapons." Although the government and military knew the Soviet Union also was working on the H-bomb, they felt the development could be up to two years away. In fact, the Soviet Union exploded its first hydrogen bomb in August 1953, less than a year later.[27]

The world had changed dramatically since Americans celebrated the end of the world war in 1945. Yet even then, many scientists, elected officials, military personnel, media, and other informed Americans understood the dangers ahead. As early as 1946, Harold Urey, nuclear physicist and part of the Manhattan Project that developed America's atomic bomb, had forewarned the current scenario in testimony before the Atomic Energy Commission. "I wish to present the probable future course and development of atomic bombs," Urey told the commission, "assuming that no prohibition of the manufacture of such bombs on an international scale is introduced and also assuming that a war does not break out during the course of developments." He divided the future into three stages. In the first stage, the United States would be the only nation to have atomic weapons. By the second stage, the U.S. would possess a fair-sized stockpile of atomic bombs, although other countries would begin to develop their own bombs. "Ours will be the best," Urey pointed out, "unless the scientists and engineers of other countries discover some better ideas that we may have overlooked." In the third stage, the U.S. and other countries would have sufficient atomic bombs to destroy each other with equally effective bombs. "As this situation develops," he said, "tensions will increase, slowly at first and finally beyond anything we have ever seen, or experienced."[28] By 1952, the world had entered the third stage, with the United States and the Soviet Union playing the major roles in an atomic standoff—both capable of inflicting massive destruction on the other. To punctuate this point, General Hoyt Vanderberg, the Air Force chief of staff, had gone on record as indicating that 70 percent of enemy airplanes would penetrate U.S. defenses. Moreover, the AEC's annual 1951 report stated, "Fissionable materials, the atomic explosives plutonium and uranium-235, are going into weapons at a record rate."[29]

President Truman decided not to run for re-election in March, giving way to Adlai Stevenson to run as the Democratic Party's nominee against Eisenhower, who won the presidency in one of the nation's biggest landslides: 442 electoral votes to 89, with 39 states voting for "Ike" and just nine states voting for Stevenson. On November 18, Truman invited the president-elect to meet at the White House, with the agenda focused primarily on Korea and the newest weapon in the nation's arsenal, the hydrogen bomb. Eisenhower assumed his office on January 20, 1953, at perhaps the peak of postwar tensions between the West and Communist powers—the Soviet Union, China, and North Korea.[30] Truman reflected these tensions in his final State of the Union address to Congress, delivered January 7, 1953, two weeks before Eisenhower's inauguration. He noted the privilege of holding the office for nearly eight years, and acknowledged the many accomplishments during his tenure, such as an expanding economy and the low unemployment rate, and pledged his support for the incoming president. Then, in a more serious tone, he talked at length about the international tensions with the Soviet Union and Communism, stressing that "the world is divided." He went on:

> The world is divided, not through our fault or failure, but by Soviet design. They, not we, began the cold war.... From 1945 to 1949, the United States was sole possessor of the atomic bomb. That was a great deterrent and protection in itself. But when the Soviets produced an atomic explosion—as they were bound to do in time—we had to broaden the whole basis of our strength. We had to endeavor to keep our lead in atomic weapons. We had to strengthen our armed forces generally and to enlarge our productive capacity—our mobilization base. Historically, it was the Soviet atomic explosion in the fall of 1949, nine months before the aggression in Korea, which stimulated the planning for our program of defense mobilization.... The war of the future would be one in which man could extinguish millions of lives at one blow, demolish the great cities of the world, wipe out the cultural achievements of the past—and destroy the very structure of a civilization that has been slowly and painfully built up through hundreds of generations. Such a war is not a possible policy for rational men. We know this, but we dare not assume that others would not yield to the temptation science is now placing in their hands.[31]

It is within this context that the FCDA proposed to launch a massive educational program to inform, educate, and, above all, motivate Americans to join civil defense programs. The FCDA's proposal exemplified its original mission described in Truman's Executive Order 10186. Issued December 1, 1950, the order outlined the mission as preparing Americans for the possibility of an atomic war; promoting the development of and standards for civil defense measures and equipment; disseminating civil defense information and exchanging such information with foreign countries; conducting or arranging for training programs in such areas as civil defense organization, operation, and techniques for state and local civil defense leaders and specialists; assisting and encouraging states and foreign countries to form mutual agreements or pacts (with the consent of Congress) to meet emergencies or disasters from enemy attacks that cannot be met or controlled adequately by the local forces; and making appropriate provision for necessary civil defense communications.[32]

Over a ninth-month period, from January to September 1952, three convoys, each comprised of ten 32-foot semi-trailers carrying identical Alert America exhibits, visited 82 cities in 36 states. More than one million men, women, and children visited the exhibit, although millions more read about it, often in front-page articles of the local newspaper; attended presentations at schools and other gatherings; listened to radio coverage and public service announcements; and, in some areas, watched local television news and special programs about the exhibit. Many host cities also held Alert America parades and special civic events related to civil defense. Mayors declared "Civil

CITY INFORMATION ON ALERT AMERICA CONVOYS

City visited	Approx. attendance	City visited	Approx. attendance
Akron, Ohio	4,015	Newark, N. J.	5,582
Albany, N. Y.	5,902	New Haven, Conn.	6,950
Atlanta, Ga.	11,169	New London, Conn.	7,333
Baltimore, Md.	13,470	New Orleans, La.	22,523
Binghamton, N. Y.	4,321	New York, N. Y.	46,724
Birmingham, Ala.	8,143	Norfolk, Va.	8,000
Boston, Mass.	5,122	Oakland, Calif.	28,864
Bridgeport, Conn.	4,000	Omaha, Nebr.	20,387
Buffalo, N. Y.	3,285	Peoria, Ill.	7,397
Canton, Ohio	6,947	Philadelphia, Pa.	9,156
Charleston, W. Va.	1,997	Phoenix, Ariz.	17,500
Chattanooga, Tenn.	15,227	Pittsburgh, Pa.	6,127
Chicago, Ill.	22,476	Pittsfield, Mass.	4,118
Cleveland, Ohio	3,350	Portland, Oreg.	25,207
Columbus, Ohio	6,800	Providence, R. I.	18,382
Dallas, Tex.	3,047	Richmond, Va.	4,370
Denver, Colo.	11,243	Rochester, N. Y.	4,163
Detroit, Mich.	7,446	Rock Island, Ill.	10,036
Duluth, Minn.	6,829	Sacramento, Calif., State Fair	114,845
Fall River, Mass.	15,654	St. Louis, Mo.	23,711
Fort Eustis, Va.	1,847	St. Paul, Minn.	5,654
Fort Worth, Tex.	4,616	Salt Lake City, Utah, State	
Gary, Ind.	4,892	Fair	74,824
Grand Rapids, Mich.	7,886	San Diego, Calif.	27,889
Greenville, S. C.	8,004	San Francisco, Calif.	12,784
Hartford, Conn.	20,021	Savannah, Ga.	9,640
Houston, Tex.	12,101	Schenectady, N. Y.	9,165
Hutchinson, Kans.	7,020	Seattle, Wash.	30,542
Indianapolis, Ind.	10,809	Springfield, Ill.	11,515
Jackson, Miss.	8,963	Springfield, Mass.	5,169
Jacksonville, Fla.	6,180	Stamford, Conn.	3,100
Kansas City, Mo.	16,446	Syracuse, N. Y.	3,065
Lincoln, Nebr., Lancaster		Topeka, Kans.	11,965
County Fair	20,329	Trenton, N. J.	11,350
Los Angeles, Calif.	52,051	Utica, N. Y.	6,000
Louisville, Ky.	2,862	Washington, D. C.	32,000
Madison, Wis.	11,340	Waterbury, Conn.	7,000
Manchester, N. H.	9,659	Wichita, Kans.	12,005
Memphis, Tenn.	8,440	Wilmington, Del.	10,700
Milwaukee, Wis.	18,075	Winston-Salem, N. C.	9,470
Mineola, N. Y.	5,000	Worcester, Mass.	5,225
Nashville, Tenn.	17,351	Youngstown, Ohio	4,200

The FCDA's *1952 Annual Report* included a list of the 82 cities visited by the Alert America convoys, with attendance figures. Convoys stopped in 36 states, plus Washington, D.C., and had more than one million visitors.

Defense Week" or "Alert America Week" in recognition of the exhibit. Local civil defense organizations launched recruiting drives. Civic leaders and organizations supported the program and private industry provided funding and services. More emphasis was placed on civil defense training in elementary and secondary schools, and adults enrolled in an expanding number of civil defense training courses. Public officials became more active and involved in the funding of civil defense staffs, equipment, and activities. According to the FCDA's *1952 Annual Report*, local committees formed to promote Alert America often maintained their active interest and participation in civil defense, with many continuing to serve in their local civil defense organization after the exhibit had moved on to another city. Several cities introduced or expanded recruiting drives and the training of civil defense instructors, as well as increased the number of training facilities. The nation's military held maneuvers, participated in parades, sponsored displays, and provided flyovers to signal the exhibit's opening day.

In reviewing the nation's newspapers, it is apparent that the FCDA's Office of Public Affairs along with the Valley Forge Foundation did an excellent job of promoting the exhibit. Moreover, it is evident that Americans were receptive to what was billed as "The Show That May Save Your Life." "In performing their mission of rapidly creating greater public understanding and participation in civil defense," read the FCDA's report, "the Alert America Convoys have been judged as the largest, most comprehensive and most dramatic mobile exhibits ever used in this country by any agency—public or private."[33] It is hard to discredit the FCDA's claim. Clearly, the Alert America exhibit represented an unprecedented government campaign.

* * *

To promote the FCDA's efforts in educating Americans about the importance of civil defense, of which Alert America represented a major component, Millard Caldwell, FCDA administrator, wrote a 12-part syndicated series in 1952 for newspapers across the nation. Titled "U.S. Needs Civil Defense," the series could be purchased for 10 cents from the Superintendent of Documents in Washington, D.C.

U.S. Needs Civil Defense
By Millard Caldwell, FCDA Administrator

Air Force Chief Says Enemy Bombers Can Attack America
(First in the series)

General Hoyt Vandenberg, Chief of Staff of the United States Air Force, has made a startling statement—one which most Americans find hard to believe. He has said that at best we could knock down only 30 out of every 100 enemy planes attacking the United States. That means that at least 7 out of 10 would get through. Despite our traditional attitude that "it can't happen here," we must believe these facts.

This does not mean that our Air Force is ineffective. We have an excellent air force and our anti-aircraft defenses are good. In the last war, the Germans also were well equipped with defense weapons, but they were not able to stop our attacking bombers. On the average, we lost fewer than 10 out of each 100 planes. That gives us something to think about!

We know that everything possible will be done to stop the enemy at our borders, and to prevent sabotage within, but we also can be sure that, in case of war, a good percentage of enemy attacks would be successful in spite of all that we could do.

That is why we must have Civil Defense.

The wide oceans which once protected us have given way to global bombers. Today we face more kinds of attack than ever before, and our danger is much greater.

There is only one sure way to keep any enemy from knocking us out of a war. We must know how to save lives and property, restore our cities and industries, and carry on the fight no matter what kind of attacks are hurled against us.

Russia Has Bombers

Russia has hundreds of heavy, long-range bombers patterned after our B-29s which could get through most of our defense setups. We know that Russia has atomic bombs and that their heavy, long-range bombers are capable of delivering them anywhere in the United States at any time the Kremlin dictates.

She can wage biological warfare for she has scientists capable of preparing diseases for use against people, plants, and animals, and trained secret agents who could spread them.

It is certain that she has the major war gases, including the new and deadly nerve gas developed by German Experts who were taken into Russia at the end of the last war.

That is not all we must plan against. In some types of biological warfare fifth columnists could begin work without waiting for a war to start. Saboteurs, too, could attack from within and wreck our defenses and war production output.

Hit Without Warning

All these enemy weapons could hit us without warning.

The outcome of modern war is not necessarily decided by armies in the field. Wars today can be won or lost on the home front. The home front cannot be hidden, it cannot retreat—not if we are to survive as a free people.

Millions of Americans must be trained in civil defense before this country can be sure it is ready for enemy attack. Meanwhile, that attack might come at any moment.

We have no time to lose in preparation to ward off such an attack. Your home, your job, your family, your own life may be at stake.

Civil defense is the sure way—the only organized way—for survival on the home front.

Rural America Has Important Part in Protecting Home Front

(Second in the series)

Even if forewarned of war, our armed forces cannot prevent attack, for there is no sure way of keeping enemy planes from getting through our defenses.

The enemy's first objective would be to upset the war efforts of the civilian population, as well as to destroy property and to kill and injure people. His aim would be to make you quit, leave your jobs, desert your homes and start panic among you. Panic can take a tremendous toll of lives. It also can bring production to a stand-still.

It is the task of civil defense to organize and train millions of Americans so that each one will be prepared to render the best protective service at the moment it is needed.

Your aim should be to accept that training so that you will know how to rescue the trapped and injured, know how to work with volunteer fire-fighting units, know how to prevent panic and know how to perform any of the specific duties of civil defense, particularly those you have indicated, in your training, that you are best qualified to do.

There are ways to save thousands of people from the effects of blast, radioactivity and heat from the atomic bomb. There are ways to take shelter, to rescue the trapped and injured, and ways to cut fire loses to a minimum. Organized civil defense can do those things.

The atomic bomb is too expensive to use purposely on a farm community. However, this relative freedom from attack only adds to the responsibility of the people who live in such areas. Civilians away from the target area will be better able, mentally and physically, to cope with situations of disaster.

Farm People Equipped

With cars, trucks and tractors available, farm people are well equipped to aid any stricken area within their reach. Mobile support, rescue and evacuation work are phases of civil defense that rural folk are especially qualified to do. To do any of them without confusion and delay, you must be organized and trained.

It is imperative that farm families learn about biological warfare and how to watch for it. While you are protecting your family and your livestock from infections and your crops from infestations, you are cooperating with the civil defense program.

There are ways of keeping disease from spreading, and of protecting our food and water supplies. Civil defense, working with existing health agencies and physicians, attends to that job.

We should be prepared to cope with poison gases. And we can be, for there are good defenses against them. There are ways of sharply reducing losses from gas attacks, and civil defense provides the best answers.

Civil defense services are organized to bring in help from outside, and to get a stricken city back into working order in the shortest possible time. It provides food, shelter and medical care for victims of attack.

Defense Takes Planning

Civil defense takes planning, organization, and a lot of hard work. There are jobs for you. Find out where you can serve your family, your community and yourself the best. Then volunteer for the work you are best suited to do.

Civil defense cannot protect every life and every home, but it will save thousands of lives—maybe your life or the life of someone dear to you.

TWO

"Paul Revere on Wheels"

Our American front lies open to attack as never before. Civilians on the home front are as vulnerable to attack as soldiers on the firing line. Our backyards of today are the potential front lines of tomorrow.—Millard Caldwell, FCDA Administrator, 1952[1]

As the caravan of ten 32-foot "trailmobiles" maneuvered down Rhode Island Avenue in Washington, D.C., on Monday, January 7, 1952, cars navigating through traffic slowed down as pedestrians hurrying along crowded sidewalks stopped to gaze, it can be imagined, with some curious, some excited, and others simply indifferent. Army personnel on loan from Fort Eustus in Virginia drove each truck, which had "Alert America" emblazoned in red, white, and blue on each side, with the increasingly familiar "CD" bridging the two words. With the temperature in the mid–30s under partly cloudy skies, the caravan wound its way through downtown, finally stopping in front of the Departmental Auditorium, located in the Federal Triangle on Connecticut Avenue between 12th Street NW and 14th Street NW, site of the Alert America exhibit. A color guard representing the various armed services stood at attention, as the Second Army's drum and bugle corps entertained the crowd. Major General Robert Rainey, director of operations for the U.S. Air Force, and John Fondahl, metropolitan police captain and civil defense director for the nation's capital, then spoke before the doors opened to the public.[2]

Many Washingtonians along the route had been anticipating the caravan for weeks. Fondahl had actively solicited local support from businesses, organizations, and the media with great success. Newspapers had published articles about the December "out-of-town tryout" of Alert America in Norfolk and Richmond, Virginia, in preparation for its official opening in the nation's capital. *The Washington Post* had been reporting on the upcoming exhibit and many of its advertisers, such as Hecht's Department Store, had been promoting Alert America. In addition, local television stations and radio stations had broadcast more than 1,000 announcements, while Boy Scouts distributed promotional materials to area hotels, theaters, and stores. The city's Board of Commissioners had also proclaimed January 7–12 as Civil Defense Week.

As people watched the trucks roll to a stop, their expectation for the unloading of materials no doubt heightened, only to be disappointed because the exhibit had already been set up, ready to welcome visitors. The trucks had traversed their way through the city merely as part of the publicity campaign to increase awareness of the "The Show That May Save Your Life," the exhibit's promotional theme.[3] The auditorium, now filled with some 7,200 square feet of displays about the atomic bomb, atomic energy, and civil defense, had been dedicated by President Franklin Roosevelt in 1935 and served as the site for the signing of the North Atlantic Treaty, creating the North Atlantic Treaty Organization (NATO), in 1949. Renamed the Andrew W. Mellon Auditorium in 1987, it stands less than a mile from the White House, the 1952 home of President Harry Truman, the man ultimately responsible for creating Alert America.[4]

The Federal Civil Defense Administration launched its campaign to promote a national civil defense program immediately after beginning operations in January 1951. Despite its efforts through the first half of year, however, the debate over the importance and viability of civil defense was anything but settled. An editorial in *The Bridgeport* (Connecticut) *Telegram*, for example, called the atomic threat illusory, going on to say, "Only an idiotic, fanatic foreign government would start an attack which would result in its own complete destruction through our retaliatory action."[5] William Perkinson, staff correspondent at *The Evening Sun* in Baltimore, Maryland, leveled his comments on the sad state of civil defense, writing, "One word—'pathetic'—can be used to describe the present status of this nation's civil-defense program. Two words—'public apathy'—can be used to describe the reason why no major city in the United States has made more than a start to prepare for the destruction that would inevitably follow an atomic attack."[6]

An editorial in *The Philadelphia Inquirer* also focused its diatribe on the civil defense program itself, rather than on its relevance: "It is no news to anyone that the Federal Civil Defense program, as it stands, has about the same consistency as fog. Fog, indeed, would be better, as it at least would blind enemy fliers." It then urged Congress to find out why civil defense was moving so slowly across the nation and how it could be implemented more quickly and made effective "before it is too little and too late, again."[7]

Based on these editorials and similar ones appearing across the nation, it is not difficult to understand why the FCDA's 12-member National Advisory Council, which included governors, mayors, publishers, and other civic leaders, concluded that there was an "appalling" lack of understanding about the dangers of an atomic war. The council stressed that civil defense cannot be mounted without advance preparation. "Civil defense must be ready at all times to meet any need which might arise," the council said. "Once the bombs hit, it will be too late."[8] To overcome the nation's apathy and lack of understanding, the council called for an "alert America" campaign—a mass educational program—"to inform the American people of their grave danger and the need for civil defense for their protection." The council went on to declare:

> Failure of the public as a whole, and the Congress and other legislative bodies to accept the terrifying facts of what inadequate civil defense would mean to our country in case of enemy attack is appalling. Every force for good and for patriotic endeavor must be brought to bear now, in this campaign to alert America.... Without a sound, large-scale civil defense program as a co-partner with the military, America could lose the next war.[9]

Frederick Payne, Republican governor of Maine, was among the council members who cautioned against the belief that only target cities would be hit; rather, the council emphasized, "No part of America is immune." Other members at the meeting included Frank Lausche, governor of Ohio; Luther Youngdahl, governor of Minnesota; Mayor William Devin of Seattle; Mayor David Lawrence of Pittsburgh; Robert Smith, publisher of the *Los Angeles Daily News*; Silliman Evans, publisher of *The Tennessean*; Dr. Mary Bethune, vice president of the National Association for the Advancement of Colored People (NAACP); Dr. Lillian Gilbreth, construction and management engineer; and George Richardson, secretary-treasurer of the International Association of Firefighters, AFL.[10] Meeting at the same time, the FCDA's Religious Advisory Committee presented its own outline of how organized religion could contribute to civil defense, recommending that each governor or state director of civil defense appoint a religious advisory committee. In addition, each locality should establish a religious executive committee with a chairman serving as a member of the primary civil defense organization. Msgr. Paul Tanner, assistant general secretary of the National Catholic Welfare Conference, told attendees that clergymen must ensure that "the right kind of people" volunteered for civil defense.[11]

Three months later, on October 15, 1951, the National Advisory Council issued its "Alert America Progress Report," which outlined six major activities to be managed by the FCDA's Office of Public Affairs: fact finding and evaluation; general public education; special projects; current information; technical information; and public liaison.[12] The first activity found that people knew about personal survival, but they had little knowledge about local volunteering activities. This reinforced the importance of the campaign to make Americans "alert" to the need of volunteering for civil defense. This, in turn, moved into perhaps the most important activity: to educate the public. The council's report called for "informing some 154 million American citizens about the fundamentals of self-protection from the various types of weapons which might be employed by an enemy against our people." Its primary effort would be the "Personal Survival Series," nine booklets covering personal survival, biological warfare, chemical warfare, what civil defense is, emergency action to save lives, firefighting for householders, preparing your home, psychological warfare defense, and "beyond the bull's-eye." The booklets would be supplemented by motion pictures, radio and television, newspaper and periodical news and features, and speakers' kits. To accomplish the goal of reaching all Americans with little expense, the Office of Public Affairs planned to enlist the support of the private sector as well as state and local governments to reprint and distribute copies of civil defense publications.[13]

An example cited by the council's report was the booklet *Survival Under Atomic Attack*, published in October 1950. Through cooperation between the FCDA and state and local governments as well as private industry, some twenty million reprints were now in circulation across the nation and several foreign countries. Civil defense educational films also were being made and distributed by the motion picture industry at no expense to the government. The FCDA released the film version of *Survival Under Atomic Attack*, narrated by Edward R. Murrow, CBS news commentator, in April 1951, and more than 4,000 copies sold in the first six months. Other films slated for production that year included *Fire Fighting for Householders*, *What You Should Know About Biological Warfare*, *Our Cities Must Fight*, *Emergency Action to Save Lives*, *Poison Gasses*, *Civil Defense for Schools*, and *Civil Defense for Industry*.[14]

Once the population was educated, state and local governments activated, and private industry mobilized, the campaign needed to turn its attention to special projects designed specifically to attract fifteen to twenty million civil defense volunteers. The center of this effort: the Alert America exhibit, which was to launch in December and travel throughout all forty-eight states over seven months. Actually, there were to be three identical exhibits, each transported by a convoy of ten semi-trailer trucks or "trailmobiles." The first convoy would begin from Washington, D.C., and travel through the Eastern Seaboard; a second convoy would cover the Midwest; and a third convoy would begin in Washington state, then travel down the West Coast and turn east and continue through the South. The plan called for the exhibit to be shown one to three days in each city, with an emphasis on the fifty-four target cities.

To ensure the convoy's success, the campaign used the "full mobilization of all the resources of advertising," which included three tasks. The first one featured the creation of a local recruiting kit, consisting of advertising, publicity, and promotional materials, to be distributed to 2,500 local civil defense directors. The second task, and one central to the overall campaign, was retaining the New York–based advertising agency, Batten, Barton, Durstine, and Osborn (BBDO), as the task force agency, with Edward Gerbic, advertising manager for Johnson & Johnson, serving as the volunteer coordinator. The third task, according to the report, was "the creation of the awareness of the threat to our national security from airborne attack and other atomic weapons and the attainment of public recognition of civil defense as the co-equal partner of the military in the common defense of the country."[15]

The campaign's fourth activity involved the dissemination of current information about the atomic threat and the importance of civil defense to magazines and newspapers, at press conferences, in interviews, on radio and television, in printed materials, and through research. The report cited articles appearing in the Hearst newspapers, *Life* magazine, and *Redbook*, as well as a full-color graphic feature titled "If an A-Bomb Falls," developed in cooperation with *The Washington Post* and Commercial Comics, Inc. In addition, more than 10,000 newspapers were offered a series of articles written by the FCDA's Millard Caldwell and based on the booklet, *This Is Civil Defense*. Caldwell and other FCDA personnel also aided the cause by appearing as guests on such television programs as *Meet the Press, American Inventory, Battle Report, Facts We Face, It's Up to You, Johns Hopkins Science Review*, and *Washington Report*. The FCDA worked in cooperation with NBC-TV on the production of *Survival*, consisting of six half-hour programs that ran from July 8 to August 19, 1951. Following these broadcasts, the agency sent a kinescope version of *Survival* to 107 television stations to use as public-service programs to the roughly 23 percent of American households that could watch. The FCDA also distributed a radio script kit, titled "This Is CD," to 2,800 radio stations throughout the nation. The kit included thirty-two pages of spot announcements, question-and-answer scripts, and dramatic scripts. Working with the FCDA's Radio Branch, commentator Frank Edwards promoted civil defense several times a week on his nationally syndicated radio program.[16]

On September 15, the FCDA conducted its first experimental use of closed-circuit television for mass training and education. Using a studio at WMAL-TV in Washington, D.C., the program was transmitted to movie theaters in four eastern cities, where civil defense volunteers, guest observers, and press representatives watched. The program featured training demonstrations of rescue operations; caring for a lost child and reuniting him with his parents in a disaster situation; and the attack warning system. The program incorporated visual aid techniques such as film, charts, animations, and live action. The program also used two-way communication for a question-and-answer session, with participants able to hear and respond.[17]

The Girl Scouts and Boy Scouts actively participated in Alert America. Scouts distributed promotional materials in advance of the exhibit and assisted as guides and hosts during the exhibit (National Archives).

The fifth activity, technical information, formed the central mission of the FCDA until 1958 when the Office of Civil and Defense Mobilization (OCDM) superseded it. The Public Affairs Office oversaw the production, publication, and distribution of a wide variety of civil defense materials, including administrative guides, instructor guides, handbooks, posters, and manuals. "These technical books," read the Progress Report, "are used for organizing, equipping, and training the 15–20 million Americans needed in the major volunteer services, such as Warden, Fire, Police, Health, Welfare, Engineering, Rescue, Communications, and Transportation."[18]

Public liaison, the sixth activity, became essential to attracting these volunteers, with the FCDA working with national organizations representing 100 million Americans, or two-thirds of the total population. "A campaign to 'Alert America' to be fully effective," read the report, "must appeal to and receive cooperation from the leadership represented by such organizations [which] afford ready-made channels of information to the 'grassroots' level."

The plan called for establishing joint activities with these organizations, citing the Religious Advisory Committee as an example of how "a few leaders, generally representative of an area, may bring their skills and energies to bear on the National civil defense program."[19] Among the many organizations lending their support were the American Legion, Veterans of Foreign Wars, Boy Scouts of America, American Hotel Association, and the Parent Teacher Association, which coordinated the publication of a pamphlet distributed to more than 28,000 local PTA chapters. Also in its first year of operation, the FCDA made presentations at various national conferences, including the National Education Association, National Fire Protection Association, American Society of Newspaper Editors, American Federation of Labor, American Red Cross, Advertising Council, American Medical Association, National Urban League, National Congress of Parents and Teachers, American Association of School Administrators, National Sheriffs Association, Municipal Finance Officers Association, American Association of University Women, and National Defense Transportation Association, to name a few.[20]

The Progress Report concluded with a summary of results from the educational program. The report pointed out that FCDA publications were being circulated through newspaper reprints, with its booklet, *Survival Under Atomic Attack*, published in full-page form by more than 200 newspapers. California announced plans to reprint three million copies of *Household First Aid Kit* and place the pamphlet in every home in the state. Radio stations in Alabama, Georgia, and Minnesota implemented regular broadcasts on civil defense, and many other states displayed photos, charts, and related materials about the atomic bomb and civil defense at state fairs and other events.[21]

Unquestionably, the FCDA achieved many of its aims in the educational program. Yet when it came time for Congress to approve President Truman's appropriations request for a national civil defense program, it balked. Caldwell had placed the need for fiscal year 1952 at $732 million, but Truman reduced this amount to $535 million. Even then, the House cut the president's request to $65.3 million, the Senate approved $97.6 million, and the final appropriation was $74.9 million, just 14 percent of Truman's request.[22] In response to the decision by Congress, Truman said, "There are no bargain basements where we can pick up America's security at cut-rate prices.... Civil defense is a vital part of our mobilization effort. It is reckless to evade, under the pretense of economy, the national responsibility for initiating a balanced federal-state civil defense program."[23] Moreover, the drastic reduction in funding had a ripple effect at the state level, as many states followed suit in reducing appropriations for civil defense. In Tennessee, the state's mayors met to decide if they should even "get out" of civil defense altogether. In Missouri, the House voted down authorization of $655,300 in state funds to match federal funds for civil defense, and the city of St. Louis appropriated only $125,000 for civil defense for 1952, when the city needed $1.3 million in funding for its civil defense program, according to Raymond Tucker, the city's civil defense director.[24]

At an August meeting called by Caldwell, the FCDA's National Advisory Council issued a warning that civil defense would only gain the support of Americans if they were convinced that being better informed, organized, and trained to protect lives and industry would result in the winning of a major war. The lack of support by Congress and the Department of Defense, however, was working against this objective, and both entities needed to reassess their commitment to the nation's defense. "If military might alone cannot win the next war," read the council's statement, "if a prepared public is essential to military success, those facts must be made known now by the Congress [and] Defense Department." The council also stressed that an effective civil defense program was both an essential and an integral part of the nation's defense. Civil defense "must become a part of the civic might of every American community and remain so until international peace becomes a reality."[25]

The council was not alone in its reaction to the cut in funding. An editorial in the *St. Louis Post-Dispatch* pointed out the conflicting message being sent by Congress, which "has done a wretched job of dealing with its responsibilities for civil defense." On the one hand, it approved massive amounts of money for the armed services "on the assumption that this nation must be prepared against a possible attack," but it cut funding for civil defense, thus "behaving as though there were all the time in the world to get ready and the attack might never come."[26] According to Secretary of the Army Frank Pace, there was not time. In an October 1951 meeting with the Atomic Energy Commission (AEC), Pace told the commission, "The threat of Russian aggression is real and immediate and we cannot permit ourselves to be caught midstream without the necessary means to protect ourselves."[27] Caldwell pledged to ask Congress for more funds in early 1952, commenting, "If I knew we have five years to prepare for atomic raids on our cities, I would be optimistic about the progress which civil defense has made in the past few months. But we cannot treat civil defense strictly as a long-range program. The danger is both immediate and long-range."[28]

Despite the lack of adequate funding, President Truman, the AEC, and the leaders of the joint congressional committee on atomic energy formally approved the Alert America convoy in October 1951 as described in the FCDA's Progress Report. Plans called for it to open in Washington, D.C., in December, with three convoys then spanning the nation to educate Americans about the atomic bomb and solicit volunteers for civil defense at the state and local levels. At the press conference to announce the convoy, Caldwell acknowledged that "more and more responsible citizens are recognizing the facts of life," but he went on to say that the average citizen was not yet "fully alert."[29] In his syndicated column, Robert S. Allen told readers, "You will soon have the chance to take a good look at the most murderous weapon in the world—the A-bomb. Perhaps even feel it, if you want to."[30]

As an immediate demonstration of support for the Alert America campaign, Captain E. A. Haisch, civil defense coordinator for Los Angeles County in California, proclaimed October 14–20 as Civil Defense Week, to be observed by all cities and communities in the county. He said an Alert America campaign was essential to inform the public of the mounting dangers in the new atomic age. "The need for civil defense does not depend on isolated world incidents or on the daily headlines," Haisch said. "The need for civil defense will continue so long as there are forces of aggression in the world. Every force for good and for patriotic endeavor must be brought to bear now in this campaign to alert America. Every organized group must act fully."[31] An editorial in *The Newark* (Ohio) *Advocate* also endorsed the FCDA's plans for Alert America, writing, "The project may help to bring home to all the people the urgent need to prepare so that any emergency will find us ready and capable of meeting it. We hope that peace can be preserved and that bombs will never fall on American cities. But preparation for civil defense can ensure that casualties will be kept at a minimum if the worst should come."[32]

To move forward with its plans, FCDA solicited the Freedoms Foundation of Valley Forge to be a partner. The Freedoms Foundation had been formed in 1949 as a highly patriotic organization that promoted moral values, constitutional rights, God, and good deeds that benefited others and the nation. Each year, it awarded more than $100,000 to individuals and schools with its Freedom Awards. Kenneth Wells, president of the foundation, was receptive to the Alert America concept but recommended that a new organization be formed solely to be responsible for designing, building, and operating the exhibit. Wells became president of the new Valley Forge Foundation, formed in October 1951. Serving as chairman was Lieutenant General Elwood Quesada, considered an expert in atomic energy having been commander of Joint Task Force Three at the Eniwetok atomic tests in the late 1940s. Dorothy Houghton, president of the General Federation of Women's Clubs, became vice chairman. Other board members included representatives from Wall Street, business, unions, universities, and religious groups. An executive from the American Heritage Foundation, sponsor of the highly successful Freedom Train that crisscrossed the nation displaying some 130 historical documents from the National Archives from 1947 to 1949, became a vice president. This addition to the board helped entice Edward H. Burdick Associates, the firm that designed the Freedom Train, to oversee the design and production of the Alert America exhibit. The AEC advised on the exhibit's content. General Motors, Ford, and International Harvester agreed to provide

In addition to the emphasis on civil defense, the Valley Forge Foundation and its president, Kenneth Wells, believed strongly that Americans needed to be reminded of their responsibility in preserving the American way of life and the fundamental belief in God. These tenets were incorporated into the Alert America exhibit (National Archives).

cars and trucks; Standard Oil contributed gas and oil; the Army provided an officer and sixteen enlisted men for each of the three convoys; and the Advertising Council agreed to create promotional materials.[33]

Historian David Krugler argues that Alert America's sponsors recognized the importance of framing civil defense as a military necessity and as a civic duty. "If civil defense appeared overly militaristic," he has written, "Americans might recoil at the thought of volunteering; worse, they might infer that if homeland defense was so vital, then the armed services should be responsible for it. If civil defense was too civil, however, if it lacked the skills and discipline paramilitary programs could impose, then doubts might arise about its efficacy."[34]

According to Wells, the Valley Forge Foundation's primary mission was to promote the importance of civil defense and to achieve the widest possible participation by American citizens. Specifically, he outlined four fundamental goals:

1. To emphasize the fact that civil defense is the constant guardian of the American way of life based on a fundamental belief in God, on constitutional government designed to serve the people, and our indivisible bundle of political and economic rights;
2. To help awaken all Americans to the urgent need for strong civil defense and to encourage each to enlist for such specialized training as may be possible;
3. To help inspire in all civil defense organizations the highest possible morale; and
4. To get every family, factory, farm, business and institution in America to set itself up as a citadel of civil defense, working in full cooperation with local civil defense authorities.[35]

Citing the importance of these goals, Caldwell dubbed Alert America as "Paul Revere on Wheels," in reference to the Revolutionary War patriot who rode through the countryside in 1775 warning the populace that the British were coming. Caldwell believed getting Americans to personally participate in the nation's civil defense program was so vast that no single government agency, including the FCDA, could succeed. "We need help," he said, "not only from all other agencies of government—federal, state and local—but from every national group and every medium of communication, to cover every corner of America and every phase of our national life."[36]

The FCDA issued the official announcement for the nationwide convoy on December 12, 1951, and newspapers across the nation picked up the release. The first two exhibits were held in December in Norfolk and Richmond, Virginia. Each served as a location of an out-of-town tryout prior to the exhibit opening in Washington, D.C. Norfolk hosted the exhibit the first week of

December; it then traveled to Richmond in mid–December for a four-day run. The *Daily Press* in Newport News, Virginia, reported, "If what happened in Norfolk during the showing there ... can be viewed as a pattern, then the Alert America operation will accomplish what it is trying to do—get folks to volunteer for civil defense work." The reference was to the fact that more than 10 percent of visitors in Norfolk had signed up as civil defense volunteers.[37]

As the caravan entered the nation's capital that Monday in January 1952, some two million Americans already had volunteered for civil defense, but the nation needed more than 17 million, according to the FCDA. Its *1951 Annual Report* identified a "trained civil defense volunteer corps" as one of its four requisites for a strong national civil defense program. The others included a well-informed public that understands what to do when disaster strikes; adequate tools and supplies for any major disaster; and "a high state of readiness—national, state, and local—for maximum use of all existing resources and personnel."[38]

The agency had based its first objective on building awareness; and within weeks of the formal unveiling of the Alert America tour, newspapers around the country began publicizing the dates the exhibit would visit their respective towns and cities. In December, five months in advance of the exhibit, *The Lansing* (Michigan) *State Journal* announced Alert America would stop in Detroit, Grand Rapids, and Lansing in April. In its December 30, 1951, issue, *The Greenville* (South Carolina) *News* ran a headline reading, "Graphic Display Showing How to Survive Atomic Warfare to Be Here February 7–10." Also that month, E. H. Bradshaw, director of civil defense for Jackson, Mississippi, released a statement picked up by the state's newspapers that Jackson would be the only city in Mississippi to host the exhibit, to run March 14–16. A month before arriving in Ohio, *The Evening Independent* in Massillon, Ohio, announced that Akron, Canton, Cleveland, Columbus, and Youngstown had been placed on the list of cities for the "Paul Revere on Wheels" exhibit, opening in Canton for a four-day showing in February. *The Portsmouth* (New Hampshire) *Herald* also publicized the convoy a month before its February stopover in Manchester. In the South, *The Anniston* (Alabama) *Star* reported in its issue of January 22, 1952, that the Alert America convoy would be in Birmingham in March, while *The Tennessean* headlined a story titled, "Alert America Exhibit, Stressing Home Mobilization, to Visit Here," in its January 9 issue announcing that Nashville would host the exhibit in March.[39]

Two days after his 1952 State of the Union address, President Truman visited the Alert America exhibit in a private showing on Friday morning, January 12, accompanied by several aides and members of the media. By all accounts, the exhibit had been a major success. Caldwell, speaking at the opening ceremonies on Monday, set the tone by saying, "Whether you die or whether I do will depend to a large extent on how well we have learned what we can do to protect ourselves and others." Two hours after the opening, some 700 people had attended the exhibit, with 370—including President Truman—signing the "Count on me" pledge cards, which indicated their willingness to learn the necessary skills for self-preservation and to consider volunteering for civil defense.[40] After seeing the exhibit, the president noted that civil defense officials had worked hard against the odds. "They have sometimes fought apathy in their own official circles," he said, "particularly in our own Congress. We have not won the war against time. We have no right to feel safe militarily or on the home front.... There are no shortcuts to civil defense preparedness. It is a tough, unpleasant but grimly necessary job."[41]

By the end of the week in its Washington, D.C., debut, Alert America had attracted more than 32,000 visitors. *The Washington Post* wrote: "The exhibit itself is so arranged that the effect is cumulative on the visitor as he passes through it. He sees the destruction of a city, of crops, of life. Then he sees how he might save himself, his family, his neighbor and areas of his city from fire ... or how he can help, by being part of Civil Defense, to rescue another city or himself from the ravages of atomic bombing.[42] Bill Henry, a newspaper columnist who had been with Truman on his tour, acknowledged that the exhibit presented "horrible possibilities of destruction," but he came away with the conclusion that the show's ultimate purpose was "to inspire you to participate in civil defense as just one of the ways of insuring for your-self and your children the wonderful characteristics which make life in this country so much better than life anywhere else on the planet."[43]

The Alert America campaign, the government hoped, would enlighten Americans about atomic energy, especially its destructive power, and con-vince them to learn more about self-preservation skills and civil defense. Working in tandem, the FCDA and Valley Forge Foundation unquestionably succeeded in building greater awareness of the atomic bomb and the impor-tance of civil defense among millions of Americans. Moreover, the words "Alert America" became a phrase often used with civil defense and other patriotic activities. Local organizations, as an example, presented talks and programs around "Alert America." Organizations and schools continued to hold meetings to watch the survival film, *Alert America*. James Conant, pres-ident of Harvard University, headed an organization created to alert America to the communist threat. The Boy Scouts even created Alert America Day as part of its "Get Out the Vote" campaign for the 1952 presidential election.[44]

On the eleventh anniversary of the attack on Pearl Harbor, December 7, 1952, President Truman addressed a national radio audience to once again emphasize the dire necessity of being on the alert for a surprise attack—an

An important objective of Alert America was to educate Americans about their central role in civil defense. This poster, titled "Civil Defense Is You," provides a breakdown of the various levels of civil defense: national, regional, state, and community (National Archives).

atomic attack. "Because of the immense destructive power of the atomic bomb," he told listeners, "we must maintain vigilance so that our cities and our industries will be less vulnerable to devastating attack. I therefore call upon all citizens who reside in communities which have been designated as possible enemy air approach areas to volunteer their services for this vital task."[45] Truman was referring to the target cities visited that year by Alert America, beginning in Wilmington, Delaware, and ending in Salt Lake City, Utah. These 82 cities had received the message in the most dramatic way that the nation faced a real atomic threat that required all Americans to learn civil defense.

* * *

U.S. Needs Civil Defense
By Millard Caldwell, FCDA Administrator

A-Bomb Would Kill All Persons Unprotected in One-Half Mile

(Third in the series)

Don't be surprised if you hear a siren blowing and learn that your community is being alerted for an imaginary atom bomb raid. If it is organized, within minutes, air raid wardens, first-aid teams, doctors, nurses, emergency rescue squads, and other civil defense units will spring into action.

Hundreds of cities, towns, and small communities in the United States today are making sure that they will be ready to do their part if, and when, the real atom bomb hits them or cities near them. These imaginary raids have shown what well-trained and coordinated civil defense personnel and equipment can do against enemy attack.

However, don't act as if the alert signal you hear is just an imaginary air raid. Act as you have been trained to act. Do whatever you have been told to do. Civil defense prepares you for that split-second decision of knowing how to act—what to do.

Within one-half mile of the center of an A-bomb explosion almost everyone without proper protection will be killed. Within the next half-mile fifty per cent of the population will not survive. From one to one-and-a-half miles away eighty-five per cent will live. Beyond two miles from the center of the explosion you will survive—but there will be work for you to do. Civil defense prepares you for that, too.

With the proper protection YOU may live, but thousands will be killed instantly and many others will be wounded and in need of immediate care. Every street within the major damage area will be completely blocked with rubble, and hundreds of persons trapped or buried in the wreckage. Fires will start within a matter of minutes—in many places at once.

Food Supply Destroyed

These are the main things which will happen, but there are others. For instance, a large part of the city's food supply might be destroyed or cut off. The water supply might be knocked out. Regular communications might stop entirely. Much of the transportation system certainly would stop. Thousands of survivors would suddenly find themselves homeless, without food, clothing, shelter, or money.

What could happen without civil defense?

Ask the Japanese—anyone of the few survivors at Hiroshima or Nagasaki. They had almost no civil defense as we know it now. When atomic bombs hit their cities, the population was almost completely unprepared. Result: the people panicked wildly. Many thousands were needlessly killed or hurt, families were scattered, and property was lost or badly damaged.

Thousands were left homeless with no one to care for them. The wounded and helpless, who might have lived, died because proper civil defense was not organized to save them.

Factories Would Be Useless

But there was something of even greater importance to a nation which was fighting for its life. The fact that there was no civil defense meant that the factories left standing after the atomic blast could not operate.

Without civil defense a nation is helpless. With it, people and production centers can get up and fight back. Casualties can be cut at least in half. Our nation can live again and fight back to win!

Civil defense is self defense for you and for our country.

One First-Aid Station Would Need 200 Workers
(Fourth in the series)

The most staggering civil defense problems are public education, training, and organization. All must be solved without delay. Immediate training for some 15,000,000 Americans, and intensive education in self-protection for 135,000,000 others are vital. Here are some facts and figures for you to think about.

Try to picture the number of trained workers that would be needed to handle an attack situation. As an example, a single first-aid station should consist of almost 200 workers. They could handle about 600 wounded people in 24 hours.

To care for those injured by one Hiroshima-size atomic bomb, nearly 100 such first-aid stations would be needed. That adds up to more than 20,000 first-aid workers needed for each atomic bomb—but it doesn't include hospital staffs.

An engineering service as large or even larger would be needed to clear away the rubble before first-aiders could reach the wounded. A highly trained rescue service would be needed to get people out of wrecked or burning buildings. A large and efficient supply service would be needed to bring food, clothing, and medicine.

Job of Helping Homeless

There would be other jobs of putting out fires, restoring utilities, caring for the homeless, gathering families together again, feeding the people, and getting the factories and community life rolling once more.

Most of the ways of meeting atomic disaster are not new or different, except in size. The biggest problem is to prepare ourselves to handle disasters greater than any that ever have struck the United States.

Remember what you read in the previous article about the Japanese at Hiroshima and Nagasaki. They were almost completely unprepared—and what happened? Their indifference in organizing an efficient civil defense should be a grim warning to us.

Here are some really important things to remember. They make up civil defense:

1. A possible enemy has the weapons now to attack us.

2. There is a defense against any attack, including atomic warfare, and civil defense is a big part of it.

3. At least 15,000,000 Americans must be trained in civil defense, and every American must learn the facts of survival.

4. Without civil defense, your city would be helpless; with civil defense, your losses could be cut in half.

5. Your State and local civil defense directors *must have your sup-port*. They have an important job for you no matter where you live.

6. Read the official civil defense booklets right away. You can double your chances of survival if you know what to do.

7. Civil defense is up to you. Get into civil defense right now.

The biggest problem before us now is to be prepared on the home front—and that problem can be met only through civil defense. Each of us must have a job to do if trouble comes—and must know how to do it.

THREE

Crossing the Delaware

Civil defense is a question of education alone. It is a matter of vital interest to all, as it is a question of learning to save your own life. You can't regiment people into it—there has got to be a desire on their part.—M. duPont Lee, Civil Defense Director, Wilmington, Delaware, 1951[1]

Shortly after the Alert America convoy left Wilmington, Delaware, where close to 11,000 people had visited the exhibit during its four days on display, Millard Caldwell, administrator of the Federal Civil Defense Administration, sent a telegram to the state's Office of Civil Defense. The telegram offered Caldwell's personal congratulations to M. (Maurice) duPont Lee, the city's civil defense director, as well as to the entire community, for promoting Alert America, held January 20–23, 1952, at the State Armory. Wilmington Mayor James Hearn had appointed Lee to the position in June 1950, six months following Lee's retirement from DuPont Company after 42 years, ending his career as general advisor to the chief engineer. Lee, already serving as president of the city's Board of Park Commissioners, accepted the newly created, nonpaying position to help build a civil defense organization to prepare the city for an atomic attack.[2] Over his two-year tenure, Lee worked diligently to establish a respected and effective civil defense program, and had been credited by the state's Civil Defense Advisory Council for creating an excellent organization—recognition also offered by Caldwell. "Reports received regarding the splendid Wilmington civil defense organization sponsorship of and arrangements for the Alert America exhibit are most gratifying," his telegram read.[3]

Wilmington represented the first stop for one of the three Alert America convoys, and was among the few cities on the FCDA's travel schedule with a population of less than 200,000 people. The 1950 census, in fact, placed the city's population at just 110,000. Wilmington, however, was the home of the DuPont Company, which had contributed to the Manhattan Project, the

59

SEE the ALERT AMERICA convoy

You've heard about it ... you've read about it. Now don't miss it! The *Alert America* Convoy is a show you'll never forget. Shows you what atomic energy is all about ... its peacetime uses for factory, farm and medicine. Its threat as a weapon of war.

SEE the inside story of atomic war

As never before, the real nature of modern warfare is dramatized before your eyes. Movies. Three-dimensional exhibits. Dioramas. You'll see what a single A-bomb could do to our community. You'll see what "Nerve Gas" and germ warfare are. You'll see how Civil Defense protects people and production.

SEE how you can protect yourself and your family

The *Alert America* Convoy helps you meet the threat of enemy aggression ... shows you the steps you can take, right now, to safeguard yourself and your family.

Continuous Showing
10 A. M. to 11 P. M.

STATE ARMORY
10TH AND DUPONT STS.—WILMINGTON

PUBLISHED AS A PUBLIC SERVICE BY

GREENWOOD BOOK SHOP

Delaware Trust Building—Fairfax Shopping Center

World War II program that developed the atomic bomb, by designing, building, and operating the Hanford, Washington, plutonium-producing plant. Then, in 1950, the company, one of the city's largest employers, agreed to build the Savannah River Plant in South Carolina as part of the nation's program to build a hydrogen bomb. The FCDA undoubtedly chose Wilmington in part because of DuPont's role in the country's atomic program. Moreover, Wilmington was Delaware's most populous city and the only major target area identified by the FCDA. Plus, the state had a well-organized and proactive civil defense program.

Governor Elbert Carvel had established the state's Office of Civil Defense in June 1950 for the purpose of implementing the necessary measures to minimize the impact of an enemy attack during war and a disaster in a time of peace. Although the Office of Civil Defense had made initial progress to enlist volunteers, focusing primarily on an eight-mile radius around Wilmington,

Newspaper advertising such as this one for Greenwood Book Shop provided a detailed description of the Alert America exhibit in Wilmington, Delaware, the first city on the cross-country tour and considered a major success by the FCDA.

the city soon launched its own initiative. Three months after Lee's appointment, Andrew Kavanaugh, Wilmington's superintendent of public safety, announced that the city would create a 1,000-member force of auxiliary police and firefighters as part of the state's civil defense program. The plan called for the city to be divided into six major defense zones, with each zone having three to four precincts, all with a full quota of auxiliary police and firefighters.[4] Two months later, Carvel acted again by calling for "thousands of volunteers" to join civil defense groups in communities throughout the state. "We are preparing now," he said, "for the possibility of an all-out conflict, and by wise and sound action during the months ahead, I feel certain that we can build an integrated program which will provide adequate protection for the people of our state. With each of us devoting ourselves to a strong individual effort, we will in turn strengthen our nation's security and survive to live again in a world of peace."[5]

In January 1951, Carvel announced a flexible civil defense program giving him wider authority to address emergency situations, and provided for the formation of the Civil Defense Advisory Council with the governor appointing members. The program also included two key provisions: There could be no political activity in civil defense operations; and both volunteers and salaried civil defense employees were required to take a loyalty oath declaring their patriotism and repudiation of the Communist Party.[6] The governor also extended to the Office of Civil Defense the authority to enter into mutual defense pacts with nearby states; and by the end of year, Delaware had formed nine mutual aid civil defense pacts—more than any other state.[7] Delaware's commitment to a strong civil defense organization again was validated with the introduction of a mobile support unit just prior to the opening of the Alert America exhibit. The unit, described as "a self-contained unit prepared to cope with any emergency," included fire and demolition equipment, first aid and medical supplies, and ladders and tools.[8] In short, the state of Delaware and the city of Wilmington, under Lee's direction, demonstrated a strong commitment to the nation's civil defense program.

Lee realized the importance of educating people about civil defense early on and addressed many state and local gatherings, often being rather blunt about the atomic threat. During the fall of 1950, he spoke before the Christina Business and Professional Women's Club, the YMCA, the Wilmington Area Girl Scout Council, the Delaware Chapter of the American Red Cross, American Legion, and Veterans of Foreign Wars. In December, he addressed a meeting of the Delaware Mayors Association, which included mayors, city managers, and council heads, on the importance of every community forming a civil defense group. He told those in attendance that each community had its own unique situation and problems to consider. But his primary message was to remind everyone that although they may reside in a smaller locality, it did not mean they were beyond the impact of an atomic bomb.[9] Monroe Park, a small community of 1,500 located near Wilmington, heeded Lee's advice by creating a civil defense program and appointing W. Dale Parker as its coordinator. Parker set his goal as 100 percent family participation, and under his direction maps were made of the area identifying fire stations, the block warden post, storage areas, and other locations deemed critical in an emergency. The community installed its own air-raid siren, formed auxiliary police and fire units, and named a block warden commander, who in turn recruited 50 volunteer wardens. The civil defense program, Parker said, had "become a great factor in building for community unity. Everyone connected with the organization seems to enjoy the fellowship with their neighbors."[10]

At a YMCA meeting in December 1950 to encourage volunteering for civil defense, Lee reminded the audience that Wilmington was one of the 58 most likely targets of an atomic attack, then pointed out that the nation faced a major challenge because 67 percent of the population was concentrated in less than 2 percent of the country's land area.[11] His warning was well-timed, coming two months after the city and the state had been part of a 19-state air-raid test conducted by the U.S. Air Force. The objective was to determine how rapidly 6,000 ground observer posts could answer a call to action. Unfortunately, the Air Force did not reveal the results to "avoid disclosing strong or weak points of the nation's air-raid warning system," according to a newspaper report.[12] The public, as a result, remained unclear about the nation's capabilities, and continued to be uneasy about the outcome of an atomic attack by the Soviet Union.

Despite his best efforts, Lee confronted the same challenge noted repeatedly by the media throughout the early 1950s: overcoming apathy. In April 1951, Bill Frank, a columnist for the city's *Morning News*, wrote an open letter to the Soviet Union's leader, Joseph Stalin, in which he lamented the state's apathy toward civil defense. After declaring that Delaware was "way behind schedule in its civil defense organization," he wrote, "Boy, but I bet you love this apathy! I can just see you grinning from ear to ear."[13] The same month, Lieutenant Colonel C. Preston Lee, the state's civil defense director, mailed letters to mayors and other officials in every city and town in Delaware expressing his fear that the civil defense program was slipping. "I am not an alarmist," the letter read. "I don't believe in frightening people. But I certainly do believe in facing the facts. We deceive no one but ourselves if we refuse to take the path of realism, unpleasant though it may be." The letter then listed the harsh realities facing all Americans, including the fact that the Soviet Union not only possessed an atomic bomb and had planes capable of reaching U.S. cities, but also that it had the capability of launching biological warfare and was "ready, willing, and able to engage in sabotage on an immense scale."[14]

The civil defense director for the Wilmington Manor community, at a May 1951 meeting, decried the same concerns, telling those attending, "If the present difficulty experienced in obtaining responsible personnel is any criteria, then it would seem that the vast majority of the citizens in this area either do not think civil defense is necessary, or are not psychologically prepared for making sacrifices of time and energy."[15] For M. DuPont Lee, though, the leaders of civil defense programs had to accept most of the blame for an apathetic public. "We cannot expect the public to take an active interest in the program," Lee told a September 1951 meeting of the governor's Civil Defense Advisory Council, "If we, as the leaders, do not make them understand the necessity for preparedness, realize what their civil defense organizations are doing, and otherwise arouse their interest, it's no use complaining over the lack of public support. It's up to us to do something about it."[16]

Lee began 1951 with a flurry of activity. In January, he obtained city funding to distribute 10,000 copies of the FCDA's pamphlet, *Survival Under Atomic Attack*, with plans to distribute up to 40,000 more.[17] In February, he took an unprecedented step by creating a biological warfare section of the city's civil defense organization. Nineteen bacteriologists, plant and animal pathologists, and biochemists formed the section under the direction of Lloyd Leach of DuPont Company. The same month, Lee met with representatives of twenty veterans' organizations to launch the city's block warden program with a goal of 3,000 men and women wardens. He named Arthur Wilson, a World War I veteran and former DuPont Company employee, as deputy civil defense director of block wardens. Commenting on the use of veterans to develop the program, Lee said, "They are adverse to communism, strikes, riots, or anything which might slow down the war effort and therefore they [are] a stabilizing influence in the community."[18] Lee also supervised the city's participation in the first statewide air-raid alert test that month—a test that proved to be a major disappointment because many of the sirens signaling the test went unheard by the public. Although the state redid the test a month later, Wilmington did not participate because the sirens in the city had not been corrected.[19] In March, Lee officially opened the new civil defense headquarters. One of his first moves was to give Frances Vernon, who would later serve on the Alert America committee, responsibility for supervising the Junior League members who registered volunteers, distributed literature on civil defense, and maintained a library of civil defense publications. In another move, he formed a speaker's bureau in October to explain the city's civil defense program to various groups, with the belief that it would persuade them to be more supportive.[20]

When the FCDA named Wilmington as one of the initial cities to host the Alert America exhibit outside Washington, D.C., Lee and his organization went to work. On January 2, 1952, in Lee's Wilmington office, John Paxton, field manager for the Valley Forge Foundation, joined Lee and Colonel Far-ragut Hall, field representative for the Delaware State Department of Civil Defense, for the formal announcement. Lee, who had dedicated the past year to creating a local organization, emphasized the show's goal of stimulating interest in the various opportunities available in the city's civil defense pro-gram. Paxton emphasized the exhibit's importance by saying, "Disaster could strike here. Since atomic blasts are aimed at industry and citizenry, not just armed forces, we are all in active partnership with those in uniform when it comes to defense. If an atomic bomb or any other disaster should befall, advance thought and preparation would save untold hardship and even lives."[21] Helping Lee on the arrangements for the convoy were Emmet Thomp-son, chief aide to Lee; Mayor Hearn; Kavanaugh; and Frances Vernon and her husband, Harcourt. To promote the exhibit, Lee formed a special com-mittee under the chairmanship of Barbara Stager.[22]

The week after the announcement, Lee, Mayor Hearn, Thompson, Stager, and five other committee members traveled to the nation's capital to visit the Alert America exhibit. After her visit, Stager commented: "While enjoying it, you absorb the message. You may have heard before, but not real-ized what it means to live in the atomic age. The convoy definitely will bring you up-to-date."[23] The real objective for the group, however, was to see the actual displays in order to make the correct logistical decisions related to set-ting up the thirteen individual units featuring motion pictures, audio record-ings, diagrams, posters, lighting and electrical equipment, and the three-dimensional diorama simulating the atomic destruction of "City X." They also had to plan for displays by Westinghouse Electric, demonstrating a Geiger counter; American Telephone and Telegraph (today known simply as AT&T), erecting the elements of an actual warning system, including obser-vation post, telephone booth, filter center, and radar screen; and the Delaware Power and Light Company and the Wilmington Water Department, display-ing posters detailing instructions for the use of gas, electricity, and water during an emergency.

In addition, plans called for a 14-foot civil defense organization chart for the city; a block warden map; an American Red Cross display; and displays of shelters, medical supplies, and food supplies.[24] The contingent learned that the exhibit required some 7,000 square feet of space, consisted of 3,700 sep-arate pieces, took more than 30 hours to set up, and needed 50 volunteers to manage its four-day operation. In addition, they had to make arrangements for parking the convoy's ten, 32-foot semi-trailers, which presented an addi-tional challenge for the small city. Even with these challenges, the local news-paper reported that the delegation returned "100 per cent afire with enthusiasm," with the show packing "a terrific wallop" that should not be missed by anyone.[25]

The Alert America exhibit, which covered the area of a basketball court, took up to 48 hours to assemble and required each city to provide a local team of workers to help set up the displays (National Archives).

The exhibit closed in Washington, D.C., on Friday, January 11. Six days later, the caravan crossed into Delaware late at night and parked at the New Castle County Airport, about nine miles from Wilmington. The following day, Friday, January 18, state police escorted the convoy of semi-trailers to the city limits, where Wilmington police escorted the trucks the rest of the way to the State Armory at Tenth and DuPont streets, where it went on display beginning Sunday. As an adjunct to the actual exhibit, Lee had received approval of the Street and Sewer Department to position four of the Alert America trucks around the city. After unloading the exhibit materials, the trucks parked in four different locations throughout downtown, including in front of the local high school.[26]

Following guidelines provided in the official *Alert America!* booklet prepared by the FCDA and Valley Forge Foundation, Mayor Hearn issued a proclamation designating the week of January 20 as Alert America Week. The proclamation, which Hearn read over local radio and television stations, reflected those issued by mayors across the country:

WHEREAS, in the interest of public understanding and public participation in the vital program of national defense, the week of Jan. 20, 1952, has been set aside as "Alert America Week," and

WHEREAS, the civilian, today, shares both the risk and responsibility for defense of the nation, in co-equal partnership with our armed forces, and

WHEREAS, we stand in desperate need of an active, determined and prepared citizenry, and

WHEREAS, "Alert America Week" coincides with the arrival of the "Alert America Exhibit," which is beginning its nationwide tour in this, "The First City of the First State,"

NOW THEREFORE I, JAMES F. HEARN, Mayor of the City of Wilmington, do hereby proclaim the week of Jan. 20 to 26, 1952, as "Alert America Week" and I urge every citizen of Wilmington over the age of 12 to visit this spectacular, free display at the State Armory in Wilmington this Sunday, Monday, Tuesday or Wednesday, as his or her first step toward becoming an "Alert American."[27]

A preview of the exhibit took place exclusively for national and state civil defense officials from 4 p.m. to 6 p.m. on Sunday. Among the dignitaries attending were Colonel Harold Battley, FCDA regional director; Clarence Keyes, executive officer of the Office of Price Stabilization for the Delaware area; Colonel D. Preston Lee, Delaware civil defense director; General N.G. Coda, Philadelphia civil defense director; and Paul Ellison, director, and Richard Funk, assistant director, of the Valley Forge Foundation. In his comments during the preview, Funk complimented the Wilmington Civil Defense Office, and specifically Lee, for the exceptional job of planning and hosting Alert America. Following a traditional ribbon-cutting ceremony, the doors opened to the public from 6 p.m. to 11 p.m., with Thompson, newly appointed as deputy civil defense director, given the primary responsibility for Alert America's four-day stay. Mrs. J. H. Tyler McConnell, head of women's activities for the city's civil defense organization, managed the volunteers, who acted as guides, interpreters, and "button pushers" (or those watching equipment using on/off controls that visitors could operate). American Telephone and Telegraph and the American Red Cross provided the representatives for their displays, while 32 members of the Wilmington Junior League managed the other local displays. McConnell worked with various women's organizations to send their members to serve as auxiliary police during the exhibit. The organizations included the Soroptomist Club, the JaneCees, the Volunteer Bureau, the American Association of University Women, and the Women's Auxiliary of the New Castle County Medical Society. Thirteen science students from the University of Delaware manned the technical exhibits.[28]

By the end of the evening, some 2,500 people had visited the exhibit. Not soon after entering, visitors heard a recorded voice say that the nation's military defenses could stop only 30 of every 100 attacking planes—an alarming statement to say the least. Yet on Monday, the morning newspaper wrote that although some phases of the exhibit were "terrifying, the overall message of the exhibit is optimistic—in that it calls upon citizens to join their local civil defense units."[29] The following day, the newspaper's editorial made clear that anyone missing the exhibit was passing up an opportunity to learn more about atomic war and civil defense. "There's no point in running away from the problem," it read. "If and when full-scale war comes to these shores, the problem of survival will still be with us." The editorial stressed that the exhibit "is not pretty," nor does it paint "a rosy picture of life on Main Street—or Market Street." Rather, the exhibit presented the "brutal facts" that collectively added up to the harsh reality that Americans needed to be prepared in order to survive. It continued:

> How prepared are we, in this modern atomic age, to meet an emergency that we pray will never come upon us? That is the challenge "Alert America" presents to every citizen of Delaware. We can rephrase the title of the exhibit and say, "Alert—Delaware!" Disaster may strike—but we can minimize disaster through our local Civil Defense units. And we cannot wait until tomorrow. If you have any doubts about the necessity of Civil Defense preparedness, attend the exhibit in the Armory at Tenth and DuPont Streets today or tomorrow.[30]

In a letter to the editor after the exhibit closed on January 23, Lee wrote that Alert America had resulted "in widespread public understanding of the civil defense need and program both locally and in the nation as a whole."[31] As would be the case in other exhibit cities, more than 20 percent of visitors, some 2,500, were children from local and area public, private, and parochial schools. Dr. Zenas Clark, administrative assistant to the Wilmington Board of Education, sent a letter to elementary and high school officials urging their attendance, and the schools responded. On the morning of January 22, students from the nearby towns of Newark, Kruse, Claymont, New Castle, and Minquadale attended, with students from Wilmington public schools attending on the following day.[32] Although children 12 and under were not allowed to visit, Clark's letter urged elementary teachers to visit the exhibit to discover "teaching devices for focusing attention upon the problems of community wide understanding and as a vehicle for increased and renewed attention upon our civil defense activities." Some teachers discovered that the annihilation of "City X" had an impact on even older students. Commented one teacher, "Our children stayed close together while touring the display and walked from the armory quietly. The atomic show left little room for levity."[33]

A week following the Alert America exhibit, on January 31, Wilmington played host to a one-day conference at the Hotel DuPont on the responsibilities of plant managers in an emergency. More than 75 representatives from state industries attended the conference, sponsored by the Delaware Department of Civil Defense and Delaware Safety Council. The keynote speaker

Visitors watched "City X" be destroyed by an atomic attack then ventured into this display of the aftermath of what might happen in their city (National Archives).

was Colonel Lawrence Wilkinson, civil defense director of New York, whose civil defense plan had become the blueprint for other states. Dr. Richard Gerstell, civil defense director of Pennsylvania and advisor to the FCDA, opened the conference with a discussion of the effects of the atomic bomb. Gerstell had authored *How to Survive an Atomic Bomb* in 1950, a book that became the definitive guide to surviving an atomic blast. "There are two things to protect," he told the plant managers, "the employees and the plant, and they are equally important.... The main responsibility will be the protection of tools, blueprints, and records, which in case of war would be difficult to replace, and the establishment of shelter areas, which would be free from flying glass and other blast effects."[34]

Although schools did not allow students under the age of 12 to attend Alert America, younger students did participate in the first citywide alert for public schools the following month. An operator at the board of education sent an alert signal to all schools by telephone at 9:50 in the morning on February 26. Once received, each school implemented its own alarm to have teachers and their students move to pre-designated shelter areas. The school district labeled the drill as a success, noting that high school students reached the shelter area in 42 seconds while elementary students reached their shelter area in 90 seconds.[35] High school students also became the focus of the city's civil defense efforts. Within days of the Alert America convoy leaving for its next stop in Baltimore, Maryland, Dr. Victor Washburn, Wilmington's health commissioner and deputy for health and medical services, announced a committee had been drawn from public, private, and parochial schools to consider recruiting boys and girls at least 15 years of age—with their parents' consent—to be trained for emergency hospital work.

The same day as Washburn's announcement, Lee launched a preliminary survey of shelter possibilities in Wilmington's mid-town buildings. Harry Stanton, deputy director of shelters, supervised teams of four persons representing the Delaware Engineering Association, the Delaware Society of Professional Engineers, and the Wilmington chapter of the American Institute of Architects. The ultimate objective was to inspect every building in a 100-block area and classify them in one of three categories: a safe shelter space; an area that could be made into a safe shelter; and an area not usable as a shelter space. Of particular note, as a reflection of the early 1950s era of McCarthyism, each team member carried a civil defense identification card as well as a notarized loyalty card declaring their allegiance to the United States.[36] In March, the same teams from the Wilmington Civil Defense Shelter Division began a survey of all the churches in Wilmington and suburban areas for the same purpose. The survey proved to be unnecessary, however, when the FCDA announced its findings the same month that churches and large auditoriums were not safe because of inadequate overhead protection. It found that office buildings, stores, schools, theaters, and factories provided the safest shelter areas in case of atomic attack.[37]

Despite Lee's best intentions and efforts, Wilmington's civil defense organization came under increasing criticism. Finally, in June, Lee resigned as director. The next day, the head of the industrial defense section, director of radiological defense, head of the church organization section, and head of the bomb shelter group all resigned. Lee admitted that several "public-spirited men" had resigned because of public indifference and constant criticism.[38] Writing in *The Morning News*, Bill Frank had been the source of much of this criticism. In his column published before Lee resigned, Frank had written: "I'm afraid that Wilmington's Defense Organization can't show much of anything that's really concrete.… I don't think Wilmington ought to kid itself. It has no working civil defense organization as of June 1952—two years after the plan was supposed to have gotten underway." He went on to claim that communications, transportation, police, fire, warden, rescue, health, evacuation, and shelter services remained in the planning stage.[39]

Lee had his supporters, however. At a city council meeting in May, councilman Frank Corsano had gone on record as saying, "This city, as a matter of fact, is very fortunate to have a man of Mr. Lee's type to head its civil defense. Just read the press and see what the county, the state, and the United States are doing about civil defense."[40] Upon receiving Lee's resignation, Mayor Hearn commented, "I have accepted with the greatest regret the resignation of Mr. Lee. He is an outstanding citizen with much civic pride, who has done a wonderful job."[41] *The News Journal*, Wilmington's evening paper, praised Lee with some reservation, writing in an editorial:

> It is regrettable that the resignation of M. duPont Lee as head of Wilmington's civil defense setup should have to occur in an atmosphere of bad feeling. Mr. Lee has served faithfully and conscientiously over a two-year period without drawing remuneration of any kind. During that two-year period, a "paper" organization has come into being. Some aspects of the organization apparently have been so well put together as to bring national mention. But there is little doubt that the important aspect of actively organizing personnel has lagged badly.[42]

Six months after the Alert America exhibit visited Wilmington, and six months after Caldwell's congratulatory telegram, Lee and his civil defense program had effectively crumbled, as described by the local newspaper. Despite receiving state and national accolades, Lee finally gave up, citing his frustration with the public's apathy—an admission that countered his long-held belief that apathy could be overcome through education and leadership. He also admitted that his organization had not been prepared to handle the 460 men and women who volunteered for civil defense during the Alert America exhibit in January.

The FCDA knew Alert America's early success was essential. And that success would ultimately be judged on whether the FCDA achieved its objective of encouraging Americans to learn more about the impact of an atomic attack, take the necessary steps to safeguard themselves and their families, and, most important, become actively involved by volunteering in civil defense programs. Although the demise of Wilmington's civil defense program had sparked a controversy one newspaper described as containing "enough fissionable material to cause an explosion," the explosion fortunately had occurred six months after Alert America's successful showing.

By the end of June 1952, the convoy had moved past its halfway point and been well received in the target cities it had visited. Approximately 700,000 people had toured the exhibit thus far, with more than 87,000 signing up for civil defense.[43] Wilmington had provided an important benchmark for other cities on the tour. Mayor Hearn and M. DuPont Lee had been very proactive in the community, and must be credited both with the turnout of some 11,000 people who visited the exhibit and with the additional thousands of people who learned more about civil defense and the atomic threat through their speaking engagements as well as through newspaper articles, radio programs, pamphlets, and supportive organizations. As the exhibit neared the end of its stay in Wilmington, *The News Journal* published an editorial titled "Time to Wake Up" that summed up the exhibit's core objective. "What the sponsors [of Alert America] aim to do," it read in part, "is wake us up to the real, perhaps imminent dangers we face from air attack by incendiary or atomic bombs, from biological weapons, from sabotage…. A lot of us have been asleep. Maybe it's time we heard the alarm clock and reached for the tools of survival."[44] As the convoy traveled on from Wilmington, along with the other two convoys making their way through the Midwest and South, Alert America did indeed awaken each city on its tour to the imminent dangers of the atomic age, often preceded with air-raid sirens, colorful parades, and low-flying military jets skimming downtown buildings.

* * *

U.S. Needs Civil Defense
By Millard Caldwell, FCDA Administrator

Home Front Protection Is Up to You and Your Family
(Fifth in the series)

Civil defense is set up by Federal and State law. But no law will work unless you back it up with action. That's why, in the end, the responsibility for civil defense is yours.

If bombs from enemy planes ever fall on your city or community, they will not fall on an organization, or a system of government. They will fall on you and your family and friends.

A solider is trained to take care of himself and to keep on fighting. As a defense of your home front, you must learn to protect yourself and keep on working. Despite every precaution, a soldier might be killed. So might you. But the more you know, and the better trained you are, the better your chances for survival.

To help protect yourself, and to make the best use of your own special ability and skill in an emergency, is the whole idea of civil defense. If you give time and thought to that, then you will be able to save yourself and others if trouble comes.

It is not up to the Federal Government to run civil defense. The Federal Civil Defense Administration does the basic planning, gives technical information to the States, pays part of the cost of equipment and shelters, and provides some kinds of emergency supplies. The operation of civil defense begins at your State line.

It Is the People's Job

It is the job of the States and Territories and their counties and cities to organize civil defense among their own people. They must build the machine and make it run. The person in charge in your State is the State Civil Defense Director. In your city it is the mayor, or your local Civil Defense Director. He and his staff organize and direct civil defense. To do this they must find and train thousands of volunteer workers. Without your help, their efforts would be useless.

Civil defense is definitely not the responsibility of the Armed Forces. Their job is to fight by carrying the attack to the enemy. Their experts have worked with the Federal Civil Defense Administration to determine which areas are most likely to be attacked, what kinds of attack to expect, and what to do about them. The Armed Forces have some definite civil defense jobs, such as making decisions on blackouts, dim-outs, camouflage and radio silence.

Air Force on Job

The Air Force operates radar screen and the ground observer system to know when its own fighter planes are needed to meet incoming bombers, and to warn civil defense officials of their approach. Once the warning has been given, the Air Force job for civil defense ends, and civil defense goes into operation. That is where you come in. That is where your training in civil defense will save lives—perhaps your life and the lives of your family.

Training Can Save Many Lives if Enemy Bombs Fall

(Sixth in the series)

Civil Defense does many things before an attack. The most important is preparedness. It gives you information on how to safeguard your home, how to fight fires, and what steps to take against atomic, biological, and chemical warfare. It arranges for shelters and operates the warning system which notifies you when to use them. It gets medical supplies and special equipment ready, trains technical services needed to restore a stricken area, and organizes mutual aid and mobile support.

There are two steps which everyone can take to get into civil defense. The first and most basic is to inform yourself what you and your family as individuals can do to protect yourselves against enemy attack. You can learn how to protect your home from fire, how to handle injuries among your family until training first aid help can be obtained, how to minimize the dangers of attacks by poison gas and biological warfare. You can do this by reading a series of booklets available from the Superintendent of Documents, Washington, D.C. They are:

"Survival Under Atomic Attack"
"What You Should Know About Biological Warfare"
"This Is Civil Defense"
"Emergency Action to Save Lives"
"Firefighting for Householders"

But this is just the beginning. The second step, and it can be taken at the same time you are studying the booklets, is to join your local civil defense organization. There you will get professional training in meeting the dangers of an enemy attack and become part of the team defending your community.

Organize Mutual Aid

One of the most important functions of civil defense before an attack is the organizing of mutual aid and mobile support. The first is help from the neighbors. No matter how well prepared a city might be, after an attack it could not take care of itself. It would have to look to neighboring suburbs, cities, and states for help. And that help must be just as well organized and trained as the civil defense organization in the city which has been knocked out. That is the meaning of mutual aid.

Mutual aid pacts to help each other in case of disaster or enemy attack have been drawn up by many cities. In operation it works like this: If your city were hit by an atomic bomb, nearby towns would send fire, police, and rescue crews to help out, or your city would do the same for other communities, for mutual aid works both ways. The same operation would take place between States, since many of them have also drawn up mutual aid pacts.

Mobile support is organized to supply more help, but on a State-wide or inter-state scale. It is made up of teams which can move rapidly. These teams would be loaded into cars, trucks, trains, or planes and rushed to the scene of disaster. Such a stricken area might be in another part of the State, instead of next door, or in another State altogether.

Mobile support groups will be manned by people on farms or in small cities and towns outside of target areas. They will assemble outside such areas and function just like the civil defense organizations in the larger cities.

Help from Neighbors

Some States do not call their mutual air or mobile support systems by the same names and not all of them are organized exactly alike. But the

important thing is, all States have a "help from and for the neighbors" operations plan.

It is your duty, no matter where you are, to serve in some civil defense
organization. You may be called upon to take your part in any one of these
civil defense operations. Be ready. Know what to do when that time comes.

FOUR

"The Show That May Save Your Life"

For Greenvillians, the businessman, the housewife and the student, today will be their greatest and possibly only opportunity to learn how to protect and help themselves and their families during and after an atomic bomb attack on this city.—Dan Halligan, The Greenville News, 1952[1]

As one of Alert America's three convoys left Wilmington, Delaware, on its way to Baltimore, Maryland, a second convoy traveled from Winston-Salem, North Carolina, to Greenville, South Carolina, another small city of 57,000. The opening reception began at 6 p.m., on Thursday, February 7, the same day as a mock air raid that began precisely at 12:30 p.m. when fire department sirens and mill whistles sounded the warning of approaching enemy bombers. Five Civil Air Patrol reconnaissance planes, timed to coincide with the sirens, flew over downtown as military personnel from Donaldson Air Force Base, located immediately south of the city, manned radar equipment to track the enemy's path. Office workers, warned in advance of the mock air raid, watched from buildings and storefronts, while crowds of men and women gathered on streets lined with American flags. *The Greenville News* had sadly announced the death of England's King George VI on its front page that morning, while reporter Dan Halligan, whose article also appeared on the newspaper's opening page, proclaimed that day as the city's "day of destiny." "Greenville will awake this morning facing the most decisive day in its 121-year-old history," he wrote. "By 1 o'clock this afternoon, Civil Defense officials will know if they are really out of the 'talking stage' and if their county-wide life-saving program is as far advanced as they hope." More important, Greenvillians—men, women, and children—would experience the "greatest and possibly only opportunity" to learn how to survive an atomic attack.[2]

75

Within minutes of the sirens' blasts, a police car, designated as the "safety car," wheeled down Main Street to warn of the impending attack. Following immediately behind were additional police cars, fire department vehicles, ambulances, a civil defense rescue car, a fleet of "commandeered" taxis, and cars from the sheriff's department—each vehicle stopping at its pre-assigned station to extinguish simulated fires or help remove the "dead" and "injured." At one of the rescue stations that had been set up in various locations, a doctor treated two boys for mythical injuries, with a nurse simulating a blood transfusion and application of first aid. As the enemy drew nearer, the Air Force radar technicians warned people by using loudspeakers mounted in front of the South Carolina National Bank Building, one of the city's notable Art Deco structures built in 1938 and located at 102 South Main Street. Students at Greenville's elementary and high schools moved quickly to shelter areas upon hearing the initial sirens. The Greenville County Civil Defense Committee swung into action with its volunteers demonstrating the use of emergency equipment set up throughout downtown, while military personnel assigned to the anti-aircraft guns pretended to shoot down the approaching planes carrying atomic bombs. Then, at 12:50, twelve Air Force planes zoomed over downtown in perfect formation at 1,000 feet to signal the "all clear," close enough that the accelerated rumble of their engines reverberated through the crowds. The mock air raid—what one reporter called "practice for World War III"—had ended as suddenly as it had begun twenty minutes earlier.[3]

Mayor J. Kenneth Cass had proclaimed February 7–10 as "Alert America Days," and worked with Paul Aughtry, Sr., the county's civil defense director, to ensure that everyone in the city, the county, and the state knew about "The Show That May Save Your Life." Greenville's success, particularly its impressive opening-day parade, established a precedent for sponsoring parades to coincide with the opening of the Alert America exhibit.

The parade began at 4:30 p.m., four hours after the air-raid drill, weaving its way from Furman University's campus through downtown Greenville, stretching for a mile and a half. Four hundred airmen from Donaldson Air Force Base marched to the rhythmic cadence of the 18th Air Force Band, along with troops from Greenville's National Guard unit and Naval reservists. Five high school bands marched, as did bands representing the American Legion, Furman University, and Camp Gordon in Augusta, Georgia. The parade featured fourteen floats representing the American Red Cross, Pilot Club, Kiwanis Club, Boy Scouts, Girls Scouts, American Legion, Civil Air Patrol, Greenville Amateur Radio Club, YMCA, Junior Chamber of Commerce, Bob Jones University, Salvation Army, and area high schools. In addition, military personnel manned five tanks and six 40-millimeter anti-aircraft guns, as well as an 80-foot radar equipment demonstration trailer. Then, following several emergency vehicles, the ten 32-foot semi-trailers with "Alert

America" colorfully painted on both sides rolled down Main Street to the delight of some 15,000 people, one-fourth of the city's population.[4]

Greenville had been the only city in South Carolina to host the exhibit, but the city promoted Alert America throughout the state. "It is hoped that officials and lay citizens of other cities and towns in the state will come to Greenville for practical and interesting lessons in civil defense that will be offered," wrote the local newspaper. "The program is well worth seeing. It is hoped that the information presented may never be called into use. But it is insurance against the worst if it should ever come."[5] Immediately after the parade ended at 6 p.m., Major General James Dozier, South Carolina's adjutant general and chairman of the state's Civil Defense Committee, formally opened the Alert America exhibit at Textile Hall.[6] Built in 1917, Textile Hall had served as the site for everything from revivalists' gatherings, conventions, and automobile shows, to pageants, basketball games, and wrestling matches. As the doors opened, local veterans groups took their positions as guards, a volunteer nurse readied herself to offer medical assistance, and volunteer guides from women's organizations greeted visitors.

In February 1952, the FCDA had just entered its second year, and Americans were still adjusting to the concept of civil defense in the atomic age. Mayor Cass had named Aughtry, president of Aughtry Motor Company, as the city's civil defense director in December 1950, although Aughtry did not begin until the following month, coinciding with the FCDA beginning its operations. Aughtry had been a first lieutenant in the infantry during World War I, fighting in France and later stationed in occupied Germany. He returned home from the service in July 1919.[7] Aughtry, like M. duPont Lee in Wilmington, had been recognized for his efforts to build a city civil defense organization, in particular his role in "the quiet but efficient manner in which industrial plants ... have been organized for protection of life and liberty."[8] He had accepted the challenge of hosting Alert America, saying, "Insofar as possible, the exhibit will give the whole story of what to do when a strike is made from the sky."[9]

By the end of his first year, he had been named director of the Greenville County Civil Defense Committee. In February 1951, he introduced a recruitment program for auxiliary police officers, including African American auxiliary officers, with a goal of 4,000 volunteers. He also introduced programs for auxiliary firefighters and wardens. He named Christy Russell, president of the Greenville Broadcasting Company, as coordinator of women's activities; the Rev. Oran Zaebst, rector of Christ Episcopal Church, as religious liaison officer; and Dr. Thomas Martin as head of the county's radiological defense and medical health section of the Greenville County Civil Defense Committee. Moreover, he enlisted the services of more than 200 nurses to be available at hospitals and first-aid casualty stations during an emergency; and he introduced a speaker's bureau for civil defense under the direction of Newton Smythe, head of WFBC, a local radio station.[10] As with Lee, Aughtry spoke before a wide range of groups about volunteerism, including the American Legion, Parent-Teachers Association, YMCA, National Society of Professional Engineers, and women's groups. At a December 1951 meeting of 75 civil defense officials and volunteers in preparation for the upcoming Alert America exhibit, M. Richard Felts, administrator for the FCDA's Southeast Region, joined Aughtry and Mayor Cass to stress the realities of the times. Felts told the gathering, "In various places, they say there is apathy toward civil defense. But I don't think there is. People just haven't taken the energy or time to sit down and think this thing out. We definitely have a threat of war hanging over our heads. I have yet to meet a man who can guarantee that a particular city will not be hit."[11]

Aughtry and Mayor Cass understood Felts' message and were committed to making the Alert America exhibit a success by planning a memorable opening day, beginning with a mock air raid, followed by a parade, and culminating with opening ceremonies at Textile Hall. At the end of its four-day run on February 10, the exhibit had drawn more than 8,000 visitors—14 percent of the Greenville population. Of more significance, almost 25 percent of the total attendance volunteered for civil defense, including firefighters, auxiliary police, wardens, rescue crews, and blood donors.[12] Commenting on the exhibit, Aughtry said, "Two hours at the exhibit is the best insurance available for anyone."[13] Greenville's success, particularly its impressive parade, had garnered interest in and generated excitement for Alert America—and captured the attention of other host cities, including Boston.

Alert America opened on Thursday, February 21, in Boston's First Corps Cadet Armory and ran through February 25. An invitation-only preview was held Wednesday evening, February 20. To mark the opening, the city conducted an air-raid drill in the morning followed by a parade beginning at noon. The parade, which took 40 minutes, began at the armory on Columbus Avenue and proceeded down Stuart Street to Washington Street, then to Boylston Street and Dartmouth Street, before returning to the armory. Mounted police, National Guardsmen, civil defense units, and all branches of the armed forces participated, along with the ten Alert America semi-trailers. Mayor John Hynes joined the parade as it passed the public library then officially opened the exhibit with a ribbon-cutting ceremony. Joseph Malone, the city's civil defense director, urged everyone to visit the exhibit not only to obtain information for their own protection but also for the protection of their city, state, and country. "A 20-minute visit to the show," Malone said, "will give more information on personal protection against the atomic bomb and civil defense in general than one could get by reading volumes on the subject."[14]

George "Pup" Phillips, Atlanta's civil defense director, also grasped the

Boston conducted an air-raid alert in the morning, followed by a parade at noon to celebrate the opening of the Alert America exhibit, which was on display February 20–25, 1952, at the First Corps Cadet Armory (National Archives).

importance of rousing the citizenry to take an interest in civil defense activities, such as the Alert America exhibit, scheduled to open February 24 in Atlanta's Municipal Auditorium. He had overseen the city's civilian defense efforts during World War II, and then was asked in July 1950 by Mayor William Hartsfield to reactivate the program for the atomic age. Although he had reservations about assuming the heavy responsibilities associated with the position, Phillips accepted.[15] The following month, he accomplished his first objective with the establishment of a seven-member Civilian Defense Advisory Committee.[16] Also that month, he attended a civil defense meeting in Washington, D.C., where he learned that Atlanta had been named a high-priority target city. At a news conference upon his return, Phillips estimated that 50,000 people might be killed if an atomic bomb hit downtown, with another 40,000 injured. He commented, "We must plan now. We must be ready if disaster comes. Those within half-mile of ground zero, the place where the bomb strikes, are virtually doomed, but those beyond that have a good chance of survival. We think we can cut down casualties by 35 percent by proper training and planning. We know we can avoid widespread panic."[17]

By the end of 1950, Phillips had established a strong civil defense organization with defense units set up in Fulton County and at city health centers. His plans for civil defense headquarters in Decatur, East Point, and Marietta, Georgia, had not been finalized but were deemed essential. "Defense against the atom bomb must be on a grand scale if it is to be successful," Phillips said at the time. "All the experts warn against centralization. If disaster should strike, a single headquarters too concentrated would be wiped out or its effectiveness destroyed. We must have several headquarters and I think four might be adequate if spaced properly."[18] Among his most impressive accomplishments in 1951 was the establishment of four decentralized control centers to serve the greater Atlanta metropolitan area. Each control center consisted of a chief and assistant, a map reader and plotter, and personnel to handle such services as communication, medical, health, radiation, fire, and police. He also launched a series of five-hour warden instructor courses for 256 Atlanta schoolteachers, who, in turn, qualified to teach an additional 3,400 teachers.[19]

In preparation for hosting Alert America, Phillips sent Mack Tucker, Jr., chairman of the exhibit program for Atlanta, along with two colleagues, to visit the Greenville display. This gave them two weeks to make final arrangements for its show. Even before their visit, however, Phillips and his team had enlisted the aid of area clubs, church groups, labor unions, women's groups, the chamber of commerce, Boy Scouts, Girl Scouts, and the local media to ensure that all Atlantans knew about Alert America. Mayor Hartsfield also did his part by proclaiming the week of February 24 as Alert America Week.[20]

More than 11,000 people visited the exhibit, which the mayor extended by one day because of "rave reviews" from visitors. Phillips named Friday as DeKalb County Day and urged the county's high school students to attend. *The Atlanta Constitution* quoted three of the reviews. A visitor from Decatur said, "It's such a good show that I came back and brought my family." A medical doctor from Lawson commented, "It gives us an understanding of how to prepare." And a local resident said simply, "It starts you thinking when you walk in the door."[21] The paper's graphic coverage of the exhibit no doubt influenced people to attend. Its Monday edition, for example, offered a gripping description of people viewing the atomic destruction of "City X," with its entrance of charred timbers and crumbling brick. "Visitors had seen in a three-dimensional model of a city a skyline blacken as air raid sirens wailed their warning, and wardens shouted orders," the article read. It then continued:

Two small children had stood close to their parents in the darkness as they watched anti-aircraft flak flash in the model sky. Over the loudspeaker, a baby whimpered its fear and suddenly a bright mushroom cloud rose in the model and the watchers saw the center of the model city dissolve into a flat bed of glowing ruins. "The time is now ... now," an urgent voice pleaded with the exhibit visitors in another booth asking for CD workers. As the voice spoke, the visitors watched intently the model figure of a ragged, gaunt-faced mother and her two children silhouetted against the flaming ruins of a city. A teenager placed his arm on the shoulder of his girl friend.[22]

To ensure that the city, even the entire state, knew about Alert America before it began, Phillips, Tucker, and Mayor Hartsfield planned a massive parade through downtown to begin at 2 p.m. on Friday, February 22—George Washington's birthday. The three-mile parade began at Peachtree and Baker streets, and then wound its way down Peachtree to Broad Street, where it turned toward Marietta Street. From there, it turned again onto Edgewood Avenue, finally ending in front of Municipal Auditorium. Thousands of Atlantans watched along the route, with office workers tossing confetti out of building windows as "multi-clad veterans doffed their hats in a reminiscent mood as the colors passed by in a Washington's birthday demonstration of American alertness."[23] Some 1,800 persons participated in the parade, but the headliner was movie actress and dancer Vera-Ellen, known for her roles in *On the Town* with Gene Kelly and *Happy Go Lucky* with Janet Jones. Representatives from all four military branches—Army, Navy, Marine Corps, and Air Force—marched along with local ROTC units and members of the Georgia National Guard. Among the 175 vehicles participating were fire engines, rescue wagons, evacuation trucks, and ambulances. Also marching or riding in cars were civil defense officials; representatives of the Atlanta Junior Chamber of Commerce, which sponsored the exhibit; and Boy Scouts, Girl Scouts, and Camp Fire Girls. Eleven bands, including the Third Army Band, 14th Air Force Band, and area high school bands, interspersed the cars, floats, and other marching units.[24]

As the parade began, military planes roared over downtown, accompanied by a formation of smaller Civil Air Patrol planes. The best was left for last, however. Two days before the parade, a three-man crew from the Lockheed plant in Marietta traveled to Wichita, Kansas, to fly back a B-47 Stratojet, touted by the local newspaper as "the only aircraft capable of delivering the H-bomb." Although initially built in Wichita, plans called for the plane also to be built at the Lockheed plant, which had reopened in January 1951 to upgrade more than 100 B-29s. On parade day, the Stratojet, with six engines generating 5,800 pounds of thrust, scraped the Atlanta skyline at just 1,200 feet to signal the parade's end, adding a thrilling punctuation mark at the end of a rather impressive parade.[25]

Another impressive parade took place in Hartford, Connecticut, where fifteen towns participated. The parade, featuring the brightly colored convoy trucks, wound its way through Hartford, East Hartford, and Manchester. Escorting the convoy were police cruisers, fire engines, rescue wagons, ambulances, and other emergency vehicles. It ended in front of the West Hartford Armory, where the exhibit was on display March 9–12.[26] Jackson, Mississippi, celebrated the opening of Alert America on Friday, March 28, with "a parade unlike anything else in this city in many a day," according to the local newspaper. Fire trucks, Red Cross trucks, medical units, and loudspeaker cars were among the participants. Also featured were high school bands, ROTC units, and a flyover by planes from Keesler Air Force Base near Biloxi.[27]

Indianapolis held two parades and a countywide air-raid test to welcome the Alert America convoy, which arrived on Saturday, March 29, from Kansas City, Missouri. As the ten semi-trailers traveled through the city that morning, airplanes from the 527 Group, Civil Air Patrol, flew cover and dropped leaflets explaining Alert America's objectives. City officials viewed the caravan as it passed City Hall on its way to the Cattle Pavilion at the state fairgrounds. At 12:30 p.m. on Monday, the first day of Alert America, the city held a second parade to draw attention to the exhibit, scheduled to close on Wednesday, April 2. The parade included police cars, fire trucks, and military vehicles, as well as a fleet of cars provided by a local Nash dealer carrying, according to a newspaper article, "a large delegation of Marion County women, busy for the last two weeks preparing to act as guides and instructors at the exhibit." Also participating were Boy Scouts, Girl Scouts, Camp Fire Girls, and the Fort Harrison military band. Coinciding with the opening ceremony at 3 p.m., the city conducted an air-raid alert with sirens and whistles sounding throughout the county.[28]

Two months later, Los Angeles, California, the twenty-sixth city on the tour, held its third annual Armed Forces parade to coincide with the opening of Alert America, scheduled to run May 17–22 at the Exposition Park Armory. *The Los Angeles Times* captured the moment: "There were trick motorcyclists, bands, massed colors, movie personalities. There were long columns of troops, soldiers, marines, sailors, Coast Guardsmen, airmen. And there were tanks, massive Sherman tanks, powerful and dustless, ready for action."[29] Prior to the parade, the city held the first test of its Red Alert air-raid warning system. At 11 a.m., more than 250 sirens sounded the "Red" alert (a three-minute warbling tone) throughout the city; ten minutes later, the sirens blared with the "White" or all-clear signal (a one-minute blast followed by two minutes of silence, then repeated for seven minutes). Overseeing the test was Rear Admiral Robert Berry (retired), the city's civil defense director, who had been appointed to his position in January 1951, immediately upon his retirement from the service.[30] Berry had served in both world wars, and commanded cruisers and other fighting ships in the Pacific campaign during

World War II. In his first official function as civil defense director, just two weeks after his appointment, he coordinated the distribution of 600,000 copies of the FCDA's booklet, *Survival Under Atomic Attack*, to every home in Los Angeles.[31] The Red Alert test had been conducted on this particular Saturday, May 17, according to Berry, to salute Armed Forces Day and the parade, to determine if there were any "dead areas" in the city where the sirens were not heard, and to signal the opening of the Alert America show that afternoon at the armory.[32]

The parade began at Washington Street and Figueroa Street at 11 a.m., and traveled south on Figueroa to Menlo Park and Exposition Boulevard. Major General William Kean, commanding general of the III Corps at Fort MacArthur, served as grand marshal of the parade, which stretched for three miles. As thousands of people watched on a warm, sunny Saturday morning, 800 men from the Army's 44th Division marched in unison, along with a battalion of Marines from Camp Pendleton and 300 sailors from the *USS Los Angeles* and the U.S. Naval Station. The Air Force Band marched and the 250th Tank Battalion of the 63rd Division manned battle-ready Sherman tanks. The Los Angeles Police Motorcycle Unit and Police Band participated, as did the Civil Air Patrol band and drill team. The Monterey Park Girl's Drum and Bugle Corps roused the crowd by playing "You Are My Sunshine" as it marched along the parade route. General J. Lawton Collins, Army chief of staff, watched from the reviewing stand, along with Mayor Fletcher Bowman and military officers representing the Navy, Marine Corps, Army, Air Force, and Coast Guard.[33]

Civil defense director Berry and Grand Marshall Kean, taking advantage of Los Angeles as the nation's movie capital, also added a bevy of stars adorning cars scattered throughout the parade, including Danny Kaye, Irene Dunne, Edward Arnold, and Marilyn Maxwell.[34] The real headliner, however, was Audie Murphy, one of the most decorated soldiers of World War II. In January 1945, at the age of 19, Murphy held off a company of German soldiers for an hour by himself, then led a counterattack while wounded and without ammunition. After the war, Murphy became an actor and had starred in eight "B" movies, most recently *The Cimarron Kid* released in February 1952. Six other Medal of Honor winners joined him in the parade: Lieutenant Richard McCool, Captain Edward Michael, Captain Raymond Harvey, Private First Class George Turner, Sergeant Louis Van Iersal, and Lieutenant Walter Ehlers. Adding the final punctuation, Jeanne Lambros, the 22-year-old Miss Alert America, led the convoy of Alert America semi-trailers at the back of the parade, which ended with 50 Air Force, Navy, and Marine Corps planes flying over downtown as the parade arrived in front of the Exposition Park Armory for the exhibit's opening ceremonies.[35] The next day, *The Los Angeles Times* wrote, "Thousands of Americans who had witnessed yesterday's armed forces

Jeanne Lambros, the 22-year-old Miss Alert America, led the convoy of Alert America semi-trailers at the back of the parade, which ended with 50 Air Force, Navy, and Marine Corps planes flying over downtown as the parade arrived in front of the Exposition Park Armory for the exhibit's opening ceremonies on May 17, 1952 (courtesy of University of Southern California, USC Libraries Special Collections).

parade, later swarmed into the armory to view the displays and dramatic demonstrations. Many pledged individual aid to the civil defense effort—so that the horrors of atomic warfare might in some measure be lessened."[36]

By the end of the six-day run, more than 52,000 people had visited Alert America, surpassing the 47,000 who had attended the show in New York City. Salt Lake City, however, hosting the exhibit September 13–21, drew some 75,000 visitors—the second largest number to visit the exhibit in any city (Sacramento drew more than 115,000).[37] To launch a successful exhibit—displayed at the state fair—the city held "the largest and most spectacular parade Salt Lake City has seen since the 1947 Centennial," according to one reporter.[38] The parade began as a jet plane skirted the city skyline at 2,000 feet and a 2,400-pound air-raid siren mounted atop the Walker Bank building in the heart of the city let loose with its warning blast. Wrote *The Salt Lake Tribune*:

> It could have been the real thing that Saturday noon incident—an air raid spewing death and destruction on the city—but, instead, it was an educational feature on civil defense highlighted by a street parade…. Most of the thousands of Salt Lakers who lined Main Street were silent as the 10-truck Alert America convoy and other components of the parade rolled past. They seemed impressed by the grim reality of a message civil defense officials were trying to present.[39]

Headlining the 39-unit parade were the ten Alert America convoy semitrailers and three accompanying cars. Other vehicles included an American Red Cross bloodmobile, ambulances, a highway patrol unit, fire department units, and cars carrying city, county, and state civil defense personnel. Entertaining the crowd were the Hill Air Force Band and the Sixth Army Kilted Band from the Presidio in San Francisco. The Marine Corps, Navy, and Utah National Guard marched, as did several bands and drill teams. In addition, the parade featured a radiological detection team from Orem, Utah, trained in decontaminating sites hit by atomic bombs. Various floats, auxiliary police units, and communications units filled out the parade.[40]

Whether a parade through downtown, a police escort into the city, a visit to a nearby community, or the sight of a convoy with ten 32-foot semitrailers motoring down the highway, Alert America most definitely had an impact. Moreover, the various events staged by cities on the tour exemplify the commitment by local organizations, public officials, private industry, and especially the media to raise public awareness of civil defense and Alert America. "War is no longer an outbreak of slaughter which can be confined to a foreign land," wrote *The Los Angeles Times* in an editorial during the exhibit's showing in the city. "But our losses will be less and our suffering considerably limited if we know what to do in the case of attack. That is the reason for the 'Alert America' exhibit."[41]

* * *

U.S. Needs Civil Defense

By Millard Caldwell, FCDA Administrator

City and Country Dwellers Have Vitally Important Jobs

(Seventh in the series)

No matter where you live—city, town, or countryside—your part in civil defense is important. If you live on a farm you are on the enemy's high priority list for some kind of biological warfare attack. Your livestock and crops may get hit by some kind of BW, and unless you are on the lookout for a possible sneak attack on what you produce, it might be too late to do anything about it. So it is of great importance to you that you know what to do in time. Civil defense will tell you.

If you live in a small town, you have a special kind of civil defense job. And it is of great importance too, for it is helping and sheltering bombed out people from some nearby city where public buildings and homes have been blasted or burned to the ground. The people in big cities are not going to panic and take to the hills, but thousands of them may have to be moved into your town for medical attention and help.

May Be Evacuation Area

There also will be young children, expectant mothers, invalids and old people to care for. Your locality might be named as an evacuation area for this purpose. If you are anywhere within reach of a major city, hospital facilities in your community surely would be targeted as reception areas for casualties. You understand now how important it is for you to take an active interest in your civil defense.

If you life in a large city, you will have a critical civil defense job to do. You will serve both as part of the civil defense team and as a member of a family which must make every effort to take care of itself. Your duties in that capacity will be very vital. If your city has more than 50,000 population, you probably live in a target area. Watch how your community organizes for civil defense. Read your newspapers, listen to radio broadcasts for information about your civil defense organization.

Expensive for Enemy

Any attack, even with regular bombs, is expensive for the enemy. Making it with atomic bombs costs a great deal more. An enemy would use atomic bombs only on targets which would pay-off in large scale damage. That means they would probably hit only the large cities, industrial centers, and other areas which would cripple our resources and upset the morale of our citizens. By looking at a population or industrial map of the United States, you can see that there are a limited number of areas which would be hit with atomic bombs.

What you know about your own community will give you some idea of its importance to the enemy. You know what industries are located there and if they are essential to the war effort. One such industry generally does not make a target area; many such industries definitely do. Ask your local civil defense director.

Yes! Civil defense is YOUR business no matter where you live.

Joining Civil Defense Can Mean Your Survival
(Eighth in the series)

The most important reason for anyone to volunteer for Civil Defense work now is that his or her life may depend on it. From that point you can add more names to the list which may be dependent on you in some hour of crisis: your own family, your relatives, your neighbors, and other friends in your community.

The protection of your own home, industrial property and war plants, public buildings, the place where you earn a living, your municipal facilities, your transportation system, farm lands, cattle, forests, harbors—everything which has to do with your life today, multiply the reasons why you should volunteer for civil defense work NOW.

Every good American will want to volunteer for civil defense. He knows it is his duty to do so, for there is no other way to recruit the millions of workers who will be needed to defeat an enemy on the home front. If we are attacked—and remember that we can be attacked—the hard, terrible task of getting our cities and industries back on their feet will fall mainly on civil defense volunteers. It is not a job for those who can't face facts or aren't willing to work. It is a job for real Americans with courage.

No one can do the civil defense job but the American people themselves. The Armed Forces have their own job to do. There are not enough people in Federal, State, or local government agencies to do the job for you. It is one of those things you will have to do yourself. And you will have to be prepared for any emergency. There will be no time to take a civil defense training course, or read booklets, when the bombs fall. All that must be done before if you want to better your chance for survival.

Service Means Survival

One local civil defense organization has adopted the slogan "Service Means Survival." It is a good slogan to remember. It sums up the meaning of civil defense. An efficient, tough, determined civil defense program can mean survival for the American people.

It's easy to find out where to volunteer for civil defense work, and the services you are qualified to perform. Visit or telephone your local civil defense headquarters or watch for announcements from your local civil defense director. Your newspapers, radio or television stations will give you information.

Your Red Cross chapter is ready to train you in first aid right now. This training is required of all civil defense volunteers. If you are not able to volunteer, you should take the latest Red Cross first aid course anyway. It is wise for you to know first aid no matter what may happen.

Red Cross Courses

The Red Cross gives courses in home nursing and nurses' aide also. It is wise to have some knowledge of these courses too. Then you might be able to save a life in your family some way, war or no war.

You can help by being a Red Cross blood donor. Thousands of pints of blood would be needed after an enemy attack.

FIVE

Convoys on the Road

It has been truthfully said that when the atom bomb was dropped on Hiroshima, an old era of the world died and a new era was born.... So within a few short years, we find ourselves moved from a safe and protected position into a potential front-line target.—Brig. Gen. Charles Thrasher, Director of Civil Defense, Kansas City, Missouri, 1952[1]

In January 1952, President Harry Truman had entered his last year in office, tensions between the United States and the Soviet Union continued to intensify, and the Korean War spilled over into another year without any sign of ending. Also that January, seven months after the FCDA's National Advisory Council voted to launch a campaign to stimulate the nation's civil defense program, three Alert America convoys left the nation's capital on a nine-month quest to bring "The Show That May Save Your Life" to the American people.

Truman, who saw Alert America during its debut in Washington, D.C., had commented that anyone seeing the exhibit would be convinced of the importance of civil defense preparedness. Senator Margaret Smith of Maine echoed the same sentiment in her nationally syndicated column. "I have great hope," Smith wrote, "that this program, which will take the facts right to the people in their home towns, will bring home to most of us the necessity of individually participating in civilian defense not just for our nation but for the members of our families, for our neighbors and friends, and for ourselves."[2] Newspaper columnist Bill Henry also urged people to attend Alert America for its more uplifting, inspirational message. He called the exhibit's most important message its emphasis on cooperation—working with your neighbors and community. Alert America, wrote Henry, "gives you just a bit of a lift and it makes you realize that we have plus values, things over and above mere possessions, which we can find real joy and inspiration in defending."[3] By the end of February, the convoys had already brought both the harsh facts about the atomic bomb's awesome power and the more positive emphasis on the importance of working together to millions of Americans in Connecticut, Delaware, Maryland, New York, and Ohio.

As one convoy arrived in Wilmington, Delaware, another one crossed the Nassau–Queens County line in New York around noon on January 16. Although unable to meet in person, Kenneth Wells had contacted Cyril Ryan, director of civil defense for Nassau County, in advance of the convoy's arrival to provide suggestions on how to improve attendance. With his preparations in place, Ryan greeted the caravan along with Army personnel, Civil Air Patrol representatives, and Air Force police from nearby Mitchel Air Force Base. Then, at 1 p.m., the county launched a full-scale test of its air-raid signal system; military jets from Fort Dix, New Jersey, flew overhead; and the red, white, and blue Alert America trucks became part of a convoy-welcoming motorcade to the armory in Hempstead. County Executive J. Russel Sprague designated January 16–20 as Alert America Week and urged all county residents to attend. Colonel Lawrence Wilkinson, chairman of the New York State Civil Defense Commission, and Lieutenant General C. R. Huebner, the state's civil defense director, along with a contingent of state and city officials, attended the opening ceremony. Civil defense officials from a dozen Northeastern states also attended. Ryan had set the county's civil defense need at a rather ambitious and unrealistic 80,000 volunteers. Although only 5,000 people visited the exhibit during its three days in Hempstead, however, the turnout did not diminish the county's commitment to its civil defense program. In fact, it designated January 22 as "Convoy Away Day" with another air-raid alert test that ended with the white, all-clear signal as the Alert America convoy left for its next stop.[4]

Boston hosted the exhibit at the First Corps Cadet Armory for five days at the end of February. On the first full day, the city held a 15-minute air-raid alert in the morning, followed by a parade that began at noon. To stress the importance of the alert, the city had announced a $500 fine or one year in prison for anyone violating orders by civil defense officials. Cars in the downtown area were not allowed to move during the alert, taxicabs had been given instructions about where to park, all city buses stopped, and subway and tunnel trains also halted operations for the short duration of the alert. Motorists had to park and lock their cars, then seek the closest shelter. In addition, the city's 55 hotels, large office buildings, and industrial plants evacuated guests and employees to shelter areas either within the facility or nearby. Civil defense officials also urged people at home to practice seeking shelter during the drill. Beginning at noon, a parade began at the armory and wove its way through downtown before returning to the site of the exhibit.[5]

The third caravan had ventured to Columbus, Ohio, where the Alert America exhibit ran for six days in January. The week prior to the opening,

George Arnold, the city's civil defense director, announced the start of classes for 100 wardens, who were to be responsible for protecting state employees working in seven government buildings.[6] Attending the exhibit's premier were civil defense representatives from the other host cities in Ohio, including Akron, Canton, Cincinnati, Cleveland, Dayton, and Youngstown, where the exhibit opened January 30 for four days.[7] Everyone associated with the convoys had a role to play in Alert America's success. In Ohio, fourteen Korean War veterans who had traveled with the caravan spoke at gatherings during the exhibit. At a meeting of the Lima, Ohio, Chapter of American Gold Star Mothers, for example, Lieutenant Vern Hedrick promoted the need for the women's involvement with the civil defense program.[8]

George Branscomb, head of the Canton Civil Defense Corps, worked with civil defense groups in neighboring Massillon and Alliance to bring Alert America to his city.[9] The exhibit ran for three days in early February at the Canton Memorial Auditorium, home to the Civil Defense Corps offices. Originally scheduled to be on display for a fourth day, personnel dismantled the exhibit a day early, with the convoy traveling on to its next stop in Cleveland. Reginald Carey, exhibit director, requested the early departure after U.S. Representative Jackson Betts, from Ohio's eighth congressional district, issued an order to remove Office of Price Stabilization posters. Carey contended that the posters were "an excursion into the realm of propaganda" because they depicted how price controls can fight inflation. Despite the early closing, however, Canton attracted 7,000 visitors—more than Cleveland, Columbus, and Youngstown.[10]

The higher attendance in Canton, as was the case in other cities, can be credited to the strong showing by local school districts. Stark County, of which Canton was the county seat, arranged to have all its schools conduct tours by junior and senior high school

THE

GREATEST SHOW

IN TOWN

IS FREE

GO SEE the Alert America Convoy! It's the show that may save your life. You'll see the "inside story" of atomic energy. Its peacetime uses. Its use as a war weapon. You'll see how Civil Defense protects you and your family from germ, gas and atomic warfare. Movies. Three-dimensional exhibits. Dioramas. A show you'll *never* forget!

 FEB. 15-18 — AKRON ARMORY
PUBLISHED AS A PUBLIC SERVICE BY
THE OHIO BELL TELEPHONE CO.

Local and regional companies, like Ohio Bell Telephone, actively supported Alert America with newspaper ads, such as this one in the *Akron Beach Journal*. The exhibit visited several Ohio cities, including Akron, Canton, Cleveland, Columbus, and Youngstown.

students.[11] In addition, the ten Alert America trucks visited surrounding communities. In Massillon, police cars, a sound truck, and members of the air-raid section of the Massillon Civil Defense Corps escorted the caravan through the city's downtown, then returned to the Canton city limits, where cruisers from the Stark County sheriff's department took over the final leg to the auditorium.[12]

The respectable showing in Canton did not assuage Branscomb's efforts to overcome what he considered an apathetic public. Named director in July 1951, Branscomb had acknowledged in December, five months after his appointment, that he had achieved little in terms of signing up volunteers and appointing an advisory council. And he blamed his poor performance on people's apathy toward civil defense, which he attributed to the belief by many that there was no defense against the atomic bomb "so why waste time and effort in preparing for a possible attack." Although he must be credited for bringing Alert America to Canton, Branscomb resigned immediately after it left the city for Cleveland and announced his intention to run for county recorder.[13]

Although the convoy's stop in Cincinnati was cancelled, the Ohio tour continued to Akron and Dayton. Summit County's civil defense command held a drill in Akron during the Alert America show to test its warning system. The first blast came from a giant rotating siren mounted atop City Hall. This was followed by a test of another air-raid warning siren and loudspeaker. Colonel Fred Cain, director of Summit County Civil Defense, called the test "a definite success" and indicated that it provided a good idea of how to establish an effective warning system. Cain estimated that forty sirens would be needed to alert the entire city.[14]

Akron drew some 4,000 visitors, bringing the state total to a disappointing 25,000, especially when compared to Providence, Rhode Island, Greenville, South Carolina, and Manchester, New Hampshire, also hosting the exhibit in February and combining for close to 35,000 visitors. In Manchester, 9,659 people attended Alert America during its brief two-day stay.[15] Yet despite Ohio's disappointing attendance, the Alert America convoy sparked civil defense organizations throughout the state to use its presence as justification for conducting civil defense exercises, including testing its systems and personnel.

During March, the Midwest convoy traveled to Kansas City and St. Louis, Missouri, and Rock Island, Illinois. Combined, the three cities accounted for approximately 56,000 visitors. The civil defense department in Kansas City, Missouri, in cooperation with its counterpart in Kansas City, Kansas, sponsored Alert America, which was set up in Municipal Auditorium. More than 16,000 people attended the exhibit, assisted by 200 guides representing twenty area organizations.[16] One of the added highlights was the pre-

Each city created extensive promotional plans to promote Alert America, including the use of billboards, such as this one for the St. Louis exhibit opening March 5 at Kiel Auditorium (General Outdoor Advertising Company, Courtesy of Harry S. Truman Library).

mier showing of thirty pieces of Signal Corps equipment being used in Korea. To promote Alert America and this special display, Mayor William Kemp sent invitations to the mayors of twenty-three communities in the greater Kansas City area to participate in the opening ceremonies. Brigadier General Charles Thrasher, director of the city's civil defense organization, named Mayor Kemp and Mayor Clark Tucker of Kansas City, Kansas, as honorary local chairmen. Following the exhibit, *The Kansas City Times* quoted Thrasher as saying, "Those who have followed scientific development, have seen the 'Alert America' show, and have had other opportunities to come in contact with the progress of atomic energy commercially, realize that any nation or group of nations which hold the sources of atomic energy will control the world."[17]

As the Midwest convoy continued on to Indianapolis, the New England convoy arrived in Hartford, Connecticut, where the exhibit ran at the West Hartford Armory March 9–12. As was typical, the day before the exhibit opened the city held a welcoming parade more than three miles long. Among the parade's 217 vehicles were police cruisers, crash trucks, and fire engines representing the fifteen area towns that sponsored the exhibit; the towns were located within the Hartford mutual aid area, which meant they would assist each other during an emergency. Also in the parade were a Red Cross life-saving boat and a public works rescue squad. The Alert America convoy and accompanying vehicles, with "red lights flashing, sirens wailing, and loud-speakers chattering incessantly" according to the *Hartford Courant*, drove some 23 miles through Hartford, East and West Hartford, and Manchester.[18]

Henry Thomas, Hartford's civil defense director, said he expected the exhibit "to touch off an intensive community and area-wide civil defense effort" and urged "every resident of the area to make attendance a must."[19] Mrs. Everett Collier, local chair for Alert America, worked with the PTA, League of Women Voters, and the American Legion Auxiliary to solicit women to volunteer as exhibit guides.[20] In addition to the 7,200-square-foot traveling exhibit, local displays included ones by the Hartford Red Cross chapter, which set up a first-aid station; the Connecticut Military Department; Boy Scouts and Girl Scouts, as well as the Catholic Youth Organization; police and fire departments of Greater Hartford; and the Southern New England Telephone Company.[21] Some 300 amateur ham operators also participated. Using three shortwave transmitters and other equipment, and working in three-hour shifts, the "hams" transmitted messages for visitors free of charge to anywhere in the world.[22]

More than 20,000 people attended the Alert America exhibit in Hartford, exceeding the total attendance of Bridgeport, New Haven, and New London combined. The city also gained 750 new civil defense volunteers, compared to 2,000 in the three previous cities. Although not a high percentage, Thomas stressed that many other visitors had taken home enrollment forms.[23] The exhibit could not have arrived at a better time in terms of its impact on civil defense awareness. A reporter had interviewed people immediately following the parade and discovered that most had not actively participated in civil defense but acknowledged that they had received literature about the need for preparedness.[24] Although Governor John Davis Lodge could not attend the exhibit, he reinforced the need for preparedness in a statement, which read: "The more that we can arm ourselves with foreknowledge, the more effectively we can cope with a civil defense emergency. With our homes, our security, and the very lives of our families at stake, we bear a fateful respon-sibility. If, God forbid, the menace should materialize, let it be said that we in Connecticut were trained and ready to meet it."[25]

To test the preparedness of residents in Pittsfield, Massachusetts, and to promote the Alert America exhibit, the city held a 15-minute air-raid alert on Saturday, March 22, a day before the exhibit began its three-day schedule. Citing that the city's civil defense program was not yet at full strength, Mayor Robert Capeless had previously voiced concerns heard all too often: "Our failure in this regard is chargeable to public apathy." He called the test the first opportunity to gauge the effectiveness of the civil defense department's extensive planning and training of the past 20 months. The police stopped all traffic within a 17-block area, had cars pull to the side of the road and park, and had drivers move to the nearest shelter. Auxiliary police directed pedestrians to public shelter areas, and volunteer wardens kept people inside until the police sounded the all clear.[26] The day after the test, which proved to be successful, the city held a private showing of the exhibit Sunday evening, with 278 Berkshire County civil defense and public officials attending. Alert America opened to the general public on Monday and drew 4,118 visitors for its brief two-day stay at the State Armory. The convoy of trucks helped publicize the exhibit by visiting nearby towns, including Adams, North Adams, Florida, Savoy, and Plainfield. School districts in Pittsfield and surrounding communities also contributed to attendance by sending students, including 84 sixth-, seventh-, and eighth-graders from Cheshire.[27] In Fall River, Massachusetts, more than 15,000 people, or one-fifth of the city's population, visited Alert America.[28]

One of the convoys wove its way to Jackson, Mississippi, where the exhibit went on display in Hangar Nine at the Jackson Municipal Airport. Following the trend in other cities, a parade the local newspaper called "unlike anything else in this city in many a day" coincided with the opening of Alert America. The parade featured police cars, fire trucks, Red Cross trucks, amateur radio groups, medical units, and high school bands. Adding to the gala was the National Guard's display of field kitchens and a flyover by planes from nearby Keesler Air Force Base in Biloxi.[29] Mississippi Governor Hugh White and Jackson Mayor Allen Thompson both declared March 24–30 as Alert America Week.[30] E. H. Bradshaw, director of Jackson's civil defense organization, reported that 2,333 visitors had signed up for civil defense out of a total attendance of 9,001—26 percent, far above the national average of 10–15 percent. The large turnout, 10 percent of Jackson's population, resulted in part from the city providing special buses for residents without cars.[31] Charles Hills, a columnist for the *Clarion-Ledger*, the local newspaper, urged people to see and hear the exhibit, which he called "one of the most amazing things we have viewed." He then added, "Someday, some of the things impressed on you by the show may come in mighty handy, who knows?" In another article, the newspaper said the exhibit was "one of the most spectacular as well as entertaining and informative to be found. It's the show that no American can afford to miss."[32]

April and May found the Alert America convoy traveling to several cities, including Detroit and Lansing, Michigan; and Binghamton, Buffalo, New York City, Rochester, Schenectady, Syracuse, and Utica, New York. Lansing hosted the exhibit for two days in April before the exhibit went on to Detroit, where it ran at the Brodhead Naval Armory. In the most impressive local demonstration, seventy volunteers in the fire department's civil defense auxiliary "poured a cascade of 24 hose streams into the Detroit River" to demonstrate their readiness skills for an emergency situation.[33] By the time Alert America reached Syracuse, which hosted the exhibit later that month at the West Jefferson Street Armory, the state's civil defense exhibit had been added. The local newspaper, *The Post-Standard*, called it a "spectacular" exhibit whose purpose was "to inform and convince the American people of the grim realities of today's threat from Kremlin aggression and modern terror weapons."[34] Among the ancillary displays were a mobile soup kitchen operated by the Onondaga County Civil Defense organization and demonstrations by the Girl Scouts, Camp Fire Girls and Red Cross. A topographical map of Syracuse showed residential and industrial areas of the city, while the Air Defense Command had a 42-foot display showing various aircraft types, a map of the Air Force signal stations, and, as described in the local newspaper, "an animated display and voice description of what happens when an air strike is scored on the West Coast."[35]

Binghamton followed Syracuse on the schedule, with Alert America running in early May at the West End Avenue Armory. The Broome County Civil Defense Office, Binghamton Junior Chamber of Commerce, and the Triple Cities Advertising and Sales Council worked together to promote the exhibit, with the goal of prompting residents to volunteer. Making Binghamton rather unique among tour cities was the addition of an atomic energy exhibit on loan from the American Museum of Atomic Energy in Oak Ridge, Tennessee. The exhibit illustrated an atomic pile; scientific elements, including neutron bullets and uranium-235; methods of separating U-235 and U-238; how isotopes are made; how new elements are created; and the atomic power plant of the future. In addition to the atomic energy exhibit, two local motorcycle clubs, the Square Deal Riders Motorcycle Club and the Tri-Cities Sports Riders, demonstrated how motorcycles offered a means of transportation and communication under conditions that, according to club officials, "make it impossible for other vehicles to operate effectively."[36]

Approximately 18,000 people visited Alert America in Binghamton, Rochester, Syracuse, and Utica. The real payoff, though, occurred in New York City, where the exhibit attracted approximately 47,000 during its seven-day stay in May at the Seventh Regiment Armory. Mayor Vincent Impellitteri had proclaimed May 13–19 as Alert America Week during a ceremony the day before the opening. Also speaking was Arthur Wallander, the city's civil defense director, who made a good news/bad news statement by declaring that one plane carrying multiple atomic bombs would "almost completely destroy the entire city of New York in a single attack." But he continued by saying the city was better prepared than two years earlier to cope with this type of attack, in large part because of the 481,000 city employees and volunteers actively participating in the civil defense program. Moreover, 733

Three volunteer supervisors in Madison, Wisconsin, prepare to help visitors at the Alert America Convoy during its run May 19–21 at the University of Wisconsin–Madison Field House. Left to right are Mrs. A.R. (Florence) Thiede of the Business and Professional Women's Club, Mrs. Ira Langlois of Amaranth, and Mrs. Mack (Mildred) Mitchell of Zor auxiliary (Wisconsin Historical Society).

public shelters had been designated, more than 66,000 air wardens had been enlisted, and 19,000 taxis had enrolled in the city's emergency taxi corps. The city celebrated the opening of Alert America with a rally held at noon in Times Square, which was closed to traffic. Singer June Valli sang the National Anthem, followed by a special pledge delivered by Jamie Smith, star of the film *Faithful City*, and Brandon de Wilde, star of *Mrs. McThing* (in which a father pledges to his son that he will volunteer for civil defense). During the exhibit, the empty convoy trucks toured the city's five boroughs to urge residents to attend.[37]

As Alert America came to an end in New York City, another convoy arrived in Madison, Wisconsin. The city council had approved a $1,000 appropriation in March to help pay for the exhibit, which was held May 19–21 at the University of Wisconsin Field House. The City-County Civil Defense Committee sponsored the exhibit, with Wisconsin Governor Walter Kohler;

Major General Ralph Olson, the state's adjutant general and director of civil defense; and Dan Anderson, publisher of the *Wisconsin State Journal*, among the honorary sponsors. The more than 200 volunteers serving as guides represented various civic and veterans organizations, including the Business and Professional Women's Clubs of Madison, American Legion Auxiliary, and VFW Auxiliary. In making the initial announcement, Richard Wilson, executive assistant of the Wisconsin Office of Civil Defense, had said, optimistically, "Towns throughout the state are expected to send bus-loads of citizens to Madison to see the exhibit." He was correct. Alert America drew 11,340 visitors during its three-day run.[38]

Close to 13,000 Minnesotans visited the exhibit during its stay in St. Paul May 26–29 and Duluth June 3–5. The week prior to the St. Paul exhibit, more than 500 Minneapolis civil defense workers cleaned up debris in a mock disaster area to demonstrate their preparedness as part of Armed Forces Day observances. St. Paul held an armed forces parade to coincide with the opening of Alert America. The 58 units in the parade included bands, drill squads, and drum and bugle corps.[39]

Hundreds of volunteers in Oakland, California, conducted what the *Oakland Tribune* called an "all-out promotion" of the Alert America exhibit, which ran June 3–6 in the Oakland Auditorium. Members of the Oakland and Berkley Junior Chambers of Commerce used colorful "advertising schemes" to get the message out. Among their efforts were the distribution of 300,000 pieces of Alert America literature, the placement of 5,000 posters and placards in area stores, and the graphic display of Alert America information on ten billboards donated by the California Outdoor Advertising Company. These billboards were in addition to the 50 billboards promoting the exhibit managed by Foster and Kleiser Company.[40] The local civil defense organization also created a speaker's bureau to give three-minute talks before service clubs. Under the direction of W. R. Paxton, a public relations officer with Standard Oil of California, the campaign's industrial committee, formed to work with area manufacturing and industrial companies, convinced East-bay firms to add announcements about Alert America in their employees' pay envelopes and their companies' billing envelopes. The committee then arranged the distribution of several thousand posters promoting Alert America to plants throughout Alameda and Contra Costa counties. School children even took home flyers to their parents.[41]

Opening ceremonies began at 7:30 p.m. on June 3, with the Sixth Army Band from the Presidio in San Francisco performing a concert in the east end of the auditorium. Simultaneously, the Sixth Army Pipe Band played near the theater entrance, where Mrs. Walter Boyd, chair of the Valley Forge Foundation, cut a red, white, and blue ribbon to officially open the exhibit. In addition to local civic and elected officials, representatives from area civil defense organizations were in attendance, along with 1,500 Legionnaires who had come to hear the evening's main speaker, Donald Wilson, national commander of the American Legion. Wilson, a World War II veteran and an attorney, minced no words, telling the gala event, "America, in the name of God, wake up! You are at the edge of the precipice of doom itself, and are being led to take the final fatal step all on the theory that you will have company of the highest quality on the way down." His remarks, carried in their entirety the next day in the *Oakland Tribune*, took uncensored aim at the government's policy of containment and its "distortions and confusion which daily have poured out of the propaganda agencies within our own government." His solution was simple:

> Power—overwhelming power—superior power—held by courageous men, determined not to be crushed, determined to be victorious—secure at home, strengthened abroad—ready to fight although desiring peace—and once launched into the fight, fighting a relentless, uncompromising fight through to death or victory—these are the men of destiny, these are the hope of the world.[42]

Wilson's emphasis on military might was reflected in the Oakland exhibit, which featured a series of military displays. The Alameda Naval Air Station loaned a 50-foot model of an aircraft carrier, while the Sixth Army provided a chemical warfare display and explosive ordnance disposal control teams and squads. The Air Force showed how the Ground Observer Corps spots enemy planes, and displayed F-84 and FX-85 fighter planes. When the exhibit closed, it had attracted 28,642 visitors, the third highest total next to New York City and Los Angeles at that juncture of the tour.[43]

Residents in Pennsylvania had two opportunities to see Alert America: Pittsburgh, which displayed the exhibit June 18–24 at the Hunt Armory; and Philadelphia, which hosted the exhibit a week earlier. Ten days before the exhibit's opening in Philadelphia, the city held its first air-raid test since World War II, in part to bring civil defense to the forefront in preparation for the Alert America show. According to *The Philadelphia Inquirer*, hundreds of people would have been killed "simply because they did not observe fundamental and simple precautions." Despite the newspaper's observation and other issues related to the test, including concerns about the capacity of the warning system to alert the entire city, officials were pleased overall. "From what I saw of the public response," said Major General Norman Cota, director of the Civil Defense Council, "our people really do recognize the nature of civil defense and are prepared to respond." He then went on to suggest that every Philadelphian who did not fully understand civil defense visit the Alert America exhibit being displayed at the Commercial Museum.[44]

Cota and Mayor Joseph Clark, Jr., set their expectations at 60,000 visitors; and to ensure a positive beginning, the mayor mailed more than 5,000 invitations to a private showing on the first night. To draw more public attention, 200 members of the Philadelphia County Council, Veterans of Foreign Wars, and VFW Auxiliary even marched to Commercial Museum for the opening gala. Unfortunately, the high expectations failed to become reality. John M. McCullough, columnist for *The Philadelphia Inquirer*, wrote extensively about the exhibit—before, during, and after. Two days before Alert America opened, he wrote, "It attempts to teach you how to live for the things you would die for. It is well worth the hour it will take you to pass through it."[45] The day after the opening, he wrote another column about Mayor Clark lamenting the rampant apathy toward civil defense. Despite all the advance efforts, fewer than 500 had attended opening night. McCullough quoted Clark as saying, "For the hundreds of thousands, even the millions of Philadelphians who are not here, it is our job to interest them in civil defense. It is our job to spread the gospel to those whose apathy does not lead them to this kind of show."[46] The next day, the newspaper commented on Clark's disappointment with the public's response to the city's air-raid drill on May 27 in an editorial titled "Time to Wake Up America":

> Must real bombs rain death and destruction upon us here in Philadelphia before our citizens are awakened to the urgent need for their cooperation and participation in Civilian Defense? … What many citizens fail to grasp is the blunt truth that preparedness is as essential for our civilian population as it is for our military forces. We expect the Army to be ready in case of peril. We must be ready too. All of us hope war will be prevented, that peace will prevail. But in a world aflame with tension and with ruthless Communist barbarians seeking its domination, it is time to wake up America, to bring home to our apathetic citizens that Civilian Defense may be their hope for survival.[47]

Despite the initial disappointment, the exhibit proved to be well received. More than 9,000 people visited Alert America, not counting special showings for 1,300 members of the Pennsylvania National Guard, nurses from Philadelphia General Hospital, and 3,200 firefighters.[48] Additionally, the convoy trucks, each equipped with small Alert America displays, toured Chester and other nearby communities to persuade people to see the exhibit at the Commercial Museum.[49]

Kenneth Wells made one of his many personal appearances the month before the Pittsburgh exhibit opened, speaking at a luncheon meeting of the chairmen of the local planning committees. He then spoke to local industrialists at a luncheon hosted by Clifford Hood, an official of U.S. Steel Company, where he emphasized that every citizen must defend every part of America. "No one has any superior immunity to enemy attack," he told the group. "Responsibility is co-equal to everybody." Two days later, Wells delivered the same message at a meeting of representatives from area women's organizations. Mrs. Everett McLaine, chairman of the Women's Civilian Defense Committee for the Alert America show and president of the Colfax Parent-Teacher Association, hosted the meeting, at which she urged women to assist with the exhibit. Despite these efforts, Melvin Hildreth, chairman of the Alert America planning committee, was among those disappointed by the turnout. Only 6,127 people visited the exhibit, even with a demonstration by the 689th Anti-Aircraft Artillery Battalion of radar equipment and an electronically controlled 90-millimeter anti-aircraft gun.[50]

The convoys continued their schedule through the summer months, visiting California, Kansas, Illinois, Nebraska, Oregon, Washington State, and West Virginia. The most successful stops occurred at state fairs. Close to 115,000 people saw the exhibit in Sacramento, California, where it had been on display at the state fairgrounds for eleven days beginning in late August. Attendance was no doubt aided by an impressive demonstration by Marines. An island with similarities to those in the Pacific during World War II, such as Okinawa and Iwo Jima, had been constructed on the infield of the state fair's racetrack. As Navy planes dived over the island providing supporting fire, Marines conducted an amphibious assault using thousands of rounds of blank ammunition. Marine frogmen also performed an underwater demolition that caused water to explode from the middle of the race-track.[51] From Sacramento, the exhibit traveled to its last stop in Salt Lake City for the Utah State Fair. Over its eight-day schedule at the fair in September, Alert America attracted some 75,000 men, women, and children.

Salt Lake City brought the total national attendance to more than one million, an impressive number when one considers that the total U.S. population at the time was about 152 million. The total impact of Alert America

Alert America was a featured attraction at the Utah State Fair in Salt Lake City and drew close to 75,000 visitors.

must be gauged not by attendance alone, however, but rather by the millions of Americans made aware of the convoy's mission and, in a broader sense, made aware of the importance of civil defense preparedness. Each venue appointed planning committees that worked diligently well in advance of the exhibit's opening. Thousands of volunteers served as guides. Schools provided transportation for their students to attend. The various branches of the armed forces performed military demonstrations and provided special displays, as did local organizations. Millions of Americans of all ages knew about Alert America; and whether or not they took the time to visit the exhibit, they assuredly knew its purpose.

* * *

U.S. Needs Civil Defense
By Millard Caldwell, FCDA Administrator

Ten Basic Services Form Core of Home Front Protection
(Ninth in the series)

The Federal Civil Defense Administration, for the sake of national uniformity, has set up these ten basic services: Warden, Fire, Police, Health, Welfare, Engineering, Rescue, Communications, Transportation, and Staff. You can imagine what a gigantic task it will be to man these various services. Some 15,000,000 volunteers are needed for this purpose.

The backbone of civil defense is the warden service. It is the source of neighborhood defense leadership before, during, and after an enemy attack. The warden's job is to help save lives and property. Before an emergency, his main duty is to help people prepare; during an emergency, he conducts people to safety; after the emergency, he helps restore order.

Wardens must be volunteers, well known, and respected in the community, whose leadership will be accepted by their neighbors and fellow workers. As a general rule, each warden post will be responsible for a residential block or factory area where about 500 people live or work. Several wardens may be assigned to such a post.

They will teach people how to protect themselves, instruct them in civil defense regulations, distribute civil defense information, keep lists of the people in their charge, and gather information about buildings and equipment in their neighborhoods.

Their records will include the home address, age, and physical condition of all persons in their charge. They also should know which people need special care and how to get in touch with their relatives and friends.

Other Important Duties

Wardens have other important duties too. If a warning sounded, they would conduct workers or the occupants of buildings to shelter areas. They would have the responsibility of helping to prevent panic among the population, rendering first aid, and performing light rescue duties. If needed, they would help other services to fight fires and clear debris.

They also would help restore the orderly life of the community immediately after an enemy attack. They would take a roll call of all people in their areas. If anyone were missing, or needed nursing or medical care, they would report the facts at once to the control center.

The warden service works directly with individuals, families, neighborhoods, and employee groups. It is the link between the specialized civil defense service and the people.

Women Have Important Role

Women must play an important part in the warden service. This is especially true of housewives, for most women are at their home posts day and night. Usually they know their own neighborhoods better than men can ever know them. Women should interest themselves in the warden service as a first step in the organization of civil defense for their neighborhood.

Outstanding men and women who can assume responsibility are urged to volunteer for the warden service.

Organizing the Home Front Means Using Many Skills

(Tenth in the series)

After the explosion of an atomic bomb, the resulting fires could cause more loss of life and property than the blast itself. Therefore, getting ready to fight fires is a big part of the civil defense job.

Atomic bombing would cause great fires in the area of the burst, and start hundreds of small fires in surrounding areas. With the regular fire fighting companies fully occupied by the main fires, people would have to put out these smaller fires on the spot. If they live in target areas they must know how to fight fires at home and at work.

At least one member of your family should be trained in the use of basic fire fighting tools and methods. Because women are at home must of the time, they are urged to learn how to put out fires in case of emergency. Teaching of householders to fight fires will be carried out by instructors trained by their local fire departments. Auxiliary or reserve firemen will be

**recruited to back up the regular companies. These volunteers will be
trained by local fire companies, using regular equipment.**

Your Warden or your local civil defense headquarters will tell you
where to volunteer for such training.

Traffic a Big Problem

The biggest police problem in event of enemy attack would be the control of traffic. Another big problem would be maintaining law and order.
These are the most important of the duties which civil defense volunteers
would help perform under the Police Service.

**Auxiliary police, which many communities now have to supplement
regular police forces in handling parades and crowds on special occasions,
will also be used in civil defense work. They will be part of the local police
departments, and under the command of regular police officers, their
authority to act being prescribed by local law.**

Civil defense will need thousands of volunteers to carry on the duties
of the Police Service. You can serve your community by volunteering today.

Good Communications Essential

No matter what kind of disaster strikes your community, much will
depend upon good communications. In the fact of enemy attack, the Communications Service would be the nerve center of civil defense for it would
relay air raid warnings promptly, direct fire, police, rescue, warden, medical,
engineering, and other services, and keep them in touch with one another.
Without this service, headquarters would not have the information necessary to control situations brought on by disaster.

Thousands of volunteers are needed to man the communications network. Any technical training in radio, television, telegraph, or telephone
work will qualify you for this service.

Neither sex nor age is a barrier to volunteering for civil defense. Retired
persons with technical training are especially valuable, such as retired policemen and firemen. There are many jobs which women can fill better than
men. Your local civil defense director will tell you what they are.

SIX

Women and Children
on Alert

*While we condemn the attempted undermining of our way of
life, we are failing to teach our children the fundamental principles of our heritage.... We must make our decision now,
whether our future course is to be socialism or the dream of
a free, new future in an atomic age.—Kenneth Wells, President, Valley Forge Foundation, 1952*[1]

"In a few awesome moments today, school children saw the heart of a
city destroyed by an atomic bomb," reported *The Indianapolis News* on March
31, 1952. Eighth-grade students from the city's Holy Trinity Catholic School,
huddled together in a darkened room at the Alert America exhibit, looked
on as a city—"City X"—slept under a "bomber's moon." Suddenly, a voice leapt
from the loudspeakers, warning of approaching enemy bombers. The children
listened intently as the bombers approached the city closer and closer, evading
anti-aircraft guns blasting away. Then, "a ball of fire appeared and poured a Nia-
gara of fire and blast on buildings that disappeared in rubble and blazing ruin."[2]

During its nine-month tour, the Alert America convoy attracted more
than one million visitors, with a sizable percentage being elementary and
high school students who knew as much or more about atomic energy as
their parents. As early as the fall of 1945, schools began to incorporate the
topics of international brotherhood, world peace, and the impact of atomic
energy—positive and destructive—into classrooms. Many of the these topics
resulted from a meeting of international educators held in Endicott, New
York, August 27–30, 1946, sponsored by the National Education Association.
Educators attending the World Conference of the Teaching Profession
approved a document titled "Recommendations on the Teaching of International Understanding," which called for a revision of the curriculum to
emphasize the importance of international affairs and to better understand

the world's diversity. Among the recommendations was the teaching of current history, which became part of the curricula as social studies and citizenship classes. "Contemporary events must be studied directly," the document read, "not only for the sake of acquiring immediately useful information, but also as a means of developing a lively and intelligent interest in world affairs. Such information and such interest in world affairs are essential for young people if they are to fulfill their duties as citizens of their country and of the world."[3]

In December 1946, the *University of Illinois Bulletin* dedicated an entire issue to a report titled "Living in the Atomic Age: A Resource Unit for Teachers in Secondary Schools." Compiled at the request of the National Committee on Atomic Information, under the direction of Harold Hand, a University of Illinois professor of education, the report provided teachers with a comprehensive list of suggestions for preparing students to live, and to survive, in the atomic age. One section, titled "Finding Out About the Atom," seemed to portend the future. It recommended that students compare the destruction of Hiroshima and Nagasaki, Japan, in 1945 with the potential impact of atomic bombs on their community or to a neighboring city. The suggestion continued: "One way to do this is to have them prepare two maps of the community or city in question and mark on one the spots of an imaginary atom bomb explosion or explosions." Students were to plot hospitals, fire stations, newspaper offices, radio stations, power stations, water works, railroad stations, factories, business areas, residential districts, schools, parks, thoroughfares, etc., on a "before" map. On the other, they were to chart the area or areas of probable destruction. Students should then use words, figures, graphs, etc., to give the details of the probable destruction. To make this exercise most effective, teachers were to emphasize aspects of social and economic life most familiar to their students during the discussion period.[4]

About the same time, Aaron Goff, a junior high school teacher in Newark, New Jersey, coined the term "atomics" to describe the integration of atomic topics into the full slate of subjects, from history, English, and science, to mathematics, art, and speech.[5] Educator Willem J. Van Der Grinten reinforced this approach in 1950, writing that teachers had the primary responsibility for preparing students for the new atomic age because "the consequences and implications of atomic energy ... affect our civilization more than anything else."[6]

On that Monday morning, the eighth-graders from Holy Trinity Catholic School watched "the familiar mushroom of smoke, dust, and vapor spread like an umbrella of death over the scene of horror." Watching the simulated destruction, one young student expressed the same sentiment as other students around the nation who had undoubtedly discussed atomic energy in their classrooms. He said quite simply, "Gee."[7]

Children were a key target audience for the Alert America message. Here a boy contemplates an atomic symbol, under the words: "Our dreams for the future of our children are framed by the symbol of the atom. What kind of world will we leave them? Will it be THIS?" The answer was atomic destruction or a world at peace (National Archives).

Schools across the country—private, public, and parochial—provided strong support for Alert America. Here, elementary students get a tour during the exhibit in New York City (National Archives).

Each city recommended that parents take their children to the exhibit and worked with school districts to provide buses for public, private, and parochial students to take tours during morning hours. Boy Scouts and Girl Scouts distributed Alert America promotional materials and volunteered as guides, while high school marching bands and drill teams participated in opening-day parades. In some cities, children represented 30 percent or more of the exhibit's total attendance, making them an essential part of Alert America's success. Women, too, played a prominent role in Alert America. The FCDA's *1951 Annual Report* made clear women were extremely important in civil defense for two primary reasons: many jobs in civil defense, such as communications, nursing, and welfare, could be best handled by women; and they were more likely to be available during the daytime—a reflection of gender stereotypes but accurate nonetheless as only 30 percent of women were in the workforce.

An FCDA booklet published in 1951, *Women in Civil Defense*, argued that if women did not help build a local civil defense organization, they must accept the blame. "Unless you, as a responsible American woman, take action, you are gambling with the safety of your family, your friends, your community, and your country," the booklet read. It then said that when women trained their families and prepared their homes for an atomic attack, they doubled their chance for survival. Moreover, when they helped to organize their community, they had "given the community and the Nation a far better chance to survive an enemy attack."[8] Another initiative aimed at women was the mailing of 55,000 copies of the FCDA's *Civil Defense Volunteer Registration Guide* to thirty-six national women's associations.[9]

In October 1951, the same month the FCDA formerly announced the upcoming Alert America traveling exhibit, the agency named regional directors of women's affairs as an additional move to attract women as volunteers. It also formed a National Advisory Committee on Women's Participation with twenty-eight members representing national women's associations with millions of members. By the end of the year, twenty-eight states had appointed their own women's civil defense advisory committees, and at least thirty-eight states had women serving in an executive civil defense position. Without question, women played an important role during the Alert America convoys' cross-country sojourn—helping millions of men, women, and children become more aware of their important roles in supporting the nation's defense.

The FCDA and the Valley Forge Foundation stressed women's importance in Alert America by strongly encouraging cities to appoint women's committees as a means to attract volunteers. To aid the efforts of these committees, special packets had been prepared containing suggested speeches, events, a discussion guide, and features for local radio, television, and newspapers. The *Alert America!* booklet distributed to host cities included a section titled "Special Role of Women" with recommended activities ranging from planning a Women's Day during the exhibit to printing library bookmarks containing the Alert America Pledge. "There was a time when women went to war, as Molly Pitcher and Joan of Arc and in an auxiliary sense went overseas in World Wars I and II," the booklet read. "Now, war comes to women far behind the troops."[10]

In January 1952, just as the Alert America caravan rolled out of the nation's capital, Mrs. John L. Whitehurst, FCDA assistant administrator in charge of civilian manpower, announced the agency's program to recruit 15 to 17 million civil defense volunteers with at least 60 percent expected to be women. "This is not just another volunteer movement," Whitehurst had said, "but a definite program to expand the present hard core of volunteers into an adequate force."[11] At a civil defense meeting in Indianapolis, Indiana, Olive Remington Goldman, FCDA assistant director for women's activities, told the 200 women in attendance, "Too many of us, particularly in the Midwest, have the mistaken idea that we are too far away from the coastal areas to worry about an attack. It is this false notion that could lead to devastation."[12]

Women's positive response to civil defense embraced their larger concerns about protecting their families, particularly their children.[13] At the same time as Whitehurst's call for volunteers, the Women's International League for Peace and Freedom issued a list of eight ways parents, primarily mothers, could minimize their children's fear of atomic bombs, beginning with helping them understand that although the threat of atomic warfare "hangs over all the world," atomic bombs are not the first or only peril the world has faced and overcome. Other recommendations by the League, founded in 1915 and still active today, included the following:

- Help them to realize that the ultimate goal is world brotherhood, not military victory.
- Instill compassion as a way to encourage them to know and understand other peoples.
- Provide opportunities for them to discuss their fears, and point out that most people are afraid sometimes.
- Provide stability and offer them a quiet and calming environment.
- Provide continuity in the family, which means having the mother at home.
- Promote "gaiety" and develop creative activities that can be employed even during difficult times.
- Emphasize that even if material possessions are destroyed, having faith will see you through.[14]

The FCDA and the Valley Forge Foundation embraced the same tenets in their overall mission for the exhibit: minimizing fear, fostering family values, maintaining a balanced perspective on atomic energy, demonstrating compassion and brotherhood, and having faith in the future.[15]

Women in Indianapolis, reflecting women throughout the country, acknowledged these tenets by preparing for their duties well in advance of the show's opening. Under the direction of Aneta Vogler, women's chairman of the city's Alert America show, representatives from the Indianapolis Council of PTA, B'Nai B'Rith, Council of Church Women, Council of Jewish Women, Council of Catholic Women, and Council of Women and Medical Auxiliary served as guides, instructors, and volunteer recruiters during the three-day exhibition.[16] *The Indianapolis Star* even gave special recognition to Barbara Ward, the assistant to Charles Broderick, civil defense director for Marion County, and recording secretary for the Alert America exhibit. "Although she's not on a plant assembly line or working the graveyard shift riveting bombers," the newspaper wrote, "Barbara's work is every bit as important, helping Mr. Broderick safeguard the county's welfare in case of an enemy attack."[17]

The Cattle Pavilion at the Indiana State Fairgrounds provided a rather unusual setting for the Alert America exhibit, which arrived in Indianapolis from Kansas City, Missouri. Broderick arranged for the 7,200-square-foot facility to house the show for three days. Following the same script as other venues, the city held a countywide air-raid test and parade to open Alert America, with Boy Scouts, Girl Scouts, and Camp Fire Girls among those participating.[18] Members of the Indianapolis Civil Air Patrol provided "air cover" for the caravan by dropping leaflets on the crowds below as they flew over downtown toward the fairgrounds. The leaflets, which explained the objectives of Alert America, were dropped too late, though.[19] The air-raid test, which preceded the parade, had been a major disappointment, with *The Indianapolis Star* declaring that residents had flunked. Colonel Martin Luchinger, air-raid director, warned, "Indianapolis people will have to get on the ball fast or someday it may be too late."[20]

Of special note at the Indianapolis exhibit was the inauguration of the state's program to distribute identification tags to all men, women, and children who requested them. On opening day, Frederick Cretors, director of the Indiana Department of Civil Defense, presented the first ID tags to Governor Henry Schricker and his wife. By the conclusion of the exhibit, some 2,500 tags had been distributed to visitors. The tags—promised not to melt below 2,500 degrees Fahrenheit, discolor the skin, lose their shape, or wear out—cost 25 cents each. According to Cretors, one of the primary purposes of the tags, which resembled a military dog tag, was to reunite lost children with their parents. "When you can put an ID tag around your neck," Cretors said, "civil defense begins to come home to you. You begin to understand that you are worth identifying as the particular person you are, regardless of what happens to you. Without an almost indestructible tag around your neck, you may be hard to name."[21] In May 1952, a month after the launch of the ID tag program, the Indiana Department of Civil Defense announced that more than 90 percent of students in the state had purchased an ID tag, with some 4,000 tags being distributed every day. In May, Sweetser High School in Grant County, the first school to sign up for the tags, reported that 93 percent of its students now wore ID tags.[22]

STATE OF INDIANA

Department of Civil Defense
Identification Tag Order Form

.... COUNTY

Accuracy is most important! Please check this identification tag order form carefully to make sure that all the information is correct.

Name of organization placing order: ....

Address to which order should be returned: ....
                                                    (Number)   (Street)

City: .... State: ....

Here is how you fill out the form:

    1. PRINT the applicant's name: ....

    ....

    List the last name, first name and middle initial, in the proper space provided.

    2. Married women should list their given name as Doe, Virginia L.—never as Mrs. John Doe.

    3. List the street or R. F. D. address and double check in all cases to be certain that the name of the town or city and state is included. Since these tags are for identification purposes, the full name of the city should be spelled out correctly.

    4. The following symbols are to be used to designate religion:
        C—for Catholic   P—for Protestant
        J—for Hebrew   Y—for all other
        S—for Christian Science   denominations

    5. List the month, day and year of birth: ....

    6. Be sure to insert the name of the county in the space provided at the top of this form.

    7. Please make certain that the information requested is complete and accurate. This is most important.

Enter the total number of ID Tags applied for: ....

Enter the total amount of remittance enclosed: ....

Make Payable to: "CIVIL DEFENSE TAGS"

(Cash and Stamps Are Not Accepted)	Money Order: ....
	Check: ....
Mail To:	Bank Draft: ....
"Civil Defense Tags" Room 203,	Date Forwarded: ....
777 North Meridian St. Indianapolis, Indiana.	Date Received at State Headquarters: ....

Indiana inaugurated a statewide program to distribute civil defense identification "dog tags" on the opening day of Alert America in Indianapolis. By the time the exhibit moved on to the next city, 2,500 people had purchased a tag for 25 cents each. The tags were guaranteed not to melt below 2,500 degrees Fahrenheit, discolor the skin, lose their shape, or wear out.

In Rock Island, Illinois, students had an opportunity to tour Alert America each morning during its three-day run from March 19 to 21. Illinois schools included Franklin, Washington, Edison, and Central junior high schools in Rock Island; Moline (Illinois) junior and senior high schools; and seventh- and eighth-graders from St. Joseph's Catholic School, and Sacred Heart and St. Mary's in Rock Island. Students from Davenport, Iowa, schools and other Iowa schools toured the exhibit on Friday, designated as Iowa Day. Fifty-two student nurses from Rock Island's St. Anthony's Hospital also had an opportunity to tour the exhibit Friday morning. Of the 2,400 visitors on the first day, 751 were from the school tour that morning.[23] According to *The Dispatch*, Moline's daily newspaper, "Controlled groups of school children flooded the armory" on the second morning. Of the 3,923 people visiting that day, 2,225 were children. Over the three days, 10,036 people visited the exhibit, including 5,846 elementary and high school students—58 percent.[24]

The show, presented in the Rock Island Armory, opened on a notable day. That morning, state and federal civil defense officials issued a statement that the Quad-City area (encompassing Rock Island and Moline, Illinois, and Davenport and Bettendorf, Iowa) had reached the critical stage as a potential enemy target. At a meeting of civil defense officials in Rock Island, Carl Gabel, regional head of the FCDA, stressed the urgency of the area's civil defense efforts. "The federal government is taking the attitude that the quicker a workable civil defense unit is set up," Gabel said, "the quicker it will be ready for a potential attack. The question is: 'If it happens tomorrow, what do we have to combat it in the way of civil defense trainees, equipment, and mutual aid pacts?'"[25]

Women constituted one answer. Women's role in civil defense had been the subject of a newspaper editorial a few days before the exhibit opened. The editorial argued that Alert America gave special attention to women's role in civil defense, going on to point out that women "are needed for enlistment in the many phases of the defense undertaking."[26] In addition to serving as guides and recruiters, women in Rock Island also participated in a demonstration of an emergency telephone center in front of the armory by Illinois Bell Telephone. The center was contained in a 31-foot, four-ton trailer with five telephone lines, two mobile telephone units, two portable telephone sets, a teletype machine, a public address system, and two field telephones. A five-ton truck, used to pull the trailer, came equipped with a generator, tools, first-aid supplies, ladders, and 10,000 feet of telephone wire.[27]

The Rev. Kenneth Hooe and his granddaughter received special recognition as the 300,000th and 300,001st visitors since the Alert America convoy began its tour in January.[28] The Valley Forge Foundation and FCDA also recognized the Rock Island exhibit for signing up 19 percent of all visitors as civil defense volunteers—compared to 10–15 percent nationwide. *The Dis-*

patch newspaper reported that Rock Island had received the "best quality and most interesting publicity" of any other exhibit city.[29]

Chicago surpassed this benchmark six weeks later. Anthony J. Mullaney, Chicago's civil defense director, had announced in advance that the Alert America exhibit had been expanded to twice its normal size. Scheduled for May 3–9, the exhibit would occupy some 30,000 square feet or the entire second half of the drill deck of the Naval Reserve Armory. "We want to develop a greater awareness of the necessity of a reasonable, common-sense civil defense program, even though the danger of war does not seem imminent," Mullaney said. "We hope that at least one in every family in Chicago will see this free show, and find out the nature of the threat that faces us, and specifically what the individual citizen can do to meet this threat."[30]

In addition to the traveling Alert America exhibit, the Chicago Civil Defense Corps included a Red Cross demonstration of a new back-pressure method of artificial respiration; a display of the Air Force's new F-86 jet fighter; the Navy's *USS Silversides* submarine, moored at the armory for public inspection; two 120-millimeter anti-aircraft guns of the 709th anti-aircraft battalion; a demonstration of air-raid sirens; and a display of new and old fire trucks, communications trailers, and debris clearing equipment, including bulldozers, cranes, and other earth-moving vehicles. The Chicago Board of Education contributed by showing an emergency outdoor mass-feeding model of a stove made of scrap material; and the city's Department of Public Works demonstrated how to determine radioactivity in drinking water by using a Geiger counter.[31]

Again, women and children played an important role in Alert America. Eight hundred women served as information clerks, guides, and registrars. As an adjunct to the exhibit, teenage boys and girls, with their parents' written permission, received free rides over the city in privately owned Civil Air Patrol planes. They could board buses at the Naval Reserve Armory and be taken directly to the airfield. Girls from Steinmetz High School helped in the Red Cross booth by demonstrating how a sickroom could be created from articles found around the house.[32]

Less than a week after the show closed in Chicago, the exhibit opened in New York City on May 13 at the Seventh Regiment Armory. Prior to the opening, Grover Whalen, the city's civil defense coordinator of recruiting and public information, held a press conference for student editors and photographers from the city's fifty-four academic and technical high schools, thirty-one vocational schools, and several parochial high schools—representing some 250,000 students combined. Whalen discussed details about Alert America and revealed that the New York City Board of Education had made arrangements for junior and senior high school students to visit the exhibit. According to the *New York Times*, the event planners had arranged

Each city hosting Alert America set aside morning hours for teachers and their students to tour the exhibit, and many school districts provided transportation for elementary and high school students. In some cities, students represented 30 percent or more of the total attendance (National Archives).

for 60,000 school children to attend the show.[33] The plans worked. For the first four days of the Alert America exhibit, which ran through May 19, some 2,000 public-school students toured the Alert America exhibit each hour between 10 a.m. and 3 p.m.; over the last three days, students from Lutheran, Catholic, Jewish, and private schools attended the exhibit.[34]

Although other cities did not approach these numbers, children still represented a major portion of all visitors to Alert America. During the four-day stay in Wilmington, Delaware, in January, some 2,500 children from public, private, and parochial schools toured the exhibit. "Our children stayed close together while touring the display, and walked from the armory quietly," one teacher said afterward. "The atomic show left little room for levity."[35] Buses transported students in sixth, seventh, and eighth grades to see Alert America during its March stopover in Pittsfield, Massachusetts.[36] Some 4,000 high school boys and girls saw the exhibit in Nashville, Tennessee, during its five-day run in March. After seeing the atomic destruction of "City X," one high school student said, "Golly. I didn't have any idea it was like that. I don't think I'll forget it." A teacher commented, "They came in here joking, but believe me, they're serious now. No one could fail to be impressed. It's a wonderful exhibit."[37] St. Louis public school children received an opportunity to tour the exhibit on opening day, March 5, in Kiel Auditorium, with students from Catholic and Lutheran schools attending on following days.[38] In its three-day stay in Phoenix, Arizona, in early May, 17,634 people saw the exhibit, including some 12,000 children—68 percent.[39] Los Angeles children "had a field day climbing in and out of great tanks, artillery pieces, and amphibious vehicles" during its May showing.[40] Then the following month, 10,000 high school students from Oakland, California, and Alameda County took chartered buses to and from the Oakland Auditorium to see the exhibit.

Responsibility for guiding these students through the Alert America exhibit rested with volunteer guides, most of whom were women. Every city on the tour, in fact, created women's committees to work with local women's organizations for volunteers. Mrs. J.H. Tyler McConnell, Wilmington's coordinator of women's activities, recruited women to serve as guides, interpreters, and auxiliary police. Among the cooperating groups were the Soroptomist Club, the JaneCees, the American Association of University Women, and the Women's Auxiliary of the New Castle County Medical Society. Thirty-two members of the Wilmington Junior League volunteered to manage various local civil defense displays. Although McConnell recommended that children below the seventh grade not visit the exhibit, she did urge elementary school teachers to attend and share their experiences with their students.[41]

In Los Angeles, Mrs. Leiland Atherton Irish served as chair of women's activities and Mrs. Clay Montfort served as chair of hostesses for the Alert America exhibit. Together, they recruited volunteer hostesses from the American Women's Voluntary Service, American Legion Auxiliary, Communications Corps, the Los Angeles Federation of Women's Clubs, Mexican Civil Defense Corps, Pilot Club, Purple Heart Auxiliary, and Volunteer Bureau of Welfare Council.[42] At the Salt Lake City exhibit, set up at the state fairgrounds, women representing the Utah Federation of Women's Clubs and many other women's groups assisted with demonstrations and helped as guides.[43] The California Federation of Women's Clubs, in a move the Berkeley Daily Gazette attributed to strengthening the awareness of their role in civil defense, voted to "wholeheartedly support" the Alert America convoy during its stops in California. The resolution, passed during the Federation's annual convention in San Jose, urged all members to visit the exhibit and to promote attendance to others.[44]

Mrs. Harry Christopher, a member of Governor McKeldin's Advisory Council for Civil Defense and president of the Maryland Federation of Women's Clubs, named sixteen representatives of area women's organizations

Women played an important part in Alert America as both volunteer guides and hosts. The FCDA targeted women as being essential in the nation's civil defense. This Los Angeles exhibit featured a typical American dining room with a sign on the table reading, "Is Your Home Prepared?" (Los Angeles Fire Department).

to assist with Alert America in Baltimore, which ran January 25–28. The organizations included Woman's Civil League, Woman's Club of Glyndon, YWCA, Maryland League of Women's Clubs, Soroptomist Club, Girl Scouts, National Council of Jewish Women, Maryland Society of Colonial Dames of America, and Business and Professional Women's Clubs of Baltimore. The week prior to the exhibit's opening, Christopher presented the awards in the "Civil Defense and Safety Contest" and highlighted the importance of the "Build Freedom With Youth" contest being sponsored by the National Federation of Women's Clubs in cooperation with the Kroger Company. Women's clubs throughout the nation promoted the contest designed to prepare youth for leadership and community service through projects "whereby youth will be helped to plan and think individually, at the same time learning to work with others toward the common goal." The "Build Freedom With Youth" contest opened February 1, 1951, and closed May 1, but awards were not announced until the spring of 1952, during the Alert America national convoy.[45]

The "Build Freedom with Youth" contest complemented the Freedom Awards issued annually by the Freedoms Foundation, parent organization of the Valley Forge Foundation. Both awards programs, as well as Alert America, stressed the importance of defending the American way of life. Through the awards, the Foundation sought to convince Americans, young and old, that civil defense was "a part of the total defense of our free American Way of Life, based on its fundamental belief in God, on constitutional government designed to serve the people and our indivisible bundle of political and economic rights."[46]

Kenneth Wells, president of both foundations, consistently linked the importance of civil defense with the preservation of democracy in a world threatened by communist aggressors. "We can and must individually hold our ideals high," Wells wrote in the *Alert America!* booklet. "The hard-driving work and power of our ideals will win out in this time of crisis. We have a sacred privilege that no thinking citizen will ignore—the privilege of serving as did George Washington at Valley Forge in 1777 and 1778—the privilege of accepting this opportunity to save and extend what is dearer than life itself—our American Way of Life. Train—Work—and Pray—for an 'Alert America'!"[47] The FCDA, as well, connected the importance of civil defense with protecting and preserving democracy. In its 1952 annual report, it stated: "There must be fuller recognition that the spiritual unity of civil defense is an important factor in the survival of our American way of life. We must have a rebirth of individual self-reliance and national neighborliness on the part of America's men, women, and children."[48]

The FCDA also made this clear in one of its first pamphlets, *This Is Civil Defense*, which reminded readers: "If the bombs from enemy planes ever fell on your city, they would not fall on a plan, or an organization, or a system of government. They would fall on you and your family and friends. If you were a soldier, you would be trained to take care of yourself and keep on fighting. As a defender of the home front, you must learn to protect yourself and keep on working."[49] It went on to warn that even though every precaution might be taken, a soldier could still be killed. For civilians, and especially women, "the more you know, and the better trained you are, the better your chances for survival."

Historian Kristina Zarlengo has argued that because of the threat of atomic bombings occurring anywhere at any time, women and children formed a new class of soldiers—"deterrence soldiers beckoned to peacetime behavior that was in concert with war prevention."[50] Zarlengo's argument rightfully describes the government's approach to civil defense. But it is important to stress that encouraging individuals to take personal responsibility for their self-preservation was the only feasible solution to an extremely complex problem: how to protect Americans if the Soviet Union actually did launch an all-out atomic attack, which, in 1952, was considered a real possibility. The FCDA's emphasis on the essential role of women serving in civil defense areas, such as warden, communications, and nursing, plus its strategy of enlisting women to assist in Alert America, had worked well. So, too, the FCDA had been successful in working with the Boy Scouts, Girl Scouts, and Camp Fire Girls to support its many projects, including Alert America. And it had succeeded in having school districts transport students to tour the exhibit during special hours. In this sense, many women and children absolutely became deterrence soldiers.

* * *

U.S. Needs Civil Defense
By Millard Caldwell, FCDA Administrator

Volunteers Are Responsible for Protecting the Home Front

(Eleventh in the series)

All persons experienced in work having to do with health or medicine, others who can be trained in special weapons defense (against atomic, biological, and chemical warfare), are needed for the civil defense Health Service. Their big job will be to care for the injured, and protect the health of a city after an attack. In addition, many more volunteers will be needed for various duties under the direction of professional people, such as doctors and nurses, in the local civil defense organizations.

The Health Service also must have thousands of persons trained in more than just first aid who can be organized for definite jobs at first aid stations, and women volunteers who have taken courses in home nursing and nurses' aide. Men will be needed as litter bearers, ambulance personnel, hospital orderlies and attendants, supply handlers, and maintenance workers.

Defense against disease and gas warfare, and against radiological contamination, will need extra food inspectors, and sanitation workers. Radiological monitoring teams will need teachers, or advance students of physics and other related subjects, as team leaders, and high school graduates who have studied elementary physics, and radio repairmen, who can serve as members of such teams.

Other volunteers are needed for clerical work, to keep records of the ill, the injured, and the dead, to aid in the procurement of blood for the blood service under the charge of the American Red Cross, and to be trained as assistants in laboratory work.

Unskilled Labor User

Help is needed for such duties as washing laboratory glassware and mopping floors. In fact, no matter what you do, Health Service can use you in the vitally important civil defense work of saving lives.

If an enemy attacks one of our cities, many persons will find themselves without food, clothing, money, and shelter. The Welfare Service provides such things and aids in locating missing persons, caring for infants, the aged, and the infirm.

It also gathers and passes on news of people who are separated from their families, contacts relatives in other cities, refers families to places where they can get special help, and registers those persons who must have individual care.

Training Courses Available

Training courses, under competent instructors, are available in the various branches of this civil defense program. Women, by background and experience, are well qualified for both these services and are urged to take a special interest in them.

Getting a Bombed Community on Its Feet Takes Organization

(Last in the series)

Getting a stricken city back into working order as soon as possible by restoring damaged facilities and clearing away debris is the job of the Engineering Service. Under their regular supervisors, but with civil defense direction, men employed by public works and utility departments or contracting firms would do the same kind of work in the event of enemy attack.

Men would be needed who can operate special equipment, such as cranes, bulldozers, dump trucks, and welding machines, and volunteers in the labor force that would help clean away wreckage and open the streets to traffic. Help would be recruited from equipment and material dealers, labor unions, engineering schools, and other groups which have skilled workmen, tools, and materials.

The Rescue Service

Rescue work is mainly an engineering job and requires some basic knowledge of shoring, rigging, and building construction. Hence, its personnel will be drawn from the building trades and similar occupations. Untrained rescue workers often make a bad situation worse by causing additional damage, creating more casualties, or becoming casualties themselves.

Rescue teams will have their own specially equipped rescue vehicles, and will be made up of eight men each. Three teams, working 8-hour shifts to provide around-the-clock operation, will be assigned to each rescue vehicle, and will be known as a rescue squad. Ability and willingness to work as a team under emergency conditions, and strength and stamina to perform that work are the requirements for the good rescue workers.

Skilled drivers are needed for the Transportation Service. In case of enemy attack, people and equipment would have to be moved carefully and rapidly: the injured to hospitals, emergency food and medical supplies to the stricken area. Women can be very useful in these operations, and many of them acted as drivers for the military and Red Cross in the last war.

The Transportation Service will teach people to drive in organized fleets under emergency condition, and give them instructions in simple repair and maintenance work if necessary. Assembly points will be set up and a mission will be assigned to every volunteer and every official vehicle.

Persons skilled in rail, air, or water transportation are also needed and should contact their local civil defense transportation service.

Will Need Volunteers

Your local civil defense headquarters will need many volunteers for staff work. No matter what job you undertake, it will be vital to your organization. You are just as important in a small job as in a big job.

It is not necessary to have any technical knowledge. By volunteering for staff work, you may give someone with technical skill the opportunity to serve where he is most needed.

All the civil defense services you have been reading about are for the purpose of protecting lives and property in the United States. Every one in every community is fitted for some job in civil defense. Select one or more for which you are best qualified and volunteer NOW.

SEVEN

The Press Responds

One of these days ... there'll be a red, white, and blue truck caravan pull up in front of some big building ... and it will unload the Alert America exhibit and, if you're smart, you'll go in and look at it. Self-preservation, they tell me, is the first law of nature, so—obey the law!—Bill Henry, *Los Angeles Times*, 1952[1]

William Mellors "Bill" Henry, a columnist for the *Los Angeles Times*, had visited the Alert America exhibit during its Washington, D.C., debut in January. In his column, "By the Way with Bill Henry," published on January 15, 1952—five months before the exhibit visited Los Angeles—Henry made clear that his readers could not afford to miss Alert America. Reflecting the viewpoints of many in the media, Henry brought to the forefront the exhibit's overriding emphasis on protecting the American way of life by becoming involved in civil defense. Despite its depiction of atomic destruction, the exhibit's fundamental point, he wrote, was "that what we really have at stake is not just our homes and our property, or even our lives. What we should seek to protect by every possible means is our American heritage. We can afford to lose everything else so long as we preserve that." His column ended with a touch of inspiration: "If they burn down your house but you still have freedom, life is still worth living!"[2]

Henry, also a radio and TV broadcaster, exemplifies the favorable newspaper coverage garnered by the Alert America exhibit as it traveled across the country. Millard Caldwell, FCDA administrator, and Kenneth Wells, president of the Valley Forge Foundation, placed media support at the top of their priority list for promoting attendance. With television still in its infancy in 1952—only 9 percent of American households had televisions—radio became the more important component in their strategy, with 90 percent of American households having at least one radio.[3] To reach this audience, the FCDA launched a radio program in January 1952 called, appropriately, *Alert America.*

American Broadcasting Company aired the program, which focused on the nation's civil defense program, to its stations nationwide.[4] Even more effective than radio, however, were daily newspapers. In the early 1950s, newspapers had some fifty-four million subscribers—more than one subscription per household in a day when many cities had morning, evening, ethnic, religious, and other special-interest newspapers.[5] With the vast majority of American households subscribing to at least one newspaper, it is evident that millions of people either read about or at least saw the headlines about the threat of atomic warfare and the role of civil defense.

Newspaper coverage of Alert America began long before Henry wrote his column on January 15, 1952. At a May 1951 meeting of 2,000 representatives of regional and national associations in Washington, D.C., attendees obtained a rather bleak update from the FCDA on the nation's state of readiness. Those attending heard not only that none of the 250 primary target areas was prepared for an atomic attack, but also that most Americans believed it was useless to do anything about such an attack.[6] The following month, on June 15, the 12-member FCDA National Advisory Council also met in the nation's capital to take action to correct this lack of readiness. The meeting ended with the council releasing a statement that to overcome Americans' lack of knowledge about the atomic bomb, an "alert America" campaign was needed to inform the public about the "grave danger" from an enemy atomic attack and that the country could lose the next war without a national civil defense program. Immediately, both Associated Press (AP) and United Press (UP) released syndicated articles on the council's actions. In a UP story distributed nationwide, the council had been quoted as saying, "Civil defense against modern weapons is not something which can be created at a moment's notice to fit a sudden need. Civil defense must be ready at all times to meet any need which might arise. Once the bombs hit, it will be too late." AP released an extensive article quoting the council's statement at length, including a not-so-subtle threat to people not supporting civil defense. "Failure to perform the duties of civil defense for reasons of apathy or disinterest," the statement read, "is as clearly treasonable behavior as would be the failure of a soldier to go to the aid of his fellows."[7]

Four months later, in October 1951, newspaper columnist Robert S. Allen reported that President Harry Truman, the Atomic Energy Commission, and a joint congressional committee on atomic energy had approved a "spectacular caravan" to tour the country to promote civil defense and provide information about the promise and perils of atomic energy.[8] *The New York Times* wrote that the FCDA was sending "a road show of exhibits of war destruction and home defense techniques across the nation to perk up civilian recruiting" because, according to the FCDA's Caldwell, the average citizen "was not yet fully alert."[9] Newspapers across the country published similar syndicated news stories as well as supportive editorials. *The Newark Advocate* in Newark, Ohio, for example, wrote: "War is never a pleasant subject for thought, and an exhibit which is designed to show possible war damage will not be entertaining. But the project may help to bring home to all the people the urgent need to prepare so that any emergency will find us ready and capable of meeting it.... If the traveling exhibits can spur our civil defense effort to such an end, they will serve a useful purpose."[10]

Senator Margaret Chase Smith of Maine, a Republican, endorsed Alert America twice in her syndicated column. On January 9, after seeing the exhibit, she wrote that it seemed "ironical, if not unbelievable—to have to try to sell us on the idea of protecting our lives, when self-preservation is a basic instinct of human beings." Expanding on the nation's apathy toward civil defense, she continued, "It is an unpleasant truth that we Americans have not awakened to the threat to our lives from potential atomic attack." But the main fault for this, she argued, rested with Congress, which had failed to support President Truman's request for funding. Two weeks later, Chase wrote another column to reinforce her concerns about the public's apathy and the lack of congressional support for civil defense. Reminding her readers that Alert America may be coming to their city, she wrote, "If it does, make every effort to see it. I guarantee that you will come away impressed—but, at any rate, better prepared mentally for your own defense and for the defense of your country."[11]

Although originally planned to open in the nation's capital in December 1951, Alert America actually opened January 7, 1952, before one of the convoys began its nationwide tour in Wilmington, Delaware. Wilmington's two newspapers, *The Morning News* and *The News Journal*, provided extensive coverage of the exhibit before and during the show, which proved to be a major success during its January 20–23 run. *The Evening Sun* focused on the show's scarier message in an article published the day following the opening ceremonies. "[L]ast night," it read, "a recorded voice said that in the event of war, military defenses could stop about 30 of every 100 attacking planes—the other 70 would get through. The gigantic display points out that where the military leaves off, civil defense takes over, and that it is every citizen's job to be prepared."[12] An editorial titled "Alert—Delaware," published in *The Morning News*, stressed that anyone not attending the Alert America exhibit was "passing up an opportunity to know the realistic facts of home front warfare."[13]

As discussed elsewhere, Caldwell traveled extensively in 1952 to speak about Alert America at national, regional, and state conferences and meetings, as well as to meet with local city and civil defense officials and volunteers, local organizations, and the media in advance of the city's Alert America exhibit. These meetings also allowed Caldwell to stress the show's larger purpose of defending the American way of life. The *Pittsburgh* (Pennsylvania)

Press provided a detailed report of Wells' talk before 75 representatives of local church, club, and school organizations in January as the Alert America tour got under way. "We must make our decision now," he told the representatives, "whether our future course is to be socialism or the dream of a free, new future in an atomic age. We are going through a major crisis and whether we resist the forces striving to undermine our freedom or extend our American way is entirely up to the individual in every community through education."[14] In April, Caldwell took the initiative by addressing the annual convention of the American Society of Newspaper Editors. He praised them for their reporting on civil defense and cited a survey by the University of Michigan that found "conclusively" that daily newspapers had made the largest information contribution to civil defense education. This contribution was critical, Caldwell told the editors, because civil defense information would "save countless thousands of lives if Russia's atomic bombs rain down on our cities." "There would be no civil defense program today," he continued, "nor can there be one in the future without the complete understanding and wholehearted support of our media … newspapers have proven to be the cornerstone in civil defense."[15]

In his dual role as president of the Freedoms Foundation, Wells also recognized the efforts of America's newspaper reporters and columnists. "It is urgent that every American rise above all the partisanship," Wells wrote in the *Alert America!* booklet, "and, realizing the common danger, prove his citizenship by actively and personally backing civil defense."[16] The foundation's Freedom Awards were presented each year on George Washington's birthday to individuals and institutions, including newspapers, contributing to the American way of life and proving his or her citizenship. The foundation awarded eleven top prizes of $1,500 each and hundreds of lower cash prizes. The 1952 awards included George Sokolsky, columnist for the *Star Press* in Muncie, Indiana, honored for his column titled "America's Spiritual Heritage"; and George Magenheimer, associate editor of the *Peoria* (Illinois) *Journal*, for an editorial titled "The Best in the World."[17]

Baltimore's two newspapers, *The Baltimore Sun* and *The Evening Sun*, provided advance coverage of Alert America, which opened January 25 for five days. Despite warnings about the more graphic elements, both newspapers urged people to see "The Show That May Save Your Life," while local companies added Alert America information to their newspaper ads—a trend followed by companies in every venue city. The *Baltimore Afro American* also promoted the exhibit, highlighting the fact that it would be demonstrating "procedures for every man, woman, and child to follow in the event of an enemy attack."[18] With the diorama of an atomic attack viewed as the focal point of the Alert America exhibit, newspapers often illuminated the destructive aspects of the show. This was evidenced by *The Evening Sun*, which

TODAY through TUESDAY
5th REGIMENT ARMORY

"THE SHOW THAT CAN SAVE YOUR LIFE!"

The
ALERT AMERICA
Convoy

Admission Free
DON'T MISS IT!

PUBLISHED AS A PUBLIC SERVICE BY

AMERICAN OIL COMPANY

In support of Alert America, many companies created special newspaper ads to encourage attendance, such as this public service ad for the Baltimore, Maryland, exhibit.

grabbed attention by publishing an article highlighting the atomic destruction of "City X," which "can shock and enlighten Baltimoreans into an appreciation of civil defense."[19] The day before Alert America opened, *The Baltimore Sun* ran a more positive article pointing out that the constructive power of the atom would be displayed as well as the destructive power, and that the show would provide information on how to prepare for an atomic attack as well as ways to contribute to the city's civil defense.[20]

The Alert America exhibit stopped in Greenville, South Carolina, on February 7 for a four-day showing, but its residents knew about the exhibit well in advance. *The Greenville News* announced its scheduled dates on December 30, 1951, following a meeting of the city's civil defense officials, John Paxton of the Valley Forge Foundation, and Colonel Harry Brown, FCDA's deputy administrator based in Atlanta. Greenville was the only city in the state to host the exhibit, which attracted some 8,000 people. The newspaper's lead paragraph asked the ultimate question—and the question to be answered by Alert America: "What should you do if an atomic bomb were dropped on Greenville?"[21] As the exhibit approached, the paper continued to publish informative articles about the parade and air-raid alert planned for opening day. Reporter Dan Halligan's article appearing on the first day took a dramatic tactic to spur people to action. Wrote Halligan: "For Greenvillians, the businessman, the housewife, and the student, today will be their greatest and possibly only opportunity to learn how to protect themselves and their families during and after an atomic bomb attack on this city."[22]

Two weeks after Greenville, another convoy rolled into Boston, where the exhibit ran from February 20 to 25 in the First Corps Cadet Armory. Saul Pett, an AP news-feature writer, provided one of the more lighthearted articles about Alert America. He wrote:

> In Boston, a dowager attending the "Alert America" exhibit demanded to know what all the fuss was about.
> "We're trying to stimulate interest in civil defense," an official explained. "We might be bombed, you know."
> "Nonsense," the lady said. "God wouldn't allow Boston to be bombed."
> With that, she stomped out, turning her back on a vivid display of what a single atom bomb could do to an American city.[23]

On a more serious note, *The Boston Globe* quoted Joseph Malone, the city's director of civil defense, as calling Alert America "a must for everyone in this atomic age." Malone stressed a viewpoint expressed repeatedly by civil defense officials across the country. "The enemy could strike with little or no warning," he said. "If we are unprepared, we are lost. But if the enemy can't crush the home front quickly, he cannot win a global war against America."[24] *The Atlanta Constitution* delivered the same message in advance of the city's scheduled February 24–28 stop. Despite the dramatic headline, "Exhibit Set Here to Cite Atom Peril," the February 14 article presented a balanced overview of the "dangers and opportunities of the atomic age."[25] But, then, the day after the exhibit opened, the newspaper ran another sizable story with yet another frightening headline, "How A-Bomb Could Raze Atlanta Shown at Exhibit." The opening sentences sounded more like the beginning of a novel: "The small group of Atlantans filed quietly out of the curtain-shrouded labyrinth of exhibits Sunday. They had seen what could happen to

Atlanta if an atom bomb fell on the Gate City, and their faces bore serious if not anxious expressions."[26]

Hartford, Connecticut, which hosted the exhibit March 9–12, drew more than 20,000 visitors, or about 11 percent of its population. The show's success can be contributed in part to the extensive coverage by the *Hartford Courant*, which published several articles in advance of its opening. Rather than the attention-grabbing headlines in some newspapers, the *Courant* primarily reported on the details of the exhibit, including additional local displays. For example, one article reported that 300 amateur radio operators would be demonstrating civil defense communications facilities and networks, and transmitting free messages from visitors to any place in the world.[27]

The Tennessean, Nashville's daily newspaper, also provided extensive advance coverage of the Alert America exhibit, which was set up on the state fairgrounds March 12–16. Lois Laycook, the newspaper's Washington correspondent, had reported the FCDA's announcement on January 9 that the exhibit would visit Nashville. Laycook called it an inspiring yet dramatic exhibit that "drives home the urgency of American home front mobilization against atomic attack."[28] The opening sentence in an article published February 15 also amplified the importance of attending: "A new call for American home-front mobilization against atomic attack will be sounded in Nashville March 12, when the 'Alert America' exhibit comes here during its tour of 70 American cities." The next week, the newspaper's headline quoted the show's theme, "The Show That Could Save Your Life," and outlined the various displays without the hyperbole of atomic warfare.[29]

Once the exhibit opened, however, *The Tennessean* continued to urge people to attend. The day after the opening ceremony, Lee McLean bylined an article titled "'Alert America' Stirs Nashville" clearly intended to spark readers into action. "More than 1,000 Alert Nashvillians," McLean wrote, "anxious to become Alert Americans, stood horror-struck last night as they watched what could be their own city destroyed by atomic attack." Governor Gordon Browning, who had attended opening night, was quoted as saying: "Our American home front lies open to attack as never before. Civilians at home are as vulnerable to attack in this modern type of warfare as are soldiers on the front line. Our backyards of today are the potential firing lines of tomorrow."[30] As if to ensure that all Nashvillians understood the importance of Alert America, the same issue ran an editorial on the urgency of knowing how to prepare for an atomic attack:

> Now doing a five-day stand here is the grimmest road show ever to hit Nashville. Offhand, that might not sound like much of a recommendation. But the "Alert America Convoy" is not here to entertain you or to reap rich rewards for its promoters. *It is here to safeguard your life!* It is here to help you understand why we cannot shrug off the possibility of atomic attack. It is here to show you how we as a nation could

minimize the effects of such an attack. It is here to show what you as an individual could do to protect yourself and your family.[31]

The editorial continued by warning that being unprepared only makes the prospect of the city being destroyed more real. "The time to prepare is now," it read, "and an excellent opportunity for helping to do so is at hand. With your life possibly hanging in the balance, what more need be said?"[32]

On the exhibit's last day in Nashville, the newspaper again published a dramatic attempt to spur people to visit. Reporter T. H. Teeter described an atomic attack coming without warning, resulting in the "white-hot heat of the sun" hovering over the darkened city, adding that "knowing what to do and when to do it is the important thing." Referring to the previous day, Teeter wrote, "Hundreds of Nashvillians filed out of the 'Alert America' exhibit ... realizing for the first time that they may be a little late in imagining such things."[33] *The Tennessean* published an even stronger message March 6, following the opening of Alert America in Chattanooga, Tennessee, where it ran March 5–8. Sergeant Alvin C. York of World War I fame—recipient of the Congressional Media of Honor for attacking a German machine gun nest, killing at least twenty-five enemy soldiers and capturing 132 Germans—made his opinion known to the 500 invited guests at the exhibit's opening reception. "It is time we were waking up," he told the audience. "If we are not ready when war comes, it is going to be a catastrophe. Those fellows are going to try and make it happen. If they can put one of those missiles on an American city, they are going to do it." When discussing the ongoing war in Korea, York said bluntly, "We are going to have to go to Moscow to win the war. Let's take an A-bomb and go up to the head of the spring and muddy the water."[34]

A month before Alert America opened in Pittsburgh, Pennsylvania, on June 18, Kenneth Wells visited the city and met with forty of the city's leading industrialists, as the newspaper described them. Although not quite as explicit as those by Alvin York, his comments were deadly serious all the same. In an article titled "America on the Alert," the *Pittsburgh Post-Gazette* summarized Wells' message: "There's a new ingredient in American life. We accept it—or we die!" The new ingredient, of course, was civil defense. "No one has any superior immunity to enemy attack," Wells was quoted as saying. "Responsibility is co-equal to everybody."[35] Across the state in Philadelphia, John McCullough of *The Philadelphia Inquirer* promoted the Alert America exhibit, scheduled for June 7–13, by emphasizing its "vital message" to the American people in an article published two days before its opening. "It attempts to teach you how to live for the things you would die for," McCullough wrote. "You would die for your family, without a second thought. You would die for some part—some right or privilege or purpose—of the United States of America. Maybe you think you wouldn't, maybe you even shrink from the thought—but you would, if the chips were down, and the calloused paw of history was sorting the men from the boys." Of course, his primary point was that it was vital that everyone attend Alert America.[36]

The Indianapolis Star provided extensive advance coverage of Alert America three months before its scheduled dates of March 31–April 2. In January, it covered the announcement by Charles Broderick, director of civil defense for Marion County, that the exhibit would be visiting Indianapolis "to awaken Americans to the dangers of atomic attack."[37] Leading up to the opening, the newspaper connected the exhibit with a dire warning about the atomic threat in two articles titled "War Exhibit Convoy Is Welcomed" and "'Alert America' Caravan Here for Defense Display." The first article said the exhibit's mission was "to arouse Hoosiers to the dangers of atomic and biological warfare and spur them to an active role in civil defense." The second article quoted Broderick as saying that visiting the Alert America exhibit "may save your life."[38]

Saving your life represented the essential message in almost all newspaper coverage of Alert America—whether articles emphasized the destructive power as shown with "City X" or focused on the more positive aspects, such as the role of civil defense. The *Oakland Tribune*, for example, published an article prior to its city's opening on June 3 titled "Show Portrays Atomic Warfare." The article described how "City X" attempts to fight back only to have "the brilliant mushroom of the atomic bomb" bloom in the sky as the city "disintegrates into fire and rubble." But it then continued to point out that the exhibit offered "outstanding photographs and artwork" highlighting America's freedoms.[39] The local newspaper in Hutchinson, Kansas, which hosted the exhibit in July, ran advertisements urging attendance and published articles about Alert America's destructive and positive aspects. The article, titled "Possible War Horrors Seen at Exhibition," pointed out that the show was "a grim reminder of what could happen here in the event of total war," but continued by pointing out that displays showed "how the individual can meet this menace, and how civil defense services are organized to protect communities."[40]

If the exhibit appeared in only one city in a state—or appeared during the state fair—newspapers throughout the state published articles about the show and the importance of attending. In September, *The Lincoln Star* promoted both Alert America and a Ground Observer Corps' Operation Skywatch exhibit at the Nebraska state fair, calling them "two outstanding, brandnew exhibits … to prepare Nebraskans for future roles in civil defense." The newspaper quoted Wendell Harding, the state's director of defense, as saying, "Chief purpose of the exhibit is to bring the job of civil defense home to the man who needs it most—the man on the street."[41] Newspapers throughout Utah, from *The Salt Lake Tribune* and *The Beaver County News* to *Helper*

The Show You'll Never Forget Will Be In

HUTCHINSON
SPORTS ARENA

Tuesday, July 29--Wednesday, July 30--Thursday, July 31

2 P.M.--10 P.M.

ADMISSION IS FREE

See the

Alert America Convoy

What is atomic energy all about? What can it do?...what are its peacetime uses?...what can Civil Defense do to protect you and your family in the event of enemy attack?

Everyone is asking these questions today. Now, the ALERT AMERICA show gives you a dramatic answer. It *shows* you... in a way you'll never forget...the "inside story" of modern war weapons—and how organized Civil Defense can beat this menace.

This is the show that may save your life. Don't miss it!

YOU'LL SEE... | **YOU'LL SEE...** | **YOU'LL SEE...** | **YOU'LL SEE...**

remarkable uses for atomic energy in times of peace...its application in the factory, on the farm, and in the field of medicine! | a scientific action diorama of enemy sabotage, and germ and gas warfare. A dramatic exhibit showing how the "war of tomorrow" may be fought! | ...and hear...and feel...a vivid dramatization of an actual A-Bomb attack. Shows what can happen to a community that is unprepared! | how organized Civil Defense in your community is working to protect lives, property, and production. Shows what you can do, now, to protect yourself!

ADMISSION FREE!

Hutchinson, Kansas, hosted Alert America July 29–31 and drew 7,000 visitors, helped by newspaper ads describing what people could expect to see.

Journal and *The Park Record*, urged residents to attend the Alert America exhibit at the state fair September 13–21, and more than 74,000 did just that.[42] A statewide syndicated article said the exhibit "combines authentic information of the Civil Defense program at all levels with dramatic presentation techniques." One of the exhibit's highlights, the article continued, was the "startling section showing the effects of an atomic bomb on a typical American city," in reference to the diorama of "City X."[43] *The Salt Lake Tribune* followed up shortly after the exhibit closed to offer its assessment, writing:

> The people of Salt Lake City and Utah deserve congratulations on their excellent response to the Alert America appeal for greater public attention to the problem of civil defense.... The day may never come in Salt Lake City when knowledge of how to protect ourselves in the event of all-out enemy attack will be put to use. We hope it will not. But we have no assurance on the matter—and it is good to know that so many Utah residents have been alerted to the problem, and that so many are prepared to do their part as volunteers to be ready for any emergency.[44]

Newspapers in the host cities, surrounding communities, and across the state provided extensive coverage of Alert America. Through news stories, columns, and editorials, newspapers not only urged people to attend the exhibit; they also promoted the importance of contributing to the nation's civil defense, from actively volunteering or enrolling in training course, to giving blood or simply cooperating during air-raid tests. Frank Evans, as an example, former civil defense director of Ingham County in Michigan, maintained the same emphasis in a guest editorial published March 23, 1952, in the *Lansing State Journal*—in advance of Alert America being shown in Detroit and Grand Rapids. Evans provided an overview of the exhibit, including its principal elements as outlined in the official *Alert America!* booklet. Then in a more personal note, he expressed his confidence in Americans responding to the call for supporting civil defense. "The American people are not the type for mass demonstration, fanfare, and drum beating," he wrote, "the sort of thing which results in waves of mass hysteria so common in today's world." Rather, the nation would survive an atomic attack in people's ability "to organize themselves into well-balanced and effective teams and the inherent determination to win in spite of seemingly insurmountable odds."[45]

Conclusion: After Effects

Should a grand slam atomic attack hit this country, as it could any minute now, it would be the civilians who really would suffer. If the enemy is able to create enough devastation at one time in dozens of our cities ... it could wreck our entire production machine and put us out of the war.—James J. Wadsworth, Acting FCDA Administrator, 1952[1]

James J. Wadsworth, FCDA's acting administrator, sent the agency's 1952 annual report to President Dwight Eisenhower shortly after his inauguration in January 1953. Wadsworth had been appointed by President Truman after Millard Caldwell's resignation the previous November. According to the report, the nation still lacked an adequate civil defense program capable of surviving an atomic attack by the Soviet Union. The Soviets could send 400 planes capable of dropping atomic bombs on any city in the United States, with an estimated 110,000 casualties resulting from each blast. The attack would be launched without warning during daylight hours, followed by psychological warfare to spread panic and weaken the resolve to fight back, and biological warfare to add disease to the devastation caused by the atomic bombings. The report noted that these assumptions were neither a dramatic overstatement nor a retreat from the reality of growing Soviet capabilities.[2] "We are making progress in civil defense but are losing ground in the face of the growing threat to our national security," Wadsworth said in the report. "Make no mistake about it. America's civil defense is not developing fast enough to meet the threat that faces us."[3]

Wadsworth reflected the same sentiments as his predecessor. Caldwell, who resigned less than two years after his appointment by President Truman, had consistently stressed that knowing the facts about civil defense meant the difference between life and death. "If we are attacked—and remember that we can be attacked—the hard, terrible task of getting our cities and industries back on their feet will fall mainly on civil defense volunteers," he had written. "It is not a job for those who can't face facts or aren't willing to work. It is a job for real Americans with courage."[4] Val Peterson, named as the new FCDA administrator by Eisenhower in February 1953, maintained the same message. "The Russians now have enough atom bombs to hit every metropolitan area in the country simultaneously," Peterson told a meeting in Baton Rouge, Louisiana. "And there is nothing we can do to stop them through the military."[5] Yet despite this reality, and all the efforts by the FCDA, including the Alert America campaign, he acknowledged regretfully that Americans remained apathetic toward civil defense. The reason? "They are living in a fool's paradise and don't believe it can happen," Peterson said.[6] A Gallup Poll conducted in August 1953 reinforced his sentiments, finding that only 17 percent of Americans believed Russia could "knock out" the nation in a surprise attack. The published findings, authored by George Gallup, read: "The great task facing the Civil Defense Administration is awakening the public to a great awareness of the dangers of an atom bomb attack on the United States."[7] Peterson was convinced that if people planned ahead, 50 percent of the casualties from any attack could be saved. "But it is a tough job to convince them that it must be done," he concluded.[8]

Petersen placed apathetic Americans in one of three categories: people preferring to let tomorrow take care of itself; people who had "wished themselves" into believing there would not be a third world war; and people who believed when the war did come it would be horrific and kill them regardless of their preparatory efforts. "This escapism and defeatism is unworthy of Americans," Peterson said in July 1953. "The enemy can't destroy this country by atom bombs or any other way, as long as we are alert. But history always has shown this country goes to sleep between wars. This time the war will hit us where we live."

Although Peterson made a valid observation, millions of Americans had not gone to sleep, but had demonstrated a real interest in learning more about civil defense, including taking advantage of the opportunity to visit Alert America. In Phoenix, Arizona, for example, some 17,000 people attended the show, with more than 5,000 volunteering for civil defense. On its first night in Nashville, 15 percent of those attending Alert America pledged their participation in the local civil defense corps. Attendance in Sacramento, California, site of the state fair, exceeded 114,000; 75,000 visited the exhibit in Salt Lake City, site of the Utah State Fair, with 8,600 volunteering for civil defense and an additional 781 giving blood. In exhibits displayed in metropolitan areas, the cities drawing the largest viewers were Washington, D.C., with 32,000; Seattle, with a total attendance of 40,000; New York City, with 47,000 visitors; and Los Angeles, which topped 52,000. Moreover, at the end of 1952, the number of civil defense volunteers had doubled from the year before, reaching four million.[9]

Nearly 47,000 people visited Alert America in New York City, which hosted the exhibit May 13–19, 1952 (National Archives).

Alert America represented a major component of the FCDA's early efforts to promote volunteerism in the national civil defense program, and the agency built upon its success to announce the Pledge for Home Defense campaign in October, just one month after the convoys ended their national tour. The FCDA's new campaign reflected the same objectives as Alert America: to encourage Americans to volunteer in civil defense organizations, enroll in civil defense classes, prepare an emergency food supply for their home shelter area, and learn the civil defense plans for their city or community. Its immediate action plan focused on family civil defense; home and family group programs; special home defense programs, including the blood program and Ground Observer Corps; Red Cross training; and local "Schools for Survival" programs. The educational phase focused on a 10-point family civil defense program covered in the FCDA pamphlet, *What You Can Do Now*. The pamphlet also contained air-raid instructions, a description of a household first-aid kit, and a list of civil defense booklets and films, with directions for obtaining them.[10]

Working with the FCDA on its Pledge for Home Defense campaign, governors and mayors across the country issued proclamations declaring November 11 (Armistice Day) through November 27 (Thanksgiving) as "A Special Time for Home Defense Action." More than 100 associations and organizations that had supported Alert America again campaigned through their local chapters in 45 states and territories. Among these groups were the American Legion, American Red Cross, National Congress of Parents and Teachers, National Federal of Business and Professional Women's Clubs, Colored Parents and Teachers Association, Camp Fire Girls, and Girl Scouts. In a speech before the Regional Conference of National Organizations on November 20, the FCDA's Wadsworth told attendees, "Our Pledge for Home Defense campaign provides another opportunity for the citizens to translate their responsibilities into action. The markings at the crossroads are clear— for you, for me, for the volunteer. The one way leads to action and preparedness, the other to uncertainty and disaster."[11] The FCDA also enlisted media's help, with 42 major consumer magazines pledging their support, and newspapers nationwide publishing articles about the program. Eighty-six television stations presented special FCDA-supplied slides, and radio stations broadcast information. Movie theaters nationwide showed the film, *Survival Under Atomic Attack*, to accompany a recruiting trailer. State and local governments, various organizations, and private industry distributed three million copies of civil defense publications. The Air Force even participated, with planes dropping leaflets over several cities that read, "This could have been a bomb—Pledge for Home Defense—Register Today!"[12]

Women, again, represented a good portion of these new volunteers, urged to action by the likes of Mamie Eisenhower and Pat Nixon, wives of the 1952 Republican presidential ticket. Mamie Eisenhower acknowledged that an atomic attack "can happen here," adding that "any housewife may be tomorrow's heroine if war comes to America…. Do everything you can possibly do to make and keep America strong on the home front. Pledge yourself for home defense." Pat Nixon also urged women to volunteer, saying, "We mothers of small children have the responsibility of teaching them the facts about survival under atomic attack in such a way that we plant facts, not fears, in their inquiring and wondering minds." She then stressed the importance of teaching children self-protection skills at home "so well and so wisely that they will respond automatically in the event of a sudden warning."[13]

Although the quantifiable results from the Pledge for Home Defense are impossible to determine, the FCDA's annual report for 1952 concluded that millions of American families had undertaken individual and group preparedness. More people had acquired self-protection booklets, and "intensified" individual participation had increased in local civil defense organizations nationwide. Many members of organizations also registered for future civil defense work, as well as pledged their support for personal and family preparedness at home. J. H. Wyse, Virginia's coordinator of civil defense, estimating that 177,000 volunteers were needed for the state's civil defense program, hoped to add to the 63,000 people who had already volunteered.[14] Joseph Downey, civil defense director for Cook County, encompassing Chicago, sought 10,000 additional volunteers to join the 8,000 already enrolled.[15] Smaller communities like Naugatuck, Connecticut, and Wisconsin Rapids, Wisconsin, indicated success with their efforts, albeit limited success. Civil defense officials in Naugatuck, with a population of 17,000, were pleased that the campaign attracted sixty volunteers, including thirty-five nurses, and resulted in many additional people agreeing to be added in the near future. Wisconsin Rapids, with a population of 13,000, gained 100 volunteers and filled 200 key positions in its county's civil defense organization.[16] In addition, cities launched new campaigns after this one ended. In Spotswood, New Jersey, twenty-two members of the local First Aid Squad joined the city's Civil Defense Council in December. Among the city's first projects was to replace the current civil defense posters with Alert America posters showcasing the various service areas accepting volunteers, such as the Warden Service, Police Service, and Welfare Service.[17] Detroit attracted 30,000 volunteers for its warden service in a subsequent campaign, which led to other cities conducting similar programs.[18]

Not only did Alert America contribute to the success of civil defense efforts throughout the United States, it also benefited Canada's civil defense program. As two convoys concluded their tours during the summer of 1952, the third traveled north to Ottawa, Canada, where it arrived on July 25. The previous day, the FCDA and Canadian government had signed a memorandum of agreement allowing civil defense agencies from both countries to operate freely across borders in the event of an atomic attack. The two countries had initiated talks the year before with the aim of pooling resources across their 3,000-mile-long shared border. Under the agreement, civil defense authorities were to keep everyone informed about any actions or regulations; materials and equipment; and training arrangements. It also allowed the exchange of personnel and training facilities, and permitted officials from both countries to confer and take immediate action if necessary. The first meeting of the Joint United States-Canadian Civil Defense Committee had taken place in Washington, D.C., on April 28, 1951. Paul Martin, minister of Canada's Health and Welfare, summarized the meeting held by saying, "The spirit of our discussions is that there be no border at all for civil defense purposes." The FCDA's Millard Caldwell, head of the U.S. delegation, commented, "We are seeking an easy interchange of people and equipment so there will be no obstacles in the way of mutual assistance."[19]

In a positive gesture in recognition of this agreement, the FCDA offered Alert America to Canada free of charge for one year. Major-General Frederic

Worthington, Canada's civil defense coordinator, announced that the exhibit would begin its tour within a month of its arrival in July. In actuality, it began in the fall of 1953, more than a year later. Much of the delay resulted from repairing worn-out displays and modifying specific aspects of the exhibit for the Canadian audience. Renamed "On Guard, Canada," the exhibit began a three-month tour in September 1953 to ten cities considered to be prime targets for attack: Montreal, Regina, Calgary, Vancouver, Edmonton, Saskatoon, Winnipeg, Windsor, Halifax, and Saint John. Although more than 100,000 Canadians visited the exhibit, it failed to result in a significant increase in volunteers. According to historian Andrew Burtch, "On Guard, Canada" might have been more impactful if the federal government and Civil Defence Canada had not demonstrated "a lack of will" to promote the exhibit's importance to the Canadian populace.[20] As a result, Burtch writes, "Civil defense was remembered by the public most often when international crises made the theoretical threat of annihilation in war frighteningly real, and it was forgotten just as quickly when these menaces passed."[21]

The threat of annihilation may have abated in Canada, but not so in the United States. By the end of 1952, nearly 2,000 operational exercises had been conducted that year at the state and local levels, including air-raid tests and alerts, mutual aid and mobile support drills, and military-supported maneuvers. One hundred sixty-three exercises—many conducted right before, during, or immediately after Alert America—involved public participation on a major scale, with an estimated 39 million people living within the area of the exercises, according to the FCDA. Another three million participated in smaller exercises, bringing the total number of men, women, and children exposed to or participating in some form of civil defense activity to 42 million—or 27 percent of the U.S. population. Two million civil defense workers joined in these various exercises and received technical training, and 125,000 volunteers took part in 204 command post specialized exercises. In addition, schools, hospitals, businesses, and manufacturing plants conducted their own civil defense drills and tests.[22] It's safe to assume, if the FCDA's figures are accurate, that some 30 percent of Americans had felt the impact of civil defense in 1952.

Boston and San Francisco both held citywide, full-scale tests in February. The Ground Observer Corps conducted numerous drills throughout the year, including one in March involving 18 northeastern and Great Lake states. As Alert America traveled through the Northeast in March, the Eastern Air Defense Command held a 12-state test of its air-raid alert system. In April, New York City and Philadelphia conducted full-scale civil defense tests, while New Jersey conducted its first statewide civil defense exercise, with five million participants. The next month, the state of Washington held a "red alert" with the assistance of 38,000 volunteers. This was followed in June by statewide tests in Connecticut and Massachusetts, with the Massachusetts test involving 63 cities and 500,000 participants. Oklahoma held the first major rural exercise in August, emphasizing biological warfare and support-area services.[23]

In the fall, Michigan, Texas, Florida, California, Virginia, New Mexico, South Carolina, Iowa, Louisiana, Missouri, Pennsylvania, and Ohio, as well as the U.S. territories of Alaska and Hawaii, all conducted exercises or air-raid tests.[24] Pennsylvania's statewide test centered on the goal of halting all non-essential activities and having the public take cover during a three-minute period. Sirens, horns, and whistles announced that an air-raid test was in progress and citizens were expected to obey rules set up by the State Council of Civil Defense. Drivers of cars pulled to the curb and people caught outside either returned to their home or entered the nearest building. Richard Gerstell, the state's civil defense director, complimented Pittsburgh and several communities across the state for their success in having the public follow instructions; however, he was more critical of Philadelphia, where people generally went on about their business.[25]

Such was not the case in New York City, which conducted its fourth citywide air-raid drill on Tuesday evening, September 30, involving thousands of participants, then conducted a simulated atomic attack on December 13. To minimize undue panic for the September drill, Arthur Wallander, the city's civil defense director, issued an advance warning that a test would begin at 7:45 p.m. Without this notice, panic no doubt would have occurred because of the added realism of two waves of Air Force bombers simulating an air attack. Several B-29 and B-25 bombers "attacked" from different directions, flying at a low altitude of 6,000 feet. As they approached, 579 air-raid sirens sounded a three-minute "red" alert warning in all five boroughs. Some 50,000 civil defense volunteers had assigned tasks, including setting up aid stations, directing people to shelter areas, and helping the "homeless" who had been gathered in temporary outdoor areas. They also performed simulated tasks of digging for victims under debris, clearing streets, and repairing broken water mains. The various exercises had been spread throughout the city, attracting hundreds of thousands of interested people, with 100,000 people crowding Times Square, one of the locations. When the test had concluded, Wallander declared, "I am satisfied with the results. The demonstration you witnessed in the Times Square area and throughout the city illustrates to all the tremendous amount of diligent planning and application since its inception."[26]

Four hundred thousand volunteers participated in the December drill, which theoretically killed 203,000 people and injured 277,000. The city's sirens sounded the alert at 8:30 a.m. Saturday morning, with New Yorkers responding according to instructions, according to Lieutenant General C. R.

Huebner, director of the New York State Civil Defense Commission. One newspaper reported, "The nation's largest metropolis became a ghost city for 15 minutes today in the biggest air raid drill since World War 2." Police halted traffic, ordering drivers to leave their cars and find shelter. Civil defense workers gave the same instructions to pedestrians. Buses pulled to the curb, as a helicopter circled overhead with its loudspeaker blaring, "Take shelter! Take shelter!"[27]

In addition to the numerous drills taking place across the country, a new association was formed, conferences were held, and cooperative agreements were implemented in the fall of 1952. The Far Western Association of Civil Defense, which included the states of Oregon, Washington, California, Utah, Nevada, Idaho, Montana, and Arizona, along with officials from Canada and Mexico, met in Phoenix in October. The association re-elected George Owen, Arizona's civil defense director, as president. Arizona Governor John Howard Pyle provided the opening remarks, telling attendees that their main job was to overcome the apathy of the average individual. "I am very conscious of the fact that civil defense must first arouse the interest of the people, which in turn will stimulate action on the part of the legislators."[28]

More than 100 civil defense directors representing 41 target cities in 22 states attended a November meeting in Columbus, Ohio, at which George Arnold became the first president of the Civil Defense Conference. The primary mission of the newly formed group—which was to work in cooperation with the National Association of State Civil Defense Directors, the American Municipal Association, and the U.S. Conference of Mayors—was to oversee the defense of these target cities, which collectively totaled 101 million people.[29] Major General Herbert Thatcher, chief of plans for the U.S. Air Force, emphasized the group's critical importance, telling the directors, "It is not only likely that the United States will be bombed. It is extremely probable." He then added that there would be no noncombatants in an atomic war and that "the foxholes would be in places like this hotel."[30] Commenting on the meeting, Richard K. Tucker, correspondent for the *Baltimore Sun*, wrote, "It has become clear that the city defense leaders, whose critical areas embrace an estimated 85 per cent of America's industrial production, feel home front defenses are a sort of 'stepchild'—lost in a welter of high-level planning and appropriations for the armed forces and European military aid."[31]

From the perspective of the overall positive response to numerous drills and exercises held nationwide, Americans had most assuredly become aware of civil defense and many had volunteered in or pledged their support for civil defense. But newspapers continued to report on the issue of apathy. In September 1952, W. M. Robertson, director of California's Civil Defense, focused his criticism on Americans' apathy in a speech at the annual convention of the California State Firemen's Association. After emphasizing the

Soviet Union's ability to deliver a devastating atomic attack on the United States, he told attendees, "What we need in this country more than anything else is a realization by the American people that we need civil defense. Civil defense, the fourth arm of national defense, now is the weakest link in our preparedness program."[32] Dorothy Mann, director of women's activities for the Michigan Office of Civil Defense, was yet another outspoken civil defense official who addressed apathy. Mann told a VFW Auxiliary meeting in October that Americans were too apathetic and totally unprepared in the event of an atomic attack, then asked, "Would you know what to do or where to go in the event of such an attack? "Would you know how many people from other areas you would be required to take care of in such an emergency?" She continued by taking direct aim at the auxiliary women in front of her, saying, "No, because you are more interested in bridge parties and shows than you are in how to take care of yourselves in such an event."[33]

Upon resigning as FCDA administrator, Caldwell had criticized what he called the Pentagon's apathy toward civil defense. He said the nation was lucky it had not yet been hit by an atomic bomb, and reminded people "this time they, not the soldiers, will be targets."[34] The same month, Edward Crenshaw, commander of Region 3 of the Pennsylvania Civil Defense Council, also resigned and blasted both official indifference and public apathy toward civil defense. In his opinion, not a single area within his region, which included Philadelphia, was "competent to operate in an emergency."[35] A newspaper editorial in December, following a civil defense test, blamed apathy on the lack of incentive:

> We don't know how to cure the apathy and we don't think the test did much to stir up interest. The best we saw was a sort of mild curiosity as to what was going on, some indignation that one's personal liberty was being interfered with by stopping traffic, and an attitude that it would last for fifteen minutes so let's sit it out. No, that's not the view of those who are actively engaged in handling all the many phases of civilian defense activities, but of the thousands who will have to be handled in the event of an actual emergency.[36]

Lieutenant General Henry Larsen, president of the National Association of State Civil Defense Directors, lashed out at President Truman for his failure to develop an effective civil defense program. At a meeting in December 1952 with President-elect Eisenhower, Larsen and the association's executive committee discussed what they deemed as critical for the nation's defense—namely, a significant increase in appropriations above the amounts approved by Congress under Truman. Although Eisenhower listened and pledged his support, he was only slightly more successful during his presidency, with Congress appropriating an annual average of $65 million for civil defense, versus average annual appropriations of $50 million under Truman.[37] For the six years ending June 30, 1956, the federal government appropriated a total of about $316 million, with $73.5 million made available in the form of grants. These grants assisted states in developing and equipping attack warnings, communications, welfare, training and education, health and special weapons defense, rescue, engineering, and other civil defense services—an almost impossible feat with the funds available.[38]

The paucity of civil defense appropriations became even more pronounced on November 1 when the United States exploded its first hydrogen bomb—a month after Great Britain successfully tested its first atomic bomb. Although most military experts believed the Soviet Union would not have an H-bomb until 1954, no one questioned its inevitability. In fact, the Soviets tested an H-bomb in August 1953, greatly escalating the threat of a devastating atomic war. Adding to the escalation, the U.S. announced in December that it now had tactical atomic rockets and guided missiles. The Atomic Energy Commission also disclosed that the United States possessed atomic warheads of different calibers capable of being delivered as aerial bombs, artillery shells, or missile charges.[39]

It was in this atmosphere that President Truman invited President-elect Eisenhower to the White House on November 18 to discuss the issues Eisenhower would soon confront, including Korea, the hydrogen bomb, and the state of the nation's civil defense efforts. More than one million spectators lined the parade route taking Eisenhower to a special reception in his honor, where Truman presented a rather blunt and stark assessment.[40] Eisenhower was to take a different approach, however. Addressing the Freedoms Foundation's annual meeting in December, Eisenhower gravitated away from Truman's approach that only through a strong national civil defense program could the United States hope to win an atomic war. In contrast, Eisenhower said the most important element was faith. "It is my conviction," he said, "that the great struggle of our times is for ... the hearts and souls of men— their very innermost souls. If we are going to be strong, we must be strong in spirit.... If we can be strong enough to sell ourselves this idea at home, we can win this ideological war."[41]

On January 7, 1953, President Truman delivered his last State of the Union address to Congress and the nation. His comments, while evoking faith in the American public, presented the world situation in more graphic terms, as he had often expressed:

> The war of the future would be one in which man could extinguish millions of lives at one blow, demolish the great cities of the world, wipe out the cultural achievements of the past—and destroy the very structure of a civilization that has been slowly and painfully built up through hundreds of generations. Such a war is not a possible policy for rational men. We know this, but we dare not assume that others would not yield to the temptation science is now placing in their hands."[42]

Two weeks later, on January 20, Dwight Eisenhower became the thirty-fourth president of the United States. In his inaugural address, he again offered a more positive view, stressing his confidence that faith and all Americans working together were the keys to a peaceful future. "No person, no home, no community can be beyond the reach of this call," he said. "We are summoned to act in wisdom and in conscience, to work with industry, to teach with persuasion, to preach with conviction, to weigh our every deed with care and with compassion. For this truth must be clear before us: whatever America hopes to bring to pass in the world must first come to pass in the heart of America."[43]

The heart of America, unfortunately, remained apathetic or indifferent toward civil defense, which makes Alert America's impact difficult to assess. To some extent, this attitude resulted from the failure of Congress to approve the requested appropriations by President Truman and President Eisenhower, a failure to which many elected and civic officials, as well as military personnel and journalists, attested. A survey conducted by the International News Service (INS) in December 1953 found the nation's ten major target cities "woefully, tragically, unprepared to cope with an enemy atomic attack." The cities—all cities visited by the Alert America convoys—included New York City, Chicago, Philadelphia, Los Angeles, Detroit, Cleveland, Baltimore, St. Louis, Boston, and Washington, D.C. According to the survey, these cities had, to one degree or another, insufficient manpower, an inability to recruit volunteers, and a shortage of equipment and supplies. This prompted Philadelphia Mayor Clark to go on record as saying, "We are gambling with national security and struggling against public apathy. Nothing on the international horizon convinces me that the danger of sudden attack is less now than a year ago."[44] Two months earlier, in an address before a civil defense conference in Gainesville, Florida, R. G. Howie, director of Florida Civil Defense, told those in attendance that Americans were not apathetic but "static because of too much indifference among their public leaders."[45] Mayors attending a White House conference in December demanded that Congress and Eisenhower appropriate more money for civil defense. Philadelphia's Mayor Clark, who attended the meeting, again spoke out, saying bluntly that civil defense was a federal problem and that only the president could end the public's apathy.[46]

Milwaukee Mayor Frank Zeidler, a strong supporter of civil defense, offered perhaps the keenest insight into apathy, commenting in 1950, "There appears in many cities a kind of helplessness once they begin to realize that they are objects marked for destruction."[47] Historians Guy Oakes and Andrew Grossman have expanded on Zeidler's observation, writing that Americans' "irrational terror of nuclear weapons" resulted in panic, apathy, and stupefaction."[48] Americans terrified by the atomic threat, in other words, reacted by attempting to avoid this threat through apathy and indifference. Many Americans undoubtedly fell into this category of simply not believing they would survive an atomic war. This fatalistic mindset, in essence, spawned the government's attempt to transform this terror into "a robust and prudent fear" that could be managed more effectively. "If the American people, motivated by a rational fear of atomic attack, were convinced that they could survive such an attack by means of careful planning, sound training, and firm moral discipline," Oakes and Grossman write, "the crucial domestic condition of national will essential to the strategy of deterrence would be satisfied."[49]

The FCDA admittedly did not alter the domestic condition of national will enough to overcome the problem of apathy. In 1955, for example, three years after Alert America, Congress moved to combat what it termed "atomic apathy" by forming a committee "to galvanize" the nation's civil defense program, which legislators deemed to be lagging.[50] A year later, without much progress in the galvanization process, journalist and radio commentator Dorothy Thompson echoed the same refrain as Zeidler's 1950 comment, writing: "The apocalyptic nature of an atomic war and its aftermath, for which all the great powers are preparing, is so beyond normal courage to contemplate that people treat it subconsciously as a sort of science-fiction story. Behind the apparent apathy is there not a resigned feeling that nothing can be done about it anyway?"[51]

Perhaps it can be argued that so-called "atomic apathy" was simply impossible to eradicate in the early atomic age—an age that witnessed the introduction of an atomic bomb, then a hydrogen bomb a thousand times more powerful within the same decade. But this does not diminish the FCDA's many accomplishments. Upon signing the Federal Civil Defense Act of 1950, which formally created the FCDA, President Truman said, "Much has been done, but much remains to be done. It will require the best efforts of all of us to get ready, and to stay ready, to defend our homes. No true American would want to give less than his best to that cause, and no one who knows the American people could ask for more."[52] The FCDA, despite the lack of adequate funding by Congress, had been effective in promoting the need for civil defense readiness. By the end of 1952, just two years after beginning its operation, the agency had launched a wide range of programs, held conferences, created regional offices, enlisted local and state support, published numerous publications, and enlisted millions of volunteers. One of its most impressive projects was Alert America, which the FCDA called a civil defense rallying point producing "more public interest in national security within a few short months than has ever been stimulated in peacetime before on behalf of any national emergency effort."[53]

From this perspective, Alert America's impact cannot—and should not—be judged exclusively on whether it eliminated the public's apathy toward the atomic bomb and civil defense; rather, Alert America should be judged more narrowly on its fulfillment of the original objective of FCDA's National Advisory Council. In its October 1951 *Progress Report*, the council stated that the campaign had been created to inform "the American people of their grave danger and the need for civil defense for their protection."[54] Not only did public and civic officials; military personnel; media; representatives of national, regional, and local organizations; and leaders from private industry promote attendance at Alert America; three convoys, each with ten 32-foot semi-trailers, supported by parades, air-raid tests, and military flyovers, conveyed the necessity of attending Alert America directly to some 43 percent of the American population in 82 target cities in 36 states. The men, women, and children in these cities and states, whether they suffered from atomic apathy or demonstrated support for civil defense, had unquestionably been informed about their grave danger. Most important, they had received the message—delivered clearly and repeatedly—that learning how to cope with this danger as well as learning how to protect themselves, their families, their communities, and their country began with a visit to "The Show That May Save Your Life."

Appendix A:
Alert America Campaign
Progress Report

On June 15, 1951, the FCDA's National Advisory Council met to discuss the current state of the nation's civil defense program, and concluded that the American public lacked an understanding of the threat of atomic war. To overcome this problem, the council moved to develop a multifaceted campaign to alert Americans to this threat and to encourage them to actively participate in civil defense. On October 23, 1951, the FCDA's Office of Public Affairs issued the following progress report on this campaign, which included the Alert America convoy as well as many other components.

Foreword

Following the June 15, 1951, meeting of the National Advisory Council, a statement was issued calling for an "Alert America" campaign to inform the American people of their grave danger and the need for Civil Defense for their protection.

The "Alert America" slogan was adopted as the underlying theme for the integrated mass educational program being development by the Office of Public Affairs through the following major activities.

Fact Finding and Evaluation

Continuing measures of public opinion are needed to determine (a) the success of all civil defense public information programs in alerting America,

(b) the speed with which progress is being made, (c) the methods that have been most effective and economical, and (d) the size of the job remaining to be done.

The base point for many Public Affairs activities was established by a study conducted by the Survey Research Center of the University of Michigan last fall. Depth interviews with representative citizens in the 11 largest cities defined a number of the problems facing civil defense. Study of the findings indicated many methods of approach.

The second study of the Survey Research Center of the University of Michigan had just been completed as far as field work is concerned. When completed, they will give some measure of the progress which has been made in the nine months between the two studies.

Early reports indicate certain general trends—for example, the personal survival information seems to be getting over. Interest in the civil defense problem has not lagged because of the current world situation. On the other hand, those interviewed had little knowledge about local volunteering activities. From what we have learned thus far, we must get the local organizations to follow through on the interest in civil defense which has been created by the personal survival information.

General Public Education

The first task in this broad area is informing some 154 million American citizens about fundamentals of self-protection from the various types of weapons which might be employed by an enemy against our people. This calls for maximum use of the mass information media to provide a backlog of basic information on personal survival. Successful achievement of this task calls for breaking down the overall problem into integral parts and getting the cooperation of private industry for reprinting and distributing additional copies of our information materials. We have attempted to do this in what we call the "Personal Survival Series," a series of nine popular basic booklets on various aspects of personal survival, supplemented by motion pictures, radio and television materials, newspaper and periodical news and features, and speakers' kits which are prepared and distributed initially by the Office of Public Affairs. State and local public affairs offices arrange for additional distribution and utilization.

The story of our "pump-priming" is an excellent example of joint industry-government cooperative efforts. Our budget allowed for the printing in October 1950, of only 225,000 copies of "Survival Under Atomic Attack"— the first in the public booklet series on personal survival—at no additional cost to the Government. Today we estimate that 20,000,000 reprints have been distributed in a dozen different treatments and in several foreign languages. This is a result of FCDA promotional efforts with state and local civil defense agencies and private industries.

Much the same story can be told in the matter of official public education films on civil defense. These are being produced by the motion picture industry at no expense to the Government. The arrangement is that private industry will supply the capital to make the films and distribute them under agreement with the Federal Civil Defense Administration, which supplies basic information and technical consultation. In six months more than 4,300 prints of all versions of the first film have been sold. This is an all-time record in the 16mm industry. This film is "Survival Under Atomic Attack," narrated by Mr. Edward R. Murrow, noted CBS news commentator. Other films now in production or contemplated include "Fire Fighting for Householders," "What You Should Know About Biological Warfare," "Our Cities Must Fight," "Emergency Action to Save Lives," "Poison Gases," "Civil Defense for Schools," "Civil Defense for Industry," and others.

Under construction now is a series of basic training films on such subjects as warden duties and rescue techniques.

The "Personal Survival Series" consists of the following basic themes:

A. Personal Survival
B. Biological Warfare
C. Chemical Warfare
D. What Civil Defense Is
E. Emergency Action to Save Lives
F. Fire Fighting for Householders
G. Preparing Your Home
H. Psychological Warfare Defense
I. Beyond the Bullseye

Special Projects

The second task is motivating some 15 to 20 million Americans to volunteer and participate in organized civil defense activities. We are trying to translate the interest aroused in civil defense through the "Personal Survival Series" to participation through other special across-the-board projects such as:

A. **The Civil Defense Convoy:** To spearhead the "Alert America" campaign at the State and local level, we plan to launch in early December the Alert America Convoy consisting of three caravans of ten motor trucks and trailers, each painted in distinctive car colors with "Alert America" on the outside of each trailer.

Each convoy will carry in 8 × 8 × 32 foot units mounted on skids, a complete dramatic exhibit. These will be designed so that they can be unloaded with portable power winches and moved into an armory auditorium or civic center in each city. When set up the exhibit will occupy a space roughly 40 × 100 feet, or about the size of a basketball court.

In 7 months the convoys will visit the principal cities in all 48 states with emphasis on the 54 target areas of the country. Convoy One would start from Washington and hit the Eastern Seaboard circuit. A second convoy would cover the Middle West and a third would start in the State of Washington, work down the Pacific Coast and swing across the South.

Allowing an average of one to three days in each city, plus necessary driving time between stops, it should be possible to cover all 48 states with the three convoys within the 7 months allowed.

B. **The Advertising Program:** We are working toward full mobilization of all the resources of advertising behind the problem of alerting America.

The first phase, a local recruiting kit of advertising, publicity, and promotion materials is ready for delivery to 2,500 local Civil Defense Directors.

National media plans are also being prepared to provide a national stimulus for Civil Defense. This will be a continuing program to alert America to the twin needs for personal Civil Defense and volunteering for organized Civil Defense. Full support is expected from national magazines, newspapers, chain radio, chain television, transportation advertising, etc.

In addition to these campaigns, advertising will be used to sell specific parts of the Federal Civil Defense program. The Advertising Council has designated Batten, Barton, Durstine and Osborn as the task force agency under the coordination of the volunteer coordinator, Edward T. Gerbic, Advertising Manager, of Johnson & Johnson.

Our third task, and it is fundamental to the previous two, is the creation of the awareness of the threat to our national security from airborne attack and other atomic weapons and the attainment of public recognition of civil defense as a co-equal partner of the military in the common defense of the country. The activities and techniques employed in the development of interest in personal protection and participation in organized programs will have a cumulative effect in this direction. Concurrently, through closer coordination of top mobilization levels in Washington, progress is also being made. Indication of this trend toward recognition is seen in the recent testimony of Secretaries Lovett and Finletter and Generals Marshall and Bradley before a Congressional committee.

Current Information

In addition to the Personal Survival Series and the Special Projects, general public education is continuously carried on through the provision of current information on all civil defense activities.

The principal media employed for the dissemination of current information are: newspapers, including press conferences, interviews and photos, radio and television, printed material and the research connection with the preparation of speeches for FCDA officials.

Typical of this continuing program are the following activities:

A. Press and Periodicals
The recent series of five articles by Don Markel in the Hearst papers.

The six-page article in LIFE, August 1951, on "What to do About Germ Warfare."

The full-color graphic feature "If an A-Bomb Falls" in cooperation with *The Washington Post* and Commercial Comics, Inc.

The article "How to Save Your Life" by William Lindsay Gresham in *Redbook*, September 1951.

Three guest columns by Governor Caldwell for Drew Pearson, Robert S. Allen, and Fulton Lewis, Jr.

Series of 12 articles based on the booklet "This Is Civil Defense" offered through mat service to 10,200 papers.

Mat service on Fire Prevention Week offered to same number of papers.

B. Television and Radio
Recent appearances of FCDA personnel on sponsored and simulated and sustaining television networks shows, such as:

Meet the Press—NBC-TV
American Inventory—NBC-TV
Battle Report—NBC-TV
Facts We Face—CBS-TV
It's Up to You—CBS-TV
Johns Hopkins Science Review—Dumont
Washington Report—Dumont

The production of "Survival" in cooperation with NBC-TV, six weekly one-half TV shows which began July 8 and concluded August 19. These have been sent by FCDA in kinescope form to 107 TV stations to use as public service programs. This is unprecedented in the TV industry—all networks and independent stations will have the same shows at very low cost to FCDA.

FCDA personnel have appeared in several national and regional network radio shows, such as:

May 22, 1951	Gannett Stations	Governor Caldwell
June 14, 1951	MBS	Governor Caldwell
June 20, 1951	Viking Network	Governor Caldwell
June 20, 1951	Pa. Network	Congressman Van Zandt's Program—Governor Caldwell
July 6, 1951	NBC	Governor Caldwell
July 13, 1951	NBC	Mr. Wadsworth
July 20, 1951	NBC	Dr. Kiefer
July 27, 1951	NBC	Colonel Talbot
August 3, 1951	NBC	Colonel Wilson
August 10, 1951	NBC	Mr. De Chant
August 14, 1951	CBS	Governor Caldwell
August 17, 1951	NBC	Mr. Jolley
August 19, 1951	MBS	Governor Caldwell
September 2, 1951	Liberty	Governor Caldwell
September 13, 1951	MBS	A. Sunderlin, CD
September 21, 1951	NBC	Mr. Randan

Congressional Networks in eight states used the Question and Answer interview with Governor Caldwell via tape. Programs were broadcast in West Virginia, Minnesota, Wisconsin, California, Connecticut, Indiana, Illinois, and Pennsylvania.

"This Is CD," a radio script kit totaling 32 pages of spot announcements, Question and Answer scripts, dramatic scripts, etc., were sent to 2,800 radio stations throughout the country. A great majority of stations are using these kits advantageously.

Many state and regional local shows have been arranged in cooperation with the FCDA Radio Branch to be broadcast over state networks. For example:

| Alabama Network | 58 stations |
| Wisconsin Network | 41 stations |

The Radio Branch has daily serviced many newsmen and commentators on all networks. For example: Frank Edwards has promoted Civil Defense as much as four times a week in recent months on his 300 MBS network stations.

In many instances radio commentators who also write news columns used our material. For example: One columnist in a weekly column which goes into 138 publications has cited Civil Defense in seven instances in two months.

In cooperation with the Advertising Council, Inc., through network and regional spot radio allocation plan, announcements of varied length on Civil Defense were made over NBC, MBS, CBS, ABC, and local cooperatives.

Theater Television Experiment—
"School for Survival"

On Saturday, September 15, FCA conducted the first experimental use of closed circuit "Theater Television" as a mass training and education medium.

A live program was televised in the studios of WMAL-TV in Washington and transmitted by coaxial cable to theaters in four Eastern Seaboard cities where Civil Defense volunteers, guest observers, and press representatives were gathered in motion picture theaters to witness the program on the large screens.

A question and answer period during the program demonstrated the feasibility of using two-way communication between the receiving theaters and the originating studio. Questions were asked from the state of the theaters, and were heard by the audiences in other cities and by a panel of FCDA experts seated before the television cameras. Answers to the questions were given immediately and heard in all theaters.

The program consisted primarily of three training demonstrations designed to show all visual aid techniques, e.g., film, charts, animations, live action. The demonstrations consisted of the new Rescue Truck, and "Tricks of the Trade" in rescue operations; the caring for a lost child and re-uniting him with his parents in a disaster situation; and the working of the attack warning system.

Sample tabulations of a questionnaire distributed to all persons attending the theaters indicate:

1. Interest in Theater Television as a medium of training and education.
2. Favorable response to the program content presented.
3. Confidence that they had learned from the training samples presented.

Further favorable reaction has been received in the form of commendatory letters from state civil defense directors; from outside observers, e.g., Gordon Dean, Chairman of the AEC, etc. The general press and trade press reported the experiment as a "success" story.

Broadcasting Magazine, trade journal of the radio and television industry, summarized advantages of the medium as follows:

"(1) It gives everyone participating, either as spectators or performers, a feeling of immediacy and a psychological lift at being part of a large group.

(2) It has great possibilities for emergency use.

(3) It permits the showing of latest defense measures and policies.

(4) It gives participants a sense of intimacy with top people in their own community and in other communities—as well as nationally.

(5) It permits questions from "grass roots" workers and instantaneous answers from top level policy makers.

(6) It is ideal for the dissemination of semi-confidential information."

Future plans for theater television, as a civil defense training and education medium, are now being prepared.

Technical Information

In addition to the general education and informational programs, the Public Affairs Office has the responsibility for producing and releasing administrative guides, instructor's guides, handbooks, and manuals of similar nature to meet the technical needs of the States and cities in organizing the Civil Defense Corps. These technical books are used for the organizing, equipping, and training the 15–20 million Americans needed in the major volunteer services, such as Warden, Fire, Police, Health, Welfare, Engineering, Rescue, Communications, and Transportation.

The production status of these technical books is shown by the following listing:

A. Printed
   1. Health Services and Special Weapons Defense
   2. Police Services
   3. Principles of Civil Defense Operations
   4. The Rescue Service
   5. The Warden Service
   6. Water Supplies for Wartime Fire Fighting
   7. Air Raid Instructions, FCDA Warning Instruction Card
   8. Civil Defense Household, First Aid Kit
   9. Fire Effects of Bombing Attacks
   10. United States Civil Defense
   11. Interim Civil Defense Instructions for Schools and Colleges
   12. Civil Defense in Industry and Institutions
B. Being Printed
   1. Fire Services
   2. The Clergy in Civil Defense
   3. Outdoor Warning Device Systems
C. In Preparation for Printing

1. Engineering Service
2. Emergency Welfare
3. Supply Service
4. Damage Control
5. Civil Defense Training and Education
6. Casualty Services Guide—Part I
7. Shelter in Existing Buildings from Atomic Attack—Part I
8. Method for Determining Shelter Needs and Shelter Areas
9. Design of Windowless Structures Exposed to Atomic Blast Loads
10. Decontamination
11. Casualty Medical Record—Part III
12. Recruitment and Utilization of Civil Defense Volunteers
13. Criteria for Determining Shelter Areas in Existing Buildings
14. Glossary of Civil Defense Terms
15. How to Instruct Civil Defense Workers
16. Basic Course in Civil Defense
17. Brief Standard Position Descriptions
18. Basic Rescue Techniques
19. Public Affairs
20. Improvement of Shelter Areas—Part II
21. Teaching Attitudes and Behavior in Civil Defense
22. How to Conduct Conferences
23. Blood and Blood Derivatives

Public Liaison

There are some 4,000 national organizations with an estimated combined membership of 100,000,000 individuals—roughly two-thirds of the total population. A campaign to "Alert America" to be fully effective must appeal to and receive cooperation from the leadership represented by such organizations. These organizations afford ready-made channels of information to the "grass root" level.

Through our Public Liaison activities we are interesting many national organizations to devote a major portion of their skills and energies to the national civil defense program through:

A. Joint Activities

The "Advisory Committee" method is being used to generate action on the part of specific types of organizations by classification of areas of interest, i.e., farm, labor, religious, business and professional, etc. In some of these areas, it is practicable to use the Advisory Committee for gathering many organizations together into a simple pattern of cooperation with the Federal

Civil Defense Administration. The Administrator's Regional Advisory Committee is an excellent example. This hardworking and effective body has demonstrated how a few leaders, generally representative of an area, may bring their skills and energies to bear on the National civil defense program. The first action of the Committee was the approval for release of a statement establishing two important problems for definition and solution: (a) the role of the individual clergyman in civil defense and (2) the utilization of church institutions in civil defense.

Through this Committee, the manual, "The Role of the Clergy in Civil Defense," now in production was originated. This Committee was also the focal point around which over 300 clergymen from all parts of the United States gathered at the Shoreham Hotel in June. As a result, many States and communities have created similar committees at those levels and an upsurge in clerical interest in civil defense has since been evidenced.

Further examples are this Division's current effort in organizing similar committees in the areas of "rural," "youth," and "labor" groups. Large conferences, such as the Conference of National Organizations held at the Hotel Statler in May, with 1,011 leaders from 286 separate organizations attending, have accelerated civil defense activity throughout the country.

Short-term projects of a highly specialized nature also afford another means of carrying on joint activities. An example is the American Hotel Association's efforts in preparation and distribution of a special "alert card" and a booklet for participation of hotels in the civil defense program and suggestions for their particular emergency action. Other examples falling in this category have involved, among others, the American Legion, the Veterans of Foreign Wars, the General Federation of Women's Clubs.

Currently we are cooperating in the observance of Fire Prevention Week, National Education Week, and United Nations Day. Currently being developed is the American Federation of Women's Auxiliaries of Labor project for a special radio transcription for national release.

B. Conventions
Arranging for FCDA participation in annual conventions of individual organizations. Speeches by key FCDA officials have been made before the following organizations since January, 1951: (partial list)

> National Education Association
> National Fire Protection Association
> General Federation of Women's Clubs
> Army War College
> U.S. Independent Telephone Association
> American Society of Newspaper Editors
> Public Relations Society of America

American Federation of Labor
Congress of Industrial Organizations
National Association of Broadcasters
American Red Cross
Advertising Council
American Federation of Advertisers
American Public Welfare Association
Veterans of Foreign Wars
Veterans of Foreign Wars Auxiliary
American Medical Association
International Association of Fire Chiefs
National Urban League
National Industrial Conference Board
National Congress of Parents and Teachers
National Health Council
American Association of School Administrators
National Sheriffs Association
Lions International
Municipal Finance Officers Association

Future speaking engagements have been scheduled before the following key organizations:

American Pharmaceutical Association
American Public Welfare Association
American Hospital Association
National Recreation Association
National Safety Council
American Legion
National Exchange Club
American College of Surgeons
National Institute of Municipal Law Officers
National Defense Transportation Association
American Association of University Women

C. Visitation

Members of the Public Liaison Staff are visiting the headquarters of all mass membership organizations for the following purposes:

1. To furnish material for use by their resources in public service programs: Publications, personnel, projects, etc.

2. To furnish appropriate staff help in developing plans for large-scale membership participation in civil defense.

Results

At the outset in this report we indicated certain early objective findings regarding the result of our public education efforts. In addition, reports from regional directors in the field also afford an indication of our progress. The following excerpts from recent reports dealing with the Public Affairs aspects of the total Federal Civil Defense Program and are significant.

From the September 6, 1951, Monthly Field Report: General Increase in Public Affairs Activity

The press in general has turned on Congress for the recent action in the House, and is now laying any lack of interest in Civil Defense on the steps of the Capitol.

Typical editorial attitude is shown by Hartford (Conn.) Courant statement, "What the House of Representatives did to the Civil Defense Administration's request for funds should not happen to a yellow dog."

And from Dallas, this one, "It took bombs on Pearl Harbor to make the American Congress and people realize the precarious state of our national defenses. They should be aware that if another war breaks out the United States will be the first target and the enemy will strike with atomic bombs." In the Seattle region, editorials have shifted from the "apathy of the people" to the "apathy of Congress."

There is obvious betterment of public relations in Regions, states, and cities where Public Affairs people are carrying out programs and where leadership is energetic. Press coverage, radio broadcasts, meetings, conferences, etc., increased slightly during the past month. Boston and Denver, with Regional P.A. officers, and New York, California, Maryland, North Carolina, Alabama, Georgia, Colorado, and Alaska and Hawaii, with Public Relations operations, are examples.

Manuals, guides, radio and other material from the National office are stimulating Public Affairs activity in critical spots. Public Affairs results show more prominently where guided organizational operations are stepped up. Loudest praises come from Tennessee, Kansas, Ohio, Illinois, Utah, Nebraska, and California. The reception in the field of "stopgap" display material for State fairs indicates the effectiveness of such "tools."

In some regions, notably Berkeley and Seattle, FCDA publications are receiving wide circulation through newspaper reprints. California is repeating with the booklet "This Is Civil Defense," its successful use of "Survival Under Atomic Attack" which was published in full-page form by more than 200 newspapers. The "Household First Aid Kit" was reprinted by newspapers in the Seattle region.

Popularity of the "Household First Aid Kit" pamphlet is demonstrated in California, too, where it is planned to place one in every home in the state. Plans are to reprint 3,000,000 of them. Cost is to be borne by state CD funds with the anticipated help of matching funds from the FCDA training and education allocation. In Arizona arrangements are being made for commercial sponsorship of 100,000 copies of "Emergency Action to Save Lives."

Best examples of increased radio and press activity come from Alabama, Georgia, Minnesota, and the Berkeley region. In Alabama, 59 radio stations are carrying short CD talks and Georgia stations broadcast more than 1,200 spot announcements in August. Forty-one of the 52 Minnesota stations are now carrying program material. In the Berkeley region press coverage totaled 969 column inches in August, as against 605 inches in July. Of the 969 inches, 623 were of national CD news. This is the first time national news has led state and local press volume.

The displays of photos and charts on biological warfare, prepared by the national office for use at state fairs, were described as "instructive, forceful and eye-catching" by the Tennessee state director. The same displays also scored hits in Kansas, Ohio, and Illinois.

Close observation at the Colorado state fair revealed that people were willing to learn by seeing rather than reading. Audiences watched motion pictures and examined photographic displays, but in many instances failed to pick up literature.

The "direct contact" is paying off. Public interest is being activated definitely by attendance of regional officers and state directors at meetings of groups of all types. Regional Director Battley of Richmond makes this observation, "The public attitude—that CD may be needed but personal interest prevent participation—is gradually being changed in areas wherein the local CD director takes his responsibility seriously, is sincerely interested in civil defense, and is determined to get his area prepared for enemy or natural disasters."

Appendix B:
The "Alert America" Program
for Your Community

To help ensure the success of the "Alert America" exhibit, the Valley Forge Foundation in cooperation with the Federal Civil Defense Administration published a 52-page booklet describing the exhibit and outlining the various means to promote it. The central article in the Alert America! *booklet, which was distributed to the cities hosting the show, follows.*

We are challenged by a deadly Enemy which seeks to destroy everything we hold dearest in life, our freedoms, our ideals, our moral standards, our spiritual values.

The United States is now locked in a major conflict fomented by the Enemy—a struggle in which we have already lost more front-line troops than the combined casualty lists of the Revolutionary War, the War of 1812, Mexican War, and the Spanish-American War.

The Enemy is master-minded by a handful of leaders in the Politburo. Ruthless fanatics, these international criminals have beaten, plundered, persecuted, tortured, imprisoned, enslaved, and murdered millions of innocent people in the Soviet Union, Latvia, Estonia, Lithuania, Poland, Czechoslovakia, Hungary, Romania, Bulgaria, Eastern Germany, China and Korea. They have incited and waged wars of aggression in Greece, Tibet, Korea, and Indo-China.

The Enemy respects only one thing—strength. Weakness invites him to strike. Strength alone will check him.

Total Strength Needs Civil Defense

The key to our progress and survival lies in the total strength of our people...

Not only must we be strong morally and spiritually...

Not only must we be strong physically and economically...

Not only must we have a strong Army, Navy, and Air Force...

WE MUST ALSO HAVE A STRONG CIVIL DEFENSE—ESPECIALLY IN THIS AGE OF ATOMIC WEAPONS. ONLY THROUGH A STRONG CIVIL DEFENSE CAN WE KEEP OUR CHERISHED FREEDOMS.

We have a strong Army, a strong Navy, and a strong Air Force; BUT OUR CIVIL DEFENSE IS WOEFULLY WEAK. BECAUSE OF THIS WEAK LINK, OUR NATION COULD PERISH.

People must be made to understand that since there is no absolute military defense against modern terror weapons, including atomic warfare, an effective Civil Defense is vital to the security of the United States. This home front preparation would provide the means whereby this country, if attacked, could get up from the rubble and fight on to victory.

An enemy attack would be aimed primarily at our industrial production centers—at the country's most critical targets. Such an attack would be against all the people of the United States. Defense against it would require the coordinated effort of the entire nation.

This grim reality was recently stressed in a speech by Millard Caldwell, Federal Civil Defense Administrator:

> Our form of active and practical patriotism that is open to everyone of us is Civil Defense—the systematic preparation to protect ourselves, our faiths, our ideals, our families, our homes, our farms and factories from the efforts of an enemy to destroy. It's not something our Armed Forces can do for us. It's something we as civilians—as patriotic American citizens—must do for ourselves. It's the first time since our frontier days that we civilians must take an active part in protecting our homes from enemy attack. If we have the kind of patriotism that our forefathers had, we can do it.

Campaign Plan

In an effort to reach every American citizen and to drive home the fact that Civil Defense is his No. 1 personal responsibility, an "Alert America" campaign was suggested in the summer of 1951 by the National Advisory Council of the Federal Civil Defense Administration. To spearhead this program, the "Alert America" Convoys were developed by the newly-formed Valley Forge Foundation and the Federal Civil Defense Administration.

The Foundation is a non-partisan, non-sectarian, non-profit organization which is acting in behalf of Civil Defense as a part of the total defense of the American way of life.

The "Alert America" Program strives to instill in every American a greater awareness of the role of Civil Defense as a co-equal partner with the Armed Forces in protecting the nation. Manned largely by unpaid part-time volunteer workers, each service of Civil Defense will work with the other for the common good and will belong to a national team—the United States Civil Defense Corps. Such cooperation demands a high level of personal participation by every citizen in meeting his Civil Defense responsibilities.

Briefly, then, the "Alert America" Program seeks to achieve two goals: (1) awareness and (2) action.

The "Alert America" Program has three parts:

1. The nationwide tour of the three "Alert America" Convoys which will visit most of the leading cities of the United States.

2. The local Civil Defense campaign preceding, coinciding with and following the Convoy and Exhibit.

3. A national campaign highlighting the "Alert America" Convoy tour as a major instrument of public education for strengthening Civil Defense.

The "Alert America" Convoys

The "Alert America" Convoys consist of three motorized units of ten 32-foot trailers, each painted in red and white with distinctive Civil Defense design. Private industry and government agencies have been most generous in contributing goods and services to the three "Alert America" Exhibits and Convoys.

Each 10-truck Convoy carries a dramatic Exhibit mounted on skids and readily handled by portable winches. When assembled, the Exhibit will be 55 by 120 feet, slightly larger than the size of most basketball courts.

The Convoys will visit the principal cities of the nation in the next six to nine months and ultimately may cover all 48 states.

In each city, the Exhibit will be set up in an armory, or exhibit hall, remaining there three to five days. Its stay will be the focal point for a local "Alert America" Week consisting of an intensive campaign of Civil Defense education and special events designed to reach every citizen in the community.

One Convoy opened in December, and visited two cities on a "shake-down cruise." On January 7, 1952, the Convoy had its formal launched in Washington, D.C. Following that, the Convoys spread out to cover the country.

The Exhibit has been designed by Edward H. Burdick, famed designer of the Freedom Train and of much of New York World's Fair. It is dramatic in its impact, using motion and three-dimensional effects throughout. Contents include striking exhibits contributed by the Federal Civil Defense Administration, the Defense Department, Atomic Energy Commission, many other government agencies, and many firms in private industry.

Exhibit Features

Half of the Exhibit drives home the reality and nature of the threat that faces us. The second half spells out specifically what the individual citizen can do to meet this threat, and how Civil Defense services are organized on the state and local level to protect our communities.

The principal elements are these:

a. Peacetime uses of atomic energy in industry, agriculture, transportation, and medicine.

b. If war does come, it will be far different from any we have known. Pictured are attack by incendiaries, sabotage, psychological, chemical, and biological warfare.

c. Multi-color films of actual atomic weapons.

d. The dramatic Atomic Attack Room—mock air raid depicting devastating assault on a typical American city.

e. The transition—with Civil Defense we can beat this menace.

f. The new concept of national defense—co-partnership of Civil Defense and the Armed Forces.

g. Structure of Civil Defense at the national, state, and local levels—with emphasis on individual and community responsibility.

h. The operations of Civil Defense forces in pre-attack and post-attack periods.

i. The peace and freedoms we cherish and protect—the motivating factor.

j. The "pay off" room. This is flexible, and may be adapted by the city Civil Defense Director to local needs. Everybody passing through the exhibit will be asked to pledge personal action—to volunteer for Civil Defense, to teach the family how to protect itself, to take first aid training, etc.

Outside the main Exhibit there is adequate space for additional features on Civil Defense. Some of them, donated by government agencies and private industry, are carried in the Convoy. Many others are supplied locally.

Among these are a live rescue truck demonstration, radiation detection equipment, and exhibits explaining the Civil Defense tie-in of other government agencies. A display of guided missiles and material on atomic energy are other attractions. Most of these are action exhibits, some of them operated by push-button devices, which the public can manipulate.

Local features in some cities include the latest fire-fighting and police equipment, demonstrations of first aid and rescue methods, and displays of emergency food, medical supplies, welfare activities, [and] control centers.

A Three-Part Campaign

The "Alert America" Community Campaign seeks to achieve impact and saturation. Its purpose is to reach every man, woman, and child in the community and to persuade them that Civil Defense is their most pressing responsibility.

The Community Campaign should be directed by a large and representative Committee of leading citizens under the leadership of the Civil Defense Director. This community "Alert America" Committee is responsible for obtaining the maximum participation by individuals, organizations, and media in all three phases of the local program. These are:

(1) The advance period of special publicity, educational and promotional events, designed to arouse the greatest possible interest in the forthcoming "Alert America" Week, the "Alert America" Convoy, and its dramatic Civil Defense Exhibit presented by local Civil Defense authorities and sponsored by the Valley Forge Foundation in cooperation with the Federal Civil Defense Administration.

(2) "Alert America" Week. This period includes the arrival of the Convoy and the public displays of the Exhibit in a large central armory, or exposition hall. "Alert America" Week is highlighted by a series of special days, such as Convoy Arrival Day, Women's Day, Veterans' Day, First Aid Day, etc.

(3) The follow-up educational period, stressing the need for continuing year-round support of local Civil Defense to protect our freedoms and to construct an enduring peace.

The visit of the "Alert America" Exhibit in each city is not an end in itself, but only the means to an end. It is the occasion for conducting an intensive program that will drive home to every man, woman, and child the immediate necessity for taking personal action in Civil Defense.

The "Alert America" Committee appointed by the Civil Defense Director has the assistance of a Field Manager of the Valley Forge Foundation who precedes the Convoy. Complete information packets containing educational material are made available to the "Alert America" Week Committee.

An educational build-up period precedes the "Alert America" Week. During this advance period newspapers, radio, television speeches, round-tables, luncheons, printed matter, posters, banners, advance displays, and special events will arouse the interest of the entire community in one of the most spectacular Exhibits ever to tour the United States.

Several weeks before the "Alert America" Convoy arrives, all organized groups and information media in the community are alerted to take an active part in making this campaign the most significant ever held in the city.

"Alert America" Week

"Alert America" Week is the period in which the Exhibit is on display. The week consist of an intensive schedule of educational and special events based on special days selected by the community "Alert America" Committee.

The purpose of "Alert America" Week is to reach every man, woman, and child in the community and get them to take personal action in Civil Defense.

According to Plan I, "Alert America" Week may consist of any of the following days or others developed by local authorities:

> Convoy Arrival Day
> Defense of Religion Day
> Women's Day
> "Young Americans" Day
> Veterans Day
> Labor and Management Day
> Agriculture Day
> Merchants Day
> Family Day
> Armed Forces Day
> Organizations Day
> Convoy Departure Day

Plan II divides the "Alert America" Week according to Civil Defense functions such as:

> Convoy Arrival Day
> Red Cross Training Day
> "Prepare Your Home" Day

Rescue Day
Warden Day, etc.
"Give Your Blood" Day
Recruitment Day
Convoy Departure Day

The community Civil Defense authorities are responsible for the follow-up educational campaign that takes place after the departure of the "Alert America" Convoy. The Valley Forge Foundation does not maintain a staff in the community; so the impact of "Alert America" Week and the "Alert America" Exhibit must be carried on by state and local Civil Defense leaders in cooperation with the organizations and individuals who participated in the local program.

Foundation Aids

The Foundation makes available to the local Civil Defense authorities and the "Alert America" Committee a vast variety of aids:

1. This Community Program Book with many detailed suggestions for maximum participation by every individual and group in the community.

2. An Advertising Kit of newspaper advertisements prepared by the Advertising Council.

3. Display Suggestions.

4. Newspaper and Magazine Packets containing fact sheets, press features, photo ideas, etc.

5. Three Radio Packets—one for the preparatory period, one for the "Alert America" Week, and one for the post-convoy campaign. There will also be free transcriptions.

6. Special Television Kit with film shorts, slides, and posters.

7. Separate Program Suggestions for Schools, Women, Veterans, Labor, Business, Industry and Agriculture, Fraternal and Professional Organizations, Churches, Young Americans, Motion Picture Theaters, and Speakers Bureau.

The Committee will receive a great deal of assistance from the Valley Forge Foundation and State and Federal Civil Defense agencies, so that the build-up period and "Alert America" Week may be certain of success. A vast variety of promotional material useful in every media is being provided. A Field Manager of the Foundation meets with the Committee several times to assist in arrangements. Major national organizations representing veterans, women, labor and management, youth, fraternal, civic and service groups have promised cooperation in the "Alert America" Campaign. They are sending advance notices to their local chapters asking that they give all possible assistance to the Committee.

Advertising Campaign Support

The Advertising Council, which for many years has been conducting public service campaigns through the cooperation of advertising agencies and industry, is supporting the "Alert America" Convoy Program by offering suggested advertisements, posters and window stickers. The Council is also rendering valuable support to the local campaign by asking their members and affiliated advertising groups in the community to cooperate generously in every phase of the "Alert America" Campaign.

Saturation—the Goal

The community and national Civil Defense program benefit from the cooperation of all groups.

The basic theme that Civil Defense is designed to protect our freedoms and to construct an enduring people will be further promoted through speeches, rallies, parades, special exhibits, banners, and a great variety of events and promotional devices.

Department stores and theaters will cooperate through displays, printed material, recruiting booths, and special events.

During these weeks, press, radio, and television will give full coverage to the "Alert America" Campaign, and the importance of personal participation to strengthen the local Civil Defense program. Special "Alert America" advertisements, sponsored by local merchants, will run in local newspapers.

We cannot stress too much the importance of women in this program. It has been pointed out there can be no successful system of Civil Defense in the United States without the all-out cooperation of American women. Present indications are that they will comprise some 60 percent of the total membership of the U.S. Civil Defense Corps.

The "Alert America" Week includes special programs for junior and senior high schools, such as excursions to the "Alert America" Convoy, classroom discussions, special assemblies, essay and oratorical contests, etc.

Local units of the Armed Forces will play an important role in the continuing exercises and special ceremonies of "Alert America" Week.

Motion picture trailers and special films will herald the coming of the

"Alert America" Convoy. Prominent local movie picture exhibitors and heads of theater associations can play a prominent part in the local program. Theaters can further participate by setting up lobby displays, providing facilities for special rallies, and generally publicizing the "Alert America" theme.

Local newspapers can be expected to provide coverage for the events built around the "Alert America" Convoy, news stories about local activities, and special exhibits, photographs, etc.

Local radio and TV stations should also carry spot announcements, special events, roundtables, forums, and other programs. Basic material for radio, TV, and newspapers will be supplied by local Civil Defense officials and Valley Forge Foundation Field Managers.

Local advertisers can prepare their own advertising or sponsor advertisements prepared by the Advertising Council.

Every organization in the community will be asked to devote all or part of its meeting during "Alert America" Week to a Civil Defense Program.

National Campaign

Apart from the community programs on the local level, there will be a national educational campaign on the Convoys conducted by the Valley Forge Foundation and the Federal Civil Defense Administration in cooperation with the Advertising Council, leading newspapers and magazines, and the major radio and television networks.

The "Alert America" Convoy Campaign will use all available media. The tested effectiveness of established public relations techniques and advertising methods will be spelled out in every detail to carry the "Alert America" message to the American public.

Accent on Action

This is not a campaign merely of words. It seeks to generate positive individual and group action in Civil Defense to protect our freedom and to construct an enduring peace.

Today the danger to our country is greater than at any time in our history. But with this danger there comes this challenge:

Now we can exercise a priceless privilege as Americans—the privilege of serving our country on the front line—in Civil Defense.

Appendix C:
Alert America!
The Time Is Now!

Among the promotional materials prepared by the Valley Forge Foundation, in cooperation with the Federal Civil Defense Administration, to promote Alert America was a brochure that unfolded into an informational poster. Titled "Alert America! The Time Is Now!" the brochure described the exhibit's goals as well as what Americans would see.

What Is the Alert America Convoy Show?

It is the spearhead of a national Civil Defense "Alert America" campaign to revolutionize public thinking about the citizen's responsibilities and dangers in modern war.... Three of these convoys are now touring the Main Streets of America carrying dramatic action exhibits with a vital, urgent story ... that YOU are Civil Defense ... and that you must act *now*, before it is too late ... or America will not have the Civil Defense program it badly needs to save our lives and our freedom and to help construct an enduring peace.

What Are the Goals of the Alert America Campaign?

1. To inform and convince 150 million American people of the grim realities of today's threat from Kremlin aggression and modern terror weapons.
2. To inform America's men, women and children of what they must do to protect themselves if war comes ... and to re-educate themselves

until self-protection becomes as instinctive with them as it is for skilled soldiers in combat.

3. To convince every American that Civil Defense is every citizen's duty.

4. To help State and local Civil Defense authorities enlist some 15 million men and women as volunteers in the growing home front army for Civil Defense.

Why Must We Americans Be Alert and Ready?

Russia now has a growing stockpile of A-Bombs, germ and gas warfare weapons.... With these terror weapons, in a grand-slam attack, the enemy could strike with little or no warning at the heart and strength of America, its people and its farm and industrial production, to try to destroy and demoralize them wherever they are.... If the enemy can't crush the home front quickly, he cannot win a global war ... against America. He knows that ... and we know it!

Can You Do Anything to Combat This Threat?

Yes—through a startling new concept of home front defense and national security, Civil Defense ... a concept which is so important that Secretary of Defense Robert Lovett says, "Civil Defense is a co-equal partner with the military in the defense of the Nation" ... General George C. Marshall warns that Civil Defense is an "urgent" matter and a "military necessity" ... Civil Defense can help keep the peace by making America strong on all fronts.... But if war does come ... with an informed public and adequate national Civil Defense ... we can cut our casualties in half ... and come back fighting!

What Will You See in the Exhibit?

You'll See... Remarkable uses for atomic energy in peace ... in the factory, on the farm ... and in the field of medicine.

You'll See... A scientific action-diorama of potential enemy sabotage, nerve gas and germ warfare.

You'll See... The inside story of atomic war ... and experience the vivid dramatization of a mock A-Bomb attack on your city.

You'll See... What you must do to protect yourself and your family.

You'll See... How America is meeting the threat ... with organized Civil

Defense … which is working now to protect people and production with its fast-growing home front army.

You'll See… The freedoms that we cherish and as individual citizens must be ready to protect.

You'll See… All this … and many other scientific, dramatic action exhibits showing the inside story of Civil Defense and modern war … and what YOU must do NOW to help America get ready … to keep the peace and preserve our freedoms!

BE AN ALERT AMERICAN—YOUR COUNTRY IS COUNTING ON YOU!

Appendix D:
Fact Sheet on
"Alert America Convoy"

Prior to the opening of the Alert America exhibit in Los Angeles, California, on May 17, 1952, the city's Office of Civil Defense released a "Fact Sheet on 'Alert America Convoy'" to its staff, volunteer committees working on the exhibit, area organizations, and city officials as part of its promotional and planning phase. The Fact Sheet, which describes the exhibit in detail, follows the same type of advance planning used in other venue cities. The plan worked in Los Angeles, which drew more than 52,000 visitors.

1. The nation-wide tour of the "Alert America Convoy" exhibit to show why this country needs a strong civil defense program to protect our freedoms and build enduring peace and to spur recruitment of volunteers, will reach Los Angeles in May.

2. It will be exhibited at the National Guard Armory, Exposition Park (Exposition Boulevard just west of Figuaroa Street), beginning Saturday, May 17th, and continuing daily through Thursday, May 22nd.

3. The opening day will be Armed Forces Day, May 17th, and there will be a parade tying in the military with the exhibit. The parade will end at the Armory and, following proper ceremonies, the exhibit will be opened to the public at 12 noon, and from there on will be open from 9 a.m. to 10 p.m. daily, according to present plans.

4. It will need a strong city-wide promotion campaign, with all segments of business industry, agriculture, newspapers, radio, television, advertising, motion picture industry, merchants, organizations, schools, churches, and all other groups within our city working together to make the visit of the convoy a success. We did it with the Freedom Train. We

can do it again with the "Alert America Convoy" if everybody gives it full support.

5. The exhibit is a product of the Valley Forge Foundation, a non-partisan and non-sectarian group of private individuals, which as secured the help and funds, equipment, and facilities from companies, individuals, and organizations and, in cooperation with the Federal Civil Defense Administration, has developed this convoy.

6. The "Alert America Convoy" consists of ten large trucks, each with a huge 32-foot trailer painted in a spectacular but uniform, distinctive design. It carries the elements of a portable exhibit, mounted on skids and handled by portable winches. When assembled, the exhibit is 95' × 155' in size. The displays are taken out of the trucks.

7. Half of the exhibit drives home the reality and nature of the threat that faces us today. The second half spells out specifically and dramatically what the individual citizen can do to meet this threat, and how Civil Defense services are organized on the Federal, State, and local levels to protect the citizen and his community. The principal elements are:

a) Peacetime uses of atomic energy in industry, agriculture, transportation, and medicine.

b) If war comes, it will be far different from any we have known. Pictured are attacks by incendiaries, sabotage, psychological, chemical, and biological warfare.

c) Multi-color films of actual atomic explosions.

d) The dramatic Atomic Attack Room—mock air raid depicting devastating assault on typical American city. This is most dramatic with spectators taken to the actual bombing of a city with all the elements that go with it, and seeing the city devastated before their eyes.

e) The transition—with Civil Defense we can beat this menace.

f) The new concept of national defense—co-partnership of Civil Defense and the Armed Forces.

g) Structure of Civil Defense at the National, State, and local levels—with emphasis on individual and community responsibility.

h) The operations of Civil Defense forces in pre-attack and post-attack periods.

i) The peace and freedoms we cherish and protect—the motivating factor.

j) The "pay-off room" where visitors are asked to volunteer for Civil Defense, teach the family now to protect itself, and to take first aid training, etc.

8. It is planned not only to display the "Alert America Convoy." But to add as additional attractions exhibits by the various Los Angeles Civil

Defense divisions of emergency service, such as Fire, Health, Block Warden, Police Auxiliary, etc., and the various elements of the military. These will be colorful as well as educational displays and demonstrations to augment the show and add color to the entire exhibit.

9. A trained crew travels with the Convoy and handles such arrangements as set-up, knock-down, information, etc.

10. Committees have been formed to carry out various functions in promoting this event. It is a big job. Every public-spirited citizen and organization in Los Angeles must get fully behind the appearance here of the Convoy if it is to be a success. We must not fail to attract many thousands to the exhibit and interest a large number in receiving this education and volunteering for civil defense duties.

Chapter Notes

Preface

1. Lowell Mellett. "Will Atom Bomb Prevent War or Stimulate Another War?" *The Ogden Standard-Examiner* (Ogden, UT), August 14, 1945: 4.

2. "Truman Leads Cheering Throngs in Capital's Wildest Celebration," *The Atlanta Constitution* (Atlanta, GA), August 15, 1952: 12.

3. "Great Loss Shared by Every American, Gov. Dewey Says," *Dayton Daily News* (Dayton, OH), April 12, 1945: 34.

4. Quoted in "Roosevelt Death Comment," *The Evening Sun* (Baltimore, MD), April 13, 1945: 6.

5. "Churchill Holds Post, Eden Flies to Funeral," *Arizona Republic* (Phoenix, AZ), April 14, 1945: 4.

6. Quoted in Jon Meacham. *The Soul of America* (New York: Random House, 2018), 172.

7. "From Caveman's Club to the Atom Bomb." *The Pantagraph* (Bloomington, IL), August 8, 1945: 4.

8. "The Atom Bomb." *Asbury Park Press* (Asbury Park, NJ), August 7, 1945: 8.

9. Jack Ramey. "Foreign Affairs." *The Cincinnati Enquirer* (Cincinnati, OH), August 12, 1945: 32.

10. Harry Truman. Proclamation 2914—Proclaiming the Existence of a National Emergency. Retrieved from http://www.presidency.ucsb.edu/ws/?pid=13684.

11. Meacham, *The Soul of America*, 172.

12. Harry Truman. Statement on Civil Defense. Retrieved from https://www.trumanlibrary.org/publicpapers/index.php?pid=606.

Introduction

1. "The Way to Win Atomic War," *The Guardian* (London, England), April 16, 1952: 10.

2. Arthur Edson, "Explaining H-Bomb to Junior," *Casper Star-Tribune* (Casper, WY), November 18, 1952: 4.

3. Tom Engelhardt, *The End of Victory Culture* (New York: Basic Books, 1995), 6.

4. Hanson Baldwin, "The Atomic Weapon," *New York Times*, August 7, 1945: 10.

5. William Graeber, *The Age of Doubt* (Boston: Twayne Publishers, 1991), 41.

6. Paul Boyer, *By the Bomb's Early Light* (New York: Pantheon Books, 1985), 25.

7. *The End of Victory Culture*: 6.

8. "Truman Text—'Our Policy Is Friendly Partnership,'" *St. Louis Post-Dispatch* (St. Louis, MO), October 27, 1945: 2.

9. "Eisenhower Hits Atomic Apathy," *The Berkshire Eagle* (Pittsfield, MA), January 18, 1947: 2; "Eisenhower Sounds Warning Against Postwar Apathy," *Salt Lake Telegram* (Salt Lake City, UT), January 18, 1947: 2.

10. Harry Truman, Truman Doctrine Address Before a Joint Session of Congress, March 12, 1947. Retrieved from http://avalon.law.yale.edu/20th_century/trudoc.asp.

11. For an overview of the Berlin blockade, NATO, and Soviet expansion, see Jeremy Isaacs and Taylor Downing, *Cold War: For Forty-Five Years the World Held Its Breath* (London: Abacus, 1998).

12. "Apathy Rides the Rails," *Hartford Courant* (Hartford, CT), June 12, 1948: 8.

13. "Bradley Scores U.S. Apathy," *Quad-City Times* (Davenport, IA), February 17, 1949: 6.

14. Straight, Michael. "The Mood of America," *St. Louis Post-Dispatch* (St. Louis, MO), July 16, 1950: 28.

15. Quoted in *By the Bomb's Early Light: 338.*

16. For more on men and women in the 1950s, see William Whyte, *The Organization Man* (New York: Simon & Schuster, 1956) and *Elaine Tyler May*, Homeward Bound (New York: Basic Books, 1988).

17. Proclamation 2914—Proclaiming the Existence of a National Emergency.

18. *Ibid.*

19. Harry Truman, Executive Order 10186. Retrieved from http://www.presidency.ucsb.edu/ws/index.php?pid=78352.

20. Federal Civil Defense Act of 1950. Retrieved from https://www.hsdl.org/?abstract&did=456688.

21. *Ibid.*

22. Millard Caldwell, "Home Front Protection Is Up to You and Your Family," *The Brockway Record* (Brockway, PA), February 15, 1952: 7.

23. *Federal Civil Defense Administration 1951 Annual Report* (Washington, D.C.: Government Printing Office, 1951), 16–17.

24. "Dangers of Atomic Attack Real, Says Defense Body," *Great Falls Tribune* (Great Falls, MT), June 17, 1951: 1.

25. "Civil Defense Goal of New Foundation," St. Louis Post-Dispatch (St. Louis, MO), October 11, 1951: 12.

26. "Alert America Show Is 'Tame' Horror," *The Tennessean* (Nashville, TN), January 13, 1952: 12.

27. For a detailed description of Alert America, see *Alert America!* booklet (Washington, D.C.: FCDA and Valley Forge Foundation, 1951).

28. *Alert America!* 3.

29. "Apathy of Public Said Civil Defense Enemy by Colonel," *Medford Mail Tribune* (Medford, OR), August 16, 1950: 6.

30. "Public's Apathy Toward Civil Defense Needs Decried in City," *The Central New Jersey Home News* (New Brunswick, NJ), August 25, 1950: 6.

31. "Defense Council Finds Way to Get Needed Volunteers," *The Central New Jersey Home News* (New Brunswick, NJ), October 7, 1950: 2.

32. Nat Finney, "Panic, Apathy Pose Civil Defense Problem," *Star Tribune* (Minneapolis, MN), August 21, 1950: 4.

33. Quoted in "Public Apathy Hobbles Civil Defense," *Dayton Daily News* (Dayton, OH), February 5, 1951: 12.

34. "Apathy to Civil Defense Plan in Area Is Attacked," *Vidette-Messenger of Porter County* (Valparaiso, IN), February 9, 1951: 1.

35. "Crusade Needed Against Apathy," *The Post-Crescent* (Appleton, WI), May 7, 1951: 2.

36. "Dewey Sees Apathy in Civil Defense Plans," *The Kingston Daily Freeman* (Kingston, NY), June 5, 1951: 1.

37. "Defense Head Sees Cure for Apathy," *Lincoln Journal Star* (Lincoln, NE), July 15, 1951: 17.

38. "Public Apathy Causes Civil Defense's Lag," *Daily Press* (Newport News, VA), December 9, 1951: 43.

39. "Apathy Toward Civil Defense Blamed on 'Brass,' Congress," *Great Falls Tribune* (Great Falls, MT), June 30, 1951: 12.

40. "No Excuse for Apathy as to Civilian Defense," *The Winona Republican-Herald* (Winona, MN), June 13, 1951: 6.

41. "Sixth V-J Day Finds Victory Not Really Won," *The Tampa Times* (Tampa, FL), August 14, 1951: 6.

42. "Apathy to Civil Defense Is Deplored; There's Task for Everyone to Perform," *The Morning Call* (Allentown, PA), December 23, 1951: 2.

43. Elton C. Fay. "Truman Fears Apathy," *The Bakersfield Californian* (Bakersfield, CA), July 5, 1951: 35.

44. Harry Truman, 1952 State of the Union Address. Retrieved from http://www.presidency.ucsb.edu/ws/index.php?pid=14418.

45. David F. Krugler, *This Is Only a Test* (New York: Palgrave Macmillan, 2006), 81.

46. "Defense Program Pushed by Truman," *Pensacola News Journal* (Pensacola, FL), January 13, 1952: 17.

47. "Apathy at the Bottom," *The Petaluma Argus-Courier* (Petaluma, CA), February 21, 1952: 6.

48. "Apathy on Civil Defense Highlights Annual Report," *Rapid City Journal* (Rapid City, SD), January 19, 1952: 3.

49. Andrew D. Grossman, *Neither Dead Nor Read* (New York: Routledge, 2001), 63, 65.

50. Dee Garrison, *Bracing for Armageddon* (New York: Oxford University Press, 2006), 43.

51. *Neither Dead Nor Read*: 65.

52. "Civil Defense Goal of New Foundation."

53. "Legion Warned Next War to Come to Main Street," *Tampa Bay Times* (Tampa, FL), October 19, 1951: 12.

Chapter One

1. "Expects 'Guts to Live in Crisis' to Avoid War," *St. Louis Post-Dispatch* (St. Louis, MO), January 21, 1952: 19.

2. "City to Show Atomic Havoc in 'City X,'" *The Evening Sun* (Baltimore, MD), January 14, 1952: 17.

3. "Alert America Exhibit Ranges from Axis Sally to A-Bomb," *The Baltimore Sun*, January 26, 1952: 22.

4. See James Isaacs, and Taylor Downing, *Cold War: For Forty-Five Years the World Held Its Breath* (London: Abacus, 1998).

5. "Tempo of War Is Stepped Up in North Korea," *The Times and Democrat* (Orangeburg, SC), March 13, 1952: 1.

6. Harry Truman, Radio and Television Address to the American People on the Situation in Korea, July 19, 1950. Retrieved from http://www.presidency.ucsb.edu/ws/?pid=13561.

7. "Soviet War 'Inevitable' Says Senator," *The Times* (Shreveport, LA), August 28, 1951: 13.

8. "Wanted: A Million Shrouds for the Bodies of Potential A-Bomb Victims," *The Courier-Journal* (Louisville, KY), June 15, 1952: 44.

9. "Priest Urges His Parishioners to Volunteer for Civil Defense," *The Central New Jersey Home News* (New Brunswick, NJ), May 1, 1952: 3; "Spiritual Aid Plan Offered in Raid Event," *The Baltimore Sun*, June 14, 1951: 3.

10. "Text of Eisenhower Statement," *The Baltimore Sun*, January 8, 1952: 8.

11. *Ibid.*

12. "Ike Will Accept Nomination," *Lincoln Journal Star* (Lincoln, NE), January 7, 1952: 1; "General Eisenhower Will Run," *Tallahassee Democrat* (Tallahassee, FL), January 7, 1952: 1; "Eisenhower, Republican, Will Run," *Redlands Daily Facts* (Redlands, CA), January 7, 1952: 1; "Gen. Eisenhower Backers Jubilant at Announcement," *Redlands Daily Facts* (Redlands, CA), January 7, 1952: 1.

13. Paul Ward, "Paris Cabinet Fall Blow to D.C. Parleys," *The Baltimore Sun*, January 8, 1952: 1; "Pleven Cabinet Falls, Is Refused Power to Trim Railway Deficit," *St. Louis Post-Dispatch* (St. Louis, MO), January 7, 1952: 1.

14. "Joy in Tokyo to Talk with Gen. Ridgway," *Delphos Daily Herald* (Delphos, OH), January 7, 1952: 1.

15. "U.S. and British Leaders Review West's Strategy," *The Cumberland News* (Cumberland, MD), January 8, 1952: 1; "Churchill, Truman Open Conferences; Study Anglo-American Policies," *The Times Standard* (Eureka, CA), January 7, 1952: 1.

16. Joint Statement Following Discussions with Prime Minister Churchill, January 9, 1952. Retrieved from http://www.presidency.ucsb.edu/ws/index.php?pid=14429.

17. Winston Churchill's "Iron Curtain" Speech, March 5, 1946. Retrieved from https://www.thoughtco.com/winston-churchills-iron-curtain-speech-1779492.

18. For more on the Berlin Blockade, China, and the Soviet Union's atomic bomb, see James Isaacs and Taylor Downing, *Cold War*.

19. Annual Message to the Congress on the State of the Union, January 9, 1952. Retrieved from http://www.presidency.ucsb.edu/ws/?pid=14418.

20. "Few U.S. Voters Fear New War," *Arizona Daily Star* (Tucson, AZ), January 21, 1955: 3.

21. "1951's Atomic Achievements Strengthen West's Power," *Medford Mail Tribune* (Medford, OR), January 2, 1952: 7.

22. "Hints of U.S. Atomic Strides Balance Red Power Estimates," *The Evening Sun* (Baltimore, MD), June 28, 1952: 3.

23. *Ibid.*

24. "World's Largest Buildings in Atomic Plants," *Chillicothe Gazette* (Chillicothe, OH), August 16, 1952: 12.

25. "1951's Atomic Achievements Strengthen West's Power."

26. "Hydrogen Bomb Plant to Cost Twice Estimate," *The Journal Times* (Racine, WI), January 30, 1952: 2.

27. For more on the development of the hydrogen bomb, see Richard Rhodes. *Dark Sun: The Making of the Hydrogen Bomb* (New York: Simon & Schuster, 1995).

28. "The World Enters Stage No. 2," *The St.*

Louis Star and Times (St. Louis, MO), September 24, 1949: 10.

29. "AEC Reports Atomic Arms Progress, Promises More Advances Yet to Come," *Asheville Citizen-Times* (Asheville, NC), January 31, 1952: 25.

30. "Capital Sets Royal Welcome for Eisenhower," *Nevada State Journal* (Reno, NV), November 18, 1952: 1.

31. Harry Truman, 1953 State of the Union. Retrieved from http://www.let.rug.nl/usa/presidents/harry-s-truman/state-of-the-union-1953.php.

32. Executive Order 10186. Retrieved from http://www.presidency.ucsb.edu/ws/index.php?pid=78352.

33. *Federal Civil Defense Administration 1952 Annual Report* (Washington, D.C.: Government Printing Office, 1952), 49.

Chapter Two

1. "Hundreds Join Civil Defense at Alert America Opening," *The Washington Post*, January 8, 1952: B1.

2. David Krugler, *This Is Only a Test: How Washington, D.C., Prepared for Nuclear War* (New York: Macmillan Palgrave, 2006), 79; Kregg Michael Fehr, "Sheltering Society: Civil Defense in the United States, 1945–1963": 48–49, dissertation retrieved from http://hdl.handle.net/2346/16965.

3. *Ibid.*; "'Alert America' Shows in Capital," *Daily Press* (Newport News, VA), December 11, 1951: 3.

4. History of auditorium retrieved from http://www.mellonauditorium.com.

5. "Civil Defense Lags," *The Bridgeport Telegram* (Bridgeport, CT), July 9, 1951: 8.

6. William Perkinson, "Nation's 'Pathetic' Civil-Defense Setup Attributed to 'Apathy' of Public," *The Evening Sun* (Baltimore, MD), April 3, 1951: 1.

7. "Money Alone Doesn't Make a Civil Defense Program." *The Philadelphia Inquirer*, August 19, 1951: 26.

8. "Dangers of Atomic Attack Real, Says Defense Body," *Great Falls Tribune* (Great Falls, MT), June 17, 1951: 1.

9. "Civil Defense Lags."

10. "Civil-Defense Advisers to Seek Fund Solution," *The Courier-Journal* (Louisville, KY), August 19, 1951: 13.

11. "Spiritual Aid Plan Offered in Raid Event," *The Baltimore Sun*, June 14, 1951: 3.

12. "Alert America Campaign: Progress Report." PHST, Official File, Box 1671, Folder 1591-C.

13. *Ibid.*, 2.

14. *Ibid.*

15. *Ibid.*, 4.

16. *Ibid.*, 5.

17. *Ibid.*, 6.

18. *Ibid.*, 7.

19. "Spiritual Aid Plan Offered in Raid Event," *The Baltimore Sun*, June 14, 1951: 3.

20. "Alert America Campaign: Progress Report," 10.

21. *Ibid.*, 11–12.

22. "Security and Congress," *The Times and Democrat* (Orangeburg, SC), November 15, 1951: 4,

23. "President Raps Slash in Funds," *Arizona Daily Star* (Tucson, AZ), November 3, 1951: 6.

24. "Mayors to Discuss Effect of Cuts on Tennessee," *The Tennessean* (Nashville, TN), August 21, 1951: 2; "The Cities Want Defense Funds," *St. Louis Post-Dispatch* (St. Louis, MO), December 15, 1951: 4; "Defeat of State Civil Defense Fund Bill Called 'Crippling Blow,'" *St. Louis Post-Dispatch* (St. Louis, MO), December 7, 1951: 3.

25. "Public in Dark on Civil Defense, Advisers State," *The Tennessean* (Nashville, TN), August 21, 1951: 1.

26. "The Cities Want Defense Funds."

27. Robert S. Allen, "A-Bomb Army Coming," *Alton Evening Telegraph* (Alton, IL), October 2, 1951: 4.

28. "To Seek More U.S. Funds for Civil Defense," *The Star Press* (Muncie, IN), November 19, 1951: 2.

29. "Defense Exhibit Going on the Road," *New York Times*, October 12, 1951: 20.

30. "A-Bomb Army Coming."

31. "Officials Proclaim Civil Defense Week," *The Signal* (Santa Clarita, CA), October 18, 1951: 7.

32. "Civil Defense on Wheels," *The Newark Advocate* (Newark, OH), October 22, 1951: 4.

33. "Civil Defense Goal of New Foundation," *St. Louis Post-Dispatch* (St. Louis, MO), October 11, 1951: 12.

34. *Krugler*: 80.

35. "Civil Defense Goal of New Foundation."

36. *Alert America!* (Valley Forge Foundation/Federal Civil Defense Administration, 1952), 3.

37. "'Alert America' Shows in Capital," *Daily Press* (Newport News, VA), December 11, 1951: 3.

38. *Federal Civil Defense Administration 1951 Annual Report* (Washington, D.C.: Government Printing Office, 1951), 1.

39. "'Alert America' Convoy Booked for Canton Visit," *The Evening Independent* (Massillon, OH), January 16, 1952: 2; "Graphic Display Showing How to Survive Atomic Warfare to Be Here February 7–10," *The Greenville News* (Greenville, SC), December 30, 1951: 4; "Truck Convoy to Promote CD Due in Manchester," *The Portsmouth Herald* (Portsmouth, NH), January 30, 1952: 2; "'Alert America Convoy' Due in City April 10," *Lansing State Journal* (Lansing, MI), December 12, 1951: 25; "'Alert America Convoy' Will Come to Alabama," *The Anniston Star* (Anniston, AL), January 22, 1952: 2; "Big Civil Defense Exhibits Coming," *The Star-Herald* (Kosciusko, MS), December 27, 1951: 7; "Alert America Exhibit, Stressing Home Mobilization, to Visit Here," *The Tennessean* (Nashville, TN), January 9, 1952: 22.

40. "Hundreds Join Civil Defense at Alert America Opening," *The Washington Post*, January 8, 1952: B1; Krugler, 81.

41. "Truman Sees Civil Defense Progress," *The Baltimore Sun*, January 13, 1952: 2.

42. "'Alert America' Exhibit Ready as Graphic Civil Defense Aid," *The Washington Post*, January 6, 1952, M9.

43. Bill Henry, "By the Way," *Los Angeles Times*, January 15, 1952: 23.

44. "Woman's Club," *Helper Journal* (Helper, UT), November 27, 1952: 5; "Ostertag Deplores Lag in Volunteers for CD," *Democrat and Chronicle* (Rochester, NY), December 11, 1952: 25; "Alert America Group to See Ike Monday," *The Tennessean* (Nashville, TN), December 21, 1952: 18.; "2 Oakland Eagle Aeries to Merge at Dinner Meet," *Oakland Tribune* (Oakland, CA), September 7, 1952: 54; "Scouts Will Alert America Tomorrow to Get Out and Vote," *The Ogden Standard-Examiner* (Ogden, UT), October 31, 1952: 16.

45. Harry Truman, Statement by the President on the Need for "Operation Skywatch," December 7, 1952. Retrieved from https:// www.trumanlibrary.org/publicpapers/index. php?pid=2105&st=civil+defense&st1=.

Chapter Three

1. "City Defense Director Blames Apathy on Leaders, Not Public," *The News Journal* (Wilmington, DE), September 14, 1951: 4.

2. "Maurice DuPont Lee Heads Civil Defense," *The News Journal* (Wilmington, DE), June 30, 1950: 4.

3. "Caldwell Praises Handling of 'Alert America' Exhibit Here," *The News Journal* (Wilmington, DE), January 23, 1952: 1.

4. "Auxiliary Police, Firemen Planned," *The Morning News* (Wilmington, DE), September 26, 1950: 17.

5. "Carvel Calls for Volunteers to Fill Civil Defense Jobs," *The Morning News* (Wilmington, DE), December 20, 1950: 1.

6. "Flexible Civil Defense Bill Prepared for Early Action," *The News Journal* (Wilmington, DE), January 12, 1951: 6.

7. "Permanent Civil Defense Set-up for State Planned," *The Morning News* (Wilmington, DE), November 15, 1950: 1.

8. "Delaware Leads U.S. in Civil Defense Pacts," *The News Journal* (Wilmington, DE), February 6, 1952: 2; "Civil Defense Mobile Unit Being Formed," *The News Journal* (Wilmington, DE), January 9, 1952: 1.

9. "Arousing All to War Peril Stressed at Mayors' Meet," *The News Journal* (Wilmington, DE), December 18, 1950: 14.

10. "Monroe Park Defense Work Building Community Unity," *The Morning News* (Wilmington, DE), April 26, 1951: 5.

11. "Atomic Attack Topic of Talk," *The News Journal* (Wilmington, DE), December 13, 1950: 43.

12. "Delaware Gets Air Raid Test in 19-State Surprise Alarm," *The News Journal* (Wilmington, DE), October 25, 1951: 25.

13. Bill Frank, "Frankly Speaking," *The Morning News* (Wilmington, DE), April 17, 1951: 16.

14. Bill Frank, "Frankly Speaking," *The Morning News* (Wilmington, DE), April 20, 1951: 12.

15. "Leader Assails Defense Apathy," *The News Journal* (Wilmington, DE), May 8, 1951: 1.

16. "City Defense Director Blames Apathy on Leaders, Not Public."

17. "City to Purchase Bomb Pamphlets for

Distribution," *The Morning News* (Wilmington, DE), January 19, 1951: 1.

18. "Biological War Civilian Defense Unit Organized," *The Morning News* (Wilmington, DE), February 7, 1951: 1; "Arthur K. Wilson Will Head 3,000 Block Wardens," *The Morning News* (Wilmington, DE), February 8, 1951: 1; "Block Warden Organization Explained at City Meeting," *The Morning News* (Wilmington, DE), February 9, 1951: 37.

19. "Raid Alarm Heard in Suburbs, Not City," *The News Journal* (Wilmington, DE), February 10, 1951: 1.

20. "Junior League Will Hear Civil Defense Leader," *The Morning News* (Wilmington, DE), March 10, 1951: 18; "Civil Defense Bureau Set Up," *The News Journal* (Wilmington, DE), October 25, 1951: 6.

21. "Big 'Alert America Convoy' to Boost Civil Defense Here," *The Morning News* (Wilmington, DE), January 3, 1952: 1.

22. "CD Group to Aid 'Alert Convoy,'" *The Morning News* (Wilmington, DE), January 8, 1952: 4.

23. "Local Delegation Enthusiastic Over Defense Convoy Preview in Washington," *The Morning News* (Wilmington, DE), January 9, 1952: 2.

24. "Local Groups Plan Exhibits in 'Alert America' Convoy," *The Morning News* (Wilmington, DE), January 15, 1952: 18; "Big 'Alert America Convoy' to Boost Civil Defense Here," *The Morning News* (Wilmington, DE), January 3, 1952: 1.

25. *Ibid.*

26. "'Alert America' Exhibit Approved," *The Morning News* (Wilmington, DE), January 16, 1952: 2.

27. "Mayor's Proclamation Asks Alertness for Civil Defense," *The Morning News* (Wilmington, DE), January 18, 1952: 7.

28. "Volunteers to Serves as Aides for 'Alert America' Exhibit," *The News Journal* (Wilmington, DE), January 17, 1952: 7.

29. "A-Bomb Attack Portrayed for 2,500 at Defense Exhibit," *The Morning News* (Wilmington, DE), January 21, 1952: 1.

30. "Alert—Delaware!" *The Morning News* (Wilmington, DE), January 22, 1952: 14.

31. "10,700 Saw It," *The News Journal* (Wilmington, DE), February 6, 1952: 14.

32. "Caldwell Praises Handling of 'Alert America' Exhibit Here."

33. "Today Last Day of Defense Show," *The Morning News* (Wilmington, DE), January 23, 1952: 34.

34. "Defense Leader Will Speak Here," *The Morning News* (Wilmington, DE), January 11, 1952: 27.

35. "Schools' Alert Called Success," *The News Journal* (Wilmington, DE), February 26, 1952: 1.

36. "Civil Defense Wants Shelters," *The News Journal* (Wilmington, DE), January 25, 1952: 11.

37. "CD Plans Survey of Churches Here," *The Morning News* (Wilmington, DE), March 18, 1952: 11; "Office Buildings Safest in Raids," *The News Journal* (Wilmington, DE), March 24, 1952: 22.

38. "M. DuPont Lee Quits as City CD Director," *The Morning News* (Wilmington, DE), June 18, 1952: 1; "Civil Defense Body Pledges Its Full Duty," *The News Journal* (Wilmington, DE), June 19, 1952: 1.

39. Bill Frank, "Frankly Speaking," *The Morning News* (Wilmington, DE), June 9, 1952: 10.

40. "Corsano, Dayton in Heated Debate on Civil Defense," *The Morning News* (Wilmington, DE), May 2, 1952: 1.

41. "Col. Dunn to Head City, County CD," *The Morning News* (Wilmington, DE), June 21, 1952: 15.

42. "Whither Civil Defense," *The News Journal* (Wilmington, DE), June 18, 1952: 20.

43. "'Alert America' Signs Civil Defense Workers," *The Paris News* (Paris, TX), May 22, 1952: 14.

44. "Time to Wake Up," *The New Journal* (Wilmington, DE), January 19, 1952: 6.

Chapter Four

1. Dan Halligan, "Air Alert, Parade and Exhibit in City," *The Greenville News* (Greenville, SC), February 7, 1952: 1.

2. *Ibid.*

3. "Air Alert, Parade and Exhibit in City"; "Greenville's Civil Defense Plan to Get Test Tomorrow," *The Greenville News* (Greenville, SC), February 6, 1952: 7; "Civil Defense Exhibit Opens 4-Day Stand," *The Greenville News* (Greenville, SC), February 8, 1952: 1; Caroline Arlington, "Greenville Parade," *The Greenville News* (Greenville, SC), February 10, 1952: 27.

4. "Air Alert, Parade and Exhibit in City."

5. "Civil Defense Program," *The Greenville News* (Greenville, SC), February 7, 1952: 4.

6. "Civil Defense Exhibit Opens 4-Day Stand."

7. "Select Head for Defense," *The Greenville News* (Greenville, SC), December 13, 1950: 1.

8. "Home Front Defense," *The Greenville News* (Greenville, SC), February 5, 1951: 4.

9. "Graphic Display Showing How to Survive Atomic Warfare to Be Here February 7–10," *The Greenville News* (Greenville, SC), December 30, 1951: 4.

10. "Civil Defense Police Set Up," The Greenville News (Greenville, SC), February 8, 1951: 8; "Zaebst Appointed to Head Civil Defense Phase Here," *The Greenville News* (Greenville, SC), August 4, 1951: 2; "Division Head to Report at Civil Defense Meeting," *The Greenville News* (Greenville, SC), October 4, 1951: 5; "Has Vital Role in Civil Defense," *The Greenville News* (Greenville, SC), July 8, 1951: 3; "CD Speakers to Offer Services," *The Greenville News* (Greenville, SC), September 26, 1951: 2.

11. "Urgency for Civil Defense Stressed at Local CD Meet," *The Greenville News*, December 18, 1951: 3.

12. "8,004 See 'Alert Exhibit'; 1,896 Volunteers as Workers," *The Greenville News* (Greenville, SC), February 11, 1952: 2.

13. "Air Alert, Parade and Exhibit in City."

14. "Heavy Fine for Failure to Obey Raid Test Signal," *The Boston Globe*, February 20, 1952: 36; "Alert America Show Expected to Attract Thousands to Boston," *The Boston Globe*, February 24, 1952: 1; "Parade Thursday to Open Exhibit for Civil Defense," *The Boston Globe*, February 17, 1952: 24.

15. Herman Hancock, "Mayor Asks Revival of Civilian Defense," *The Atlanta Constitution* (Atlanta, GA), July 15, 1950: 10.

16. Herman Hancock, "Civil Defense Advisors to Meet on Atom Peril," *The Atlanta Constitution* (Atlanta, GA), August 16, 1950: 23.

17. "Atlanta Seen as A-Bomb Target; 50-Mile Defense Area Sought," *The Atlanta Constitution* (Atlanta, GA), August 15, 1950: 3.

18. "4 Atom Defense Units Held Necessary Here," *The Atlanta Constitution* (Atlanta, GA), August 23, 1950: 2.

19. "Civil Defense Organizers Set Up Hapeville Center," *The Atlanta Constitution* (Atlanta, GA), May 15, 1951: 12; "Transport Snag Delays Schools' Air Raid Trials," *The Atlanta Constitution* (Atlanta, GA), November 6, 1951: 7.

20. "Exhibit Set Here to Cite Atom Peril," *The Atlanta Constitution* (Atlanta, GA), February 14, 1952: 8.

21. "'Alert America' Exhibit Held Over Here Through Friday," *The Atlanta Constitution* (Atlanta, GA), February 27, 1952: 8.

22. "How A-Bomb Could Raze Atlanta Shown at Exhibit," *The Atlanta Constitution* (Atlanta, GA), February 25, 1952: 6.

23. "Alert America Parade Slated for 2 p.m. Today," *The Atlanta Constitution* (Atlanta, GA), February 22, 1952: 5; "Parade Here Buzzed by Stratojet," *The Atlanta Constitution* (Atlanta, GA), February 23, 1952: 1.

24. "Superjet to Fly Over CD Parade," *The Atlanta Constitution* (Atlanta, GA), February 21, 1952: 17; "Alert America Parade Slated for 2 p.m. Today"; "Parade Here Buzzed by Stratojet."

25. "Parade Here Buzzed by Stratojet."

26. "38 Trucks Haul Defense Spectacle to West Hartford for Four-Day Show," *Hartford Courant* (Hartford, CT), March 8, 1952: 7; "Towns Will Join in City CD Parade," *Hartford Courant* (Hartford, CT), March 4, 1952: 3.

27. "Open 'Alert America' Exhibit Here Friday," *Clarion-Ledger* (Jackson, MS), March 25, 1952: 12; "Paul Revere Travels in Truck, Puts on Super Show in Jackson," *Clarion-Ledger* (Jackson, MS), March 28, 1952: 1.

28. "Convoy to 'Alert America,' Air Escort, to Parade Today," *The Indianapolis Star* (Indianapolis, IN), March 29, 1952: 15; "Parades, Screaming Sirens to Greet Defense Caravan," *The Indianapolis Star* (Indianapolis, IN), March 27, 1952: 21.

29. "Thousands March Here in Armed Forces Parade," *Los Angeles Times*, May 18, 1952: 1.

30. "City Defense Post Goes to Admiral Berry," *Los Angeles Times*, January 17, 1951: 1.

31. "Defense Booklet Distribution Begins as Berry Takes Office," *Los Angeles Times*, February 6, 1951: 25.

32. "Red Alert Air Raid System Given Test," *Los Angeles Times*, May 18, 1952: 1.

33. "Thousands March Here in Armed Forces Parade."

34. "Military Might Will Parade on Armed Forces Day Sat., May 17," *The Signal* (Santa Clarita, CA), May 15, 1952: 8.

35. *Ibid.*

36. "Children Have Field Day at Alert America Display," *Los Angeles Times*, May 18, 1952: 3.

37. *Federal Civil Defense Administration 1952 Annual Report* (Washington, D.C.: Government Printing Office, 1952).

38. "Alert America Parade Set," *Salt Lake Tribune* (Salt Lake City, UT), September 13, 1952: 17.

39. "Siren Alerts S.L. as Fighter Spews Death, Destruction," *Salt Lake Tribune* (Salt Lake City, UT), September 14, 1952: 20.

40. "Spectacular Parade Saturday to Feature 'Alert America,'" *Salt Lake Tribune* (Salt Lake City, UT), September 9, 1952: 23.

41. "Alert America," *Los Angeles Times*, May 16, 1952: 35.

Chapter Five

1. "Strategy for the Atomic Age Involves Study of Red Pressure Around World," *The Kansas City Times* (Kansas City, MO), May 8, 1952: 40.

2. "Merry-Go-Round," *The Express* (Lock Haven, PA), January 16, 1952: 4; Margaret Chase Smith, "Civil Defense to Be Pictured in New Motorcades Set to Tour United States," *The Daily Times* (Davenport, IA), January 9, 1952: 10.

3. Bill Henry, "By the Way with Bill Henry," *Los Angeles Times*, January 15, 1952: 21.

4. "Jets to Zoom Welcome Today to 'Alert America' Motorcade," *The Brooklyn Daily Eagle* (Brooklyn, NY), January 16, 1952: 5; "Raid Alarm Tests Planned as Part of 'Alert America,'" *The Brooklyn Daily Eagle* (Brooklyn, NY), January 11, 1952: 4; "Nassau Showing Set for CD Film, 'Alert America,'" *The Brooklyn Daily Eagle* (Brooklyn, NY), January 4, 1952: 7.

5. "Heavy Fine for Failure to Obey Raid Test Signal," *The Boston Globe*, February 20, 1952: 36; "Alert America Show Expected to Attract Thousands to Boston," *The Boston Globe*, February 24, 1952: 1; "Parade Thursday to Open Exhibit for Civil Defense," *The Boston Globe*, February 17, 1952: 24.

6. "CD Drills Start for Wardens of State

Buildings," *The Newark Advocate* (Newark, OH), January 15, 1952: 11.

7. "Alert America Exhibit Opens Ohio Stopover," *The Sandusky Register* (Sandusky, OH), January 23, 1952: 11.

8. "'Alert America' Unit to Visit Youngstown," *The Salem News* (Salem, OH), January 23, 1952: 2; "Gold Star Mothers Attend State Session," *Lima News* (Lima, OH), January 24, 1952: 14.

9. "Auto Caravan Planned for Alert America," *The Evening Independent* (Massillon, OH), February 2, 1952: 2.

10. "OPS Posters Removed from CD Display," *The Circleville Herald* (Circleville, OH), February 8, 1952: 1; "Convoy Told Not to Show OPS Posters," *The Evening Independent* (Massillon, OH), February 8, 1952: 2.

11. "Canton Gets CD Exhibit for 4 Days," *The Akron Beacon Journal* (Akron, OH), January 30, 1952: 2.

12. "'Alert America' Convoy Booked for Canton Visit," *The Evening Independent* (Massillon, OH), January 16, 1952: 2; "Wednesday Is Massillon Day at 'Alert America' Exhibit," *The Evening Independent* (Massillon, OH), February 5, 1952: 11.

13. "Apathy Smothers Canton CD," *The Akron Beacon Journal* (Akron, OH), December 2, 1951: 3; "Canton CD Revamping Is Planned," *The Akron Beacon Journal* (Akron, OH), February 7, 1952: 6.

14. "CD to Make Siren Tests on Thursday," *The Akron Beacon Journal* (Akron, OH), February 12, 1952: 5; "City Takes Siren Test in Stride," *The Akron Beacon Journal* (Akron, OH), February 15, 1952: 5.

15. "Truck Convoy to Promote CD Due in Manchester," *The Portsmouth Herald* (Portsmouth, NH), January 30, 1952: 2.

16. "'Alert America' Unit Set," *The Kansas City Star* (Kansas City, MO), March 23, 1952: 7A.

17. "To Head Defense Show," *The Kansas City Times* (Kansas City, MO), March 12, 1952: 13; "Strategy for the Atomic Age Involves Study of Red Pressure Around the World."

18. "Towns Will Join in City CD Parade," *Hartford Courant* (Hartford, CT), March 4, 1952: 3; "CD Exhibit Opens Today at Armory in West Hartford," *Hartford Courant* (Hartford, CT), March 9, 1952: 2.

19. "Alert America Show Opens Next

Sunday," *Hartford Courant* (Hartford, CT), March 2, 1952: 36.

20. "East Hartford Day Set at Alert America Exhibit," *Hartford Courant* (Hartford, CT), March 6, 1952: 318.

21. "Alert America Show Opens Next Sunday."

22. "Ham Radio Messages to Be Sent Free," *Hartford Courant* (Hartford, CT), March 3, 1952: 1.

23. "Alert America Exhibit Seen by 20,000 Closes After Signing Up 750 for CD," *Hartford Courant* (Hartford, CT), March 13, 1952: 17.

24. "Alert America Parade Prompts CD Questions," *Hartford Courant* (Hartford, CT), March 9, 1952: 35.

25. "Alert America Exhibit Endorsed by Governor," *Hartford Courant* (Hartford, CT), March 9, 1952: 31.

26. "Rules for Practice Alert Here Tomorrow Announced," *The Berkshire Eagle* (Pittsfield, MA), March 21, 1952: 14; "Mayor Asks Co-operation for CD Alert," *The Berkshire Eagle* (Pittsfield, MA), March 20, 1952: 17.

27. "Alert America Trucks Will Be Here Monday," *North Adams Transcript* (North Adams, MA), March 21, 1954: 4; "Alert America Convoy Goal Is 3,000 CD Volunteers Here," *The Berkshire Eagle* (Pittsfield, MA), March 14, 1952: 8; "Alert America Exhibit Viewed by Cheshire Students," *The Berkshire Eagle* (Pittsfield, MA), March 25, 1952: 16.

28. "Paul Revere of Today Huge Trailer Convoy," *Alton Evening Telegraph* (Alton, IL), May 6, 1952: 14.

29. "Paul Revere Travels in Truck, Puts on Super Show in Jackson," *Clarion-Ledger* (Jackson, MS), March 28, 1952: 1.

30. "'Alert U.S. Convoy' Due Here March 28th," *Clarion-Ledger* (Jackson, MS), March 16, 1952: 3.

31. "Civil Defense Show Draws Well Here," *Clarion-Ledger* (Jackson, MS), April 6, 1952: 2; "Last Chance to See Exhibit That May Save Your Life," *Clarion-Ledger* (Jackson, MS), March 30, 1952: 4.

32. Charles Hill, "Affairs of State," *Clarion-Ledger* (Jackson, MS), March 30, 1952: 49; "Paul Revere Travels in Truck, Puts on Super Show in Jackson."

33. "CD Exhibit Scheduled," *Lansing State Journal* (Lansing, MI), March 5, 1952: 27;

"Water Barrage," *Detroit Free Press*, April 13, 1952: 4.

34. "Press Will Get Preview of 'Alert America' Show," *The Post-Standard* (Syracuse, NY), April 13, 1952: 25.

35. "CD Exhibit Opens Tomorrow in City to 'Alert America,'" *The Post-Standard* (Syracuse, NY), April 15, 1952: 6.

36. "Alert America Exhibit Opens Here Next Week," *Press and Sun-Bulletin* (Binghamton, NY), April 27, 1952: 25; "Atomic Energy Exhibit Opens at State Armory Next Monday," *Press and Sun-Bulletin* (Binghamton, NY), April 29, 1952: 3; "Cyclists Plan CD Exhibit," *Press and Sun-Bulletin* (Binghamton, NY), May 1, 1952: 9.

37. "Wallander Cites Gains in Civil Defense," *New York Times*, May 12, 1952: 9; "Show People to Aid B'way Defense Rally," *The Brooklyn Daily Eagle* (Brooklyn, NY), May 9, 1952: 11; "'Alert America' Exhibit," *New York Times*, May 15, 1952, 15.

38. "Council Votes $1,000 for U.S. Defense Show," *The Capital Times* (Madison, WI), March 3, 1952: 6; "Sponsors for Civil Defense Named," *The Capital Times* (Madison, WI), May 13, 1952: 6; "32 to Sponsor 'Alert' Convoy," *WI State Journal* (Madison, WI), May 14, 1952: 10; "Workers Ready for 'Alert America' Visit," *WI State Journal* (Madison, WI), May 18, 1952: 40.

39. "Civil Defense Unit to Stage City 'Disaster,'" *Star Tribune* (Minneapolis, MN), May 11, 1952: 19; "Defense Units Will Parade," *The Minneapolis Star*, May 22, 1952: 55.

40. "Hundreds of Volunteers Promote Defense Show," *Oakland Tribune* (Oakland, CA), May 29, 1952: 6; "Leaders to Honor Defense Convoy," *Oakland Tribune* (Oakland, CA), June 1, 1952: 14.

41. "Eastbay Firms Promote 'Alert America' Convoy," *Oakland Tribune* (Oakland, CA), May 22, 1952: 35.

42. "Legion Chief to Speak at Civil Defense Show," *Oakland Tribune* (Oakland, CA), May 26, 1952: 15; "All-Out Defense Effort Urged by Legion Chief," *Oakland Tribune* (Oakland, CA), June 4, 1952: 28.

43. "Military Exhibits Here for 'Alert America' Show," *Oakland Tribune* (Oakland, CA), June 2, 1952: 12; "Daily Knave," *Oakland Tribune* (Oakland, CA), June 13, 1952: 33.

44. "Air Raid Alert During May 27," *The*

Philadelphia Inquirer, April 3, 1952: 26; "Air-Raid Test Receives Cooperation of Public; Some Faults Uncovered," *The Philadelphia Inquirer*, May 28, 1952: 1.

45. "Civil Defense Convoy Bears Vital Message," *The Philadelphia Inquirer*, June 5, 1952: 17.

46. "'Alert America' Goal Is 60,000," *The Philadelphia Inquirer*, June 6, 1952: 10; "Clark Hits Apathy on Civil Defense," *The Philadelphia Inquirer*, June 7, 1952: 26.

47. "Time to Wake Up America," *The Philadelphia Inquirer*, June 8, 1952: 58.

48. "Clark Hits Apathy on Civil Defense," *The Philadelphia Inquirer*, June 7, 1952: 26.

49. "Defense Exhibit to Be Shown in Chester Saturday," *Chester Times* (Chester, PA), June 6, 1952: 44.

50. "Civilian Defense Drive Planned," *The Pittsburgh Press* (Pittsburgh, PA), May 21, 1952: 31; "Industry in CD Speaker's Theme," *The Pittsburgh Press* (Pittsburgh, PA), May 19, 1952: 31; "Women Organize Defense," *Pittsburgh Post-Gazette* (Pittsburgh, PA), May 21, 1952: 10; "School to Take Bomb Test," *Pittsburgh Post-Gazette* (Pittsburgh, PA), May 7, 1952: 15; "Anti-Aircraft Exhibit at 'Alert America' Show," *The Pittsburgh Press* (Pittsburgh, PA), June 22, 1952: 11.

51. "Marines Attack Set Last Day of Fair," *Lincoln News Messenger* (Lincoln, California), September 4, 1952: 2.

Chapter Six

1. "Organizations Aid in Education to Preserve Freedom," *The Pittsburgh Press* (Pittsburgh, PA), January 29, 1952: 25.

2. "City Pupils Get Taste of Atom Horror," *The Indianapolis News* (Indianapolis, IN), March 31, 1952: 16.

3. "Recommendations for the Teaching of International Understanding," *The Phi Delta Kappan* 28, 2 (October 1946), 91–95.

4. Harold Hand, "Living in the Atomic Age: A Resource Unit for Teachers in Secondary School," *University of Illinois Bulletin* 23 (December 3, 1946).

5. See Florence Gelbond, "The Impact of the Atomic Bomb on Education," *The Social Studies* 65 (March 1974), 110.

6. Willem J. Van Der Grinten, "Not Only Science Teachers," *The Clearing House*, 24, 8 (April 1950), 487.

7. *Ibid.*

8. *Ibid.*, 1–3.

9. *Federal Civil Defense Administration 1952 Annual Report* (Washington, D.C.: U.S. Government Printing Office, 1952), 62.

10. *Alert America!* (Washington, D.C.: Valley Forge Foundation and FCDA, 1951), 13.

11. "Millions of Women to Be Recruited for Civil Defense Training in 1952," *The Indianapolis Star* (Indianapolis, IN), January 23, 1952: 20.

12. "Women Warned on Atom Danger," *The Indianapolis Star* (Indianapolis, IN), August 29, 1952: 15.

13. For a detailed account of women's participation in civil defense, see Michael Scheibach, *Protecting the Home Front* (Jefferson, NC: McFarland, 2017).

14. "Letters from the People," *The Ithaca Journal* (Ithaca, NY), January 23, 1952: 6.

15. *Alert America!*: 3.

16. "Clubs Prepare for Visit of 'Alert America Convoy,'" *The Indianapolis Star* (Indianapolis, IN), March 13, 1952: 9; "Civil Defense Alert America Group Listed," *The Indianapolis Star* (Indianapolis, IN), March 13, 1952: 31; "Parades, Screaming Sirens to Greet Defense Caravan."

17. "Barbara Busy Helping with County's Defense," *The Indianapolis Star* (Indianapolis, IN), April 6, 1952: 82.

18. "'Alert America' Cavalcade Soon to Visit Fairgrounds," *The Indianapolis Star* (Indianapolis, IN), March 2, 1952: 19; "Parades, Screaming Sirens to Greet Defense Caravan," *The Indianapolis Star* (Indianapolis, IN), March 27, 1952: 21.

19. "Capital Residents 'Flunk' Air Alert," *Journal and Courier* (Lafayette, IN), April 1, 1952: 1.

20. "City Shrugs Off Air Raid Warning," *The Times* (Munster, IN), April 1, 1952: 4.

21. "Indiana Is Now Issuing ID Tags," *The Tribune* (Seymour, IN), April 16, 1952: 9; "Official Civil Defense Identification Tags Issued for Hoosier by State," *Steuben Republican* (Angola, IN), April 16, 1952: 5.

22. "Identification Tags Going at Rate of 4,000 Daily," *The Indianapolis Star* (Indianapolis, IN), May 17, 1952: 5.

23. "Officials Announce Program for Alert America Caravan," *The Dispatch* (Moline, IL), March 13, 1952: 2; "2,370 Attend Alert America

Show 1st Day," *The Dispatch* (Moline, IL), March 20, 1952: 16.

24. "Defense Show Draws 10,000," *The Dispatch* (Moline, IL), March 22, 1952: 11.

25. "Armory Doors Swing Open, Alert America Show Begins," *The Dispatch* (Moline, IL), March 19, 1952: 14.

26. "Woman's Role in Defense to Get Attention," *The Dispatch* (Moline, IL), March 11, 1952: 4.

27. "Telephone Center Part of Armory Defense Exhibit," *The Dispatch* (Moline, IL), March 20, 1952: 8.

28. "2,370 Attend Alert America Show 1st Day."

29. "Defense Show Draws 10,000."

30. "Civil Defense Show May 3–9 at Naval Reserve Armory," *The Chicago Heights Star* (Chicago Heights, IL), April 24, 1952: 34.

31. "Parade Opens Civil Defense Show by Lake," *Chicago Tribune*, May 4, 1952: 9; "Civil Defense Exhibit to Be Opened on May 3," *Suburbanite Economist* (Chicago, IL), April 23, 1952: 1; "Civil Defense Show May 3–9 at Naval Reserve Armory."

32. Open Civil Defense Corps Exhibition Next Saturday," *Suburbanite Economist* (Chicago, IL,) April 30, 1952: 23; "Steinmetz High Girls Aid Class in Home Nursing," *Chicago Tribune*, May 15, 1952: 99.

33. *Ibid.*; "Student Press Meeting," *New York Times*, May 4, 1952: 60.

34. "City to Be Alerted on Defense Perils," *New York Times*, May 11, 1952: 76.

35. "Atomic Bomb Defense Display Draws Record Throng in City," *Arizona Republic* (Phoenix, AZ), May 9, 1952: 24.

36. "'Alert America' Opens Tonight," *Oakland Tribune* (Oakland, CA), June 3, 1952: 5; "Alert America Exhibit Viewed by Cheshire Students," *Berkshire Evening Eagle* (Pittsfield, MA), March 25, 1952: 16.

37. "Children Have Field Day at Alert America Display," *Los Angeles Times*, May 18, 1952: 3.

38. "Today Last Day of Defense Show," *The Morning News* (Wilmington, DE), January 23, 1952: 34.

39. "4000 View Alert America Exhibit," *The Tennessean* (Nashville, TN), March 14, 1952: 6.

40. "Pupils to Be Given Chance to Look at Defense Exhibit," *St. Louis Post-Dispatch* (St. Louis, MO), March 4, 1952: 22.

41. "Civil Defense Topic of Talk to Junior League," *The News Journal* (Wilmington, DE), January 18, 1952: 18; "Volunteers to Serve as Aides for 'Alert America' Exhibit," *The News Journal* (Wilmington, DE), January 17, 1952: 7.

42. "Many Help with 'Alert U.S.' Exhibit," *Los Angeles Times*, May 21, 1952: 52.

43. "Springville Women Assist with Civil Defense Exhibition," *The Springville Herald* (Springville, UT), September 18, 1952: 9.

44. "Women's Clubs to Aid in Exhibit of 'Alert America' Convoy in Oakland, June 3–6," *Berkeley Daily Gazette* (Berkeley, CA), May 6, 1952: 7.

45. "'Build Freedom with Youth' to Be Sponsored by GFWC," *Tampa Bay Times* (St. Petersburg, FL), January 22, 1951: 6; "For a Stronger America," *Denton Journal* (Denton, MD), February 18, 1951: 3; "Defense and Safety Awards Slated," *The Evening Sun* (Baltimore, MD), January 16, 1952: 29; "Children of Near East Treasure Pencils," *The Evening Sun* (Baltimore, MD), April 24, 1952: 35.

46. *Alert America!*: 3

47. *Ibid.*

48. *Federal Civil Defense Administration 1952 Annual Report* (Washington, D.C.: Government Printing Office, 1952), 116.

49. *This Is Civil Defense* (Washington, D.C.: Government Printing Office, 1951), 10.

50. Kristina Zarlengo, "Civilian Threat, the Suburban Citadel, and the Atomic Age Woman," *Signs* 24/4 (Summer 1999), 940.

Chapter Seven

1. Bill Henry, "By the Way with Bill Henry," *Los Angeles Times*, January 15, 1952: 23.

2. *Ibid.*

3. "How America Adopted Radio: Demographic Differences in Set Ownership Reported in the 1930–1950 U.S. Censuses," *Journal of Broadcasting & Electronic Media* 48, 2 (June 2004), 179–195; Moving Image Section—Motion Picture, Broadcasting and Recorded Sound Division. Retrieved from https://memory.loc.gov/ammem/awhhtml/awmi10/television.html.

4. "Civil Defense Series to Be on WTJS-ABC," *The Jackson Sun* (Jackson, TN), January 23, 1952: 1.

5. "Newspaper Fact Sheet," Pew Research Center. Retrieved from http://www.journal ism.org/fact-sheet/newspapers/.

6. "A-Bomb Targets Reported Unprepared for Attack," *The Times* (Munster, IN), June 6, 1951: 3.

7. "Dangers of Atomic Attack Real, Says Defense Body," *Great Falls Tribune* (Great Falls, MT), June 17, 1951: 1; "'Alert America' Campaign Opens," *The Palm Beach Post* (West Palm Beach, FL), June 17, 1951: 27; "Defense Council Issues Warning," *The Baltimore Sun*, June 16, 1951: 2.

8. Robert S. Allen, "A-Bomb to Go on Public Display," *The Miami News* (Miami, FL), October 1, 1951: 20.

9. "Defense Exhibits Going on the Road," *New York Times*, October 12, 1951: 20.

10. "Civil Defense on Wheels," *The Newark Advocate* (Newark, OH), October 22, 1951: 4.

11. Margaret Chase Smith, "Selling America on Survival Is Role of Newest Motorcade," *Battle Creek Enquirer* (Battle Creek, MI), January 9, 1952: 6; Margaret Chase Smith, "Civil Defense Must Include Personal Mental Preparation," *Battle Creek Enquirer* (Battle Creek, MI), January 23, 1952: 6.

12. "Alert America Show Tells How Foe Could Fly into U.S.," *The News Journal* (Wilmington, DE), January 21, 1952: 1.

13. "Alert—Delaware!" *The Morning News* (Wilmington, DE), January 22, 1952: 14.

14. "Organizations Aid in Education to Preserve Freedom," *Pittsburgh Press* (Pittsburgh, PA), January 29, 1952: 25.

15. Millard Caldwell, "Editors Get Praise from Caldwell," *The Tampa Tribune* (Tampa, FL), April 18, 1952: 4.

16. *Alert America!* (Washington, D.C.: Valley Forge Foundation, 1951), 3.

17. "Muncie Star Columnist Is Honored," *Star Press* (Muncie, IN), February 27, 1952: 11; "Freedom Awards Made on G. Washington's Birthday," *Monroe News-Star* (Monroe, LA), February 22, 1952: 7.

18. "Civil Defense Convoy Arriving Here Friday," *Baltimore Afro American*, January 22, 1952: 6.

19. "Exhibit to Show Atomic Havoc in City 'X,'" *The Evening Sun* (Baltimore, MD), January 14, 1952: 17.

20. "Power of Atom to Be Exhibited," *The Baltimore Sun*, January 24, 1952: 22.

21. "Graphic Display Showing How to Survive Atomic Warfare to Be Here February 7–10," *The Greenville News* (Greenville, SC), December 30, 1951: 4.

22. Dan Halligan, "Air Alert, Parade and Exhibit in City," *The Greenville News* (Greenville, SC), February 7, 1952: 1.

23. Saul Pett, "'Alert America' Convoy Shows Vital Need for Civil Defense," *Santa Cruz Sentinel* (Santa Cruz, CA), May 21, 1952: 16.

24. "Alert America Show Expected to Attract Thousands to Boston," *The Boston Globe,* February 24, 1952: C1.

25. "Exhibit Set Here to Cite Atom Peril," *The Atlanta Constitution* (Atlanta, GA), February 14, 1952: 8.

26. "How A-Bomb Could Raze Atlanta Shown at Exhibit," *The Atlanta Constitution* (Atlanta, GA), February 25, 1952: 6.

27. "Ham Radio Messages to Be Sent Free," *Hartford Courant* (Hartford, CT), March 3, 1952: 1.

28. Lois Laycock, "Alert America Exhibit, Stressing Home Mobilization, to Visit Here," *The Tennessean* (Nashville, TN), January 9, 1952: 22.

29. "Coming Exhibit Shows Actual Defense Needs," *The Tennessean* (Nashville, TN), February 15, 1952: 26; "'Show That Could Save Your Life,'" *The Tennessean* (Nashville, TN), February 27, 1952: 26.

30. Lee McLean, "'Alert America' Stirs Nashville," *The Tennessean* (Nashville, TN), March 13, 1952: 1.

31. "Safety Is Not in the Sand," *The Tennessean* (Nashville, TN), March 13, 1952: 12.

32. *Ibid.*

33. H.B. Teeter, "Horrors of A-Bomb Could Strike You," *The Tennessean* (Nashville, TN), March 16, 1952: 9.

34. "Let's Muddy Water at Head of Stream in Moscow with A-Bomb, York Advises," *The Tennessean* (Nashville, TN), March 6, 1952: 22.

35. "America on the Alert!" *The Pittsburgh Post-Gazette* (Pittsburgh, PA), May 21, 1952: 17.

36. John McCullough, "Civil Defense Convoy Bears Vital Message," *The Philadelphia Inquirer*, June 5, 1952: 17.

37. "Civil Defense Caravan Due," *The Indianapolis Star* (Indianapolis, IN), January 18, 1952: 26.

38. "War Exhibit Convoy Is Welcomed," *The Indianapolis News* (Indianapolis, IN), March 29, 1952: 1; "'Alert America' Caravan Here for Defense Display," *The Indianapolis Star* (Indianapolis, IN), March 30, 1952: 19.

39. "Show Portrays Atomic Warfare," *Oakland Tribune* (Oakland, CA), June 1, 1952: 14.

40. "Possible War Horrors Seen at Exhibition," *The Hutchinson News Herald* (Hutchinson, Kansas), July 29, 1952: 1.

41. "Two New Exhibits at State Fair to Show Need for Civil Defense," *The Lincoln Star* (Lincoln, NE), August 24, 1952: 6.

42. "State Fair to Feature Atom Exhibit Show," *The Beaver County News* (Milford, UT), September 4, 1952: 1.

43. "'Alert America' Convoy to Be Shown at Fair," *The Times-Independent* (Moab, UT), September 4, 1952: 7.

44. "We Are Alerted," *The Salt Lake Tribune* (Salt Lake City, UT), September 25, 1952: 6.

45. Frank Evans, "Alert America," *Lansing State Journal* (Lansing, MI), March 23, 1952: 8.

Conclusion

1. "U.S. Defense Director Hails Tribune Refuge," *Chicago Tribune*, November 21, 1952: 12.

2. *Federal Civil Defense Administration 1952 Annual Report* (Washington, D.C.: Government Printing Office, 1952), 9; "Country Warned It's Vulnerable to Red Bombing," *Argus-Leader* (Sioux Falls, SD), February 16, 1953: 14.

3. W. Joyce MacFarlan, "Country Warned It's Vulnerable to Red Bombing," *Argus-Leader* (Sioux Falls, SD), February 16, 1953: 14.

4. Millard Caldwell, "Joining Civil Defense Can Mean Your Survival," *The Daily Courier* (Connellsville, PA), November 17, 1951: 2.

5. "Civil Defense Leader Lashes Public Apathy," *The Monroe News-Star* (Monroe, LA), July 16, 1953: 14.

6. *Ibid.*

7. George Gallup, "Civil Defense Apathy Continues," *Tampa Bay Tribune* (Tampa, FL), August 14, 1953: 6.

8. Glen Thompson, "Wake Up, America! Civil Defense Apathy Parlous," *The Cincinnati Enquirer* (Cincinnati, OH)), July 12, 1953: 89.

9. *Federal Civil Defense Administration 1952 Annual Report*: 47–49.

10. *Ibid.*, 62.

11. James Wadsworth, "Preparedness, the Price of Peace," *Elizabethtown Chronicle* (Elizabethtown, PA), January 9, 1953: 14.

12. *Federal Civil Defense Administration 1952 Annual Report*: 54.

13. "Big Four Urge Alertness! Any Housewife a Heroine if War Comes to America," *The Cincinnati Enquirer* (Cincinnati, OH), October 29, 1952: 1.

14. "Battle Urges Volunteers in Defense Week," *Daily Press* (Newport News, VA), November 10, 1952: 2.

15. "Open 'Pledge for Home Defense' Dive," *The Chicago Heights Star* (Chicago Heights, IL), November 11, 1952: 5.

16. "Sixty Volunteers Pledge Services to Civil Defense," *Naugatuck Daily News* (Naugatuck, CT), December 3, 1952: 10; "100 Volunteers Join Civil Defense Group," *Marshfield News-Herald* (Marshfield, WI), December 3, 1952: 18.

17. "22 First Aid Squad Members Join Spotswood Defense Unit," *The Central New Jersey Home News* (New Brunswick, NJ), December 11, 1952: 6.

18. "Parents Invited to Join Block Warden Service," *Naugatuck Daily News* (Naugatuck, CT), June 6, 1952: 8.

19. "U.S. and Canada Agree to Pool Civil Defenses," *The Evening Sun* (Baltimore, MD), March 27, 1951: 1; "U.S., Canada Slash Red Tape for Joint Border Defenses," *The Salt Lake Tribune* (Salt Lake City, UT), April 29, 1951: 2.

20. Burtch, Andrew. *Give Me Shelter* (Toronto: UBC Press, 2012), 63–76.

21. *Ibid.*: 14.

22. *Ibid.*: 24–27.

23. *Ibid.*

24. *Ibid.*

25. "State Air Raid Test Revealed Weaknesses, Including County," *The Indiana Gazette* (Indiana, PA), October 16, 1952: 33.

26. "Planes to 'Attack' City," *New York Times*, September 25, 1952: 33; "Outdoor Care Set in Event of Attack," *New York Times*, September 21, 1952: 32; "Mock Atomic Raid on City Tomorrow," *New York Times*, September 29, 1952: 25; "City Sirens to Sound at 7:45 p.m. in a Test for Civil Defense Staff," *New York Times*, September 30, 1952: 1; "Bomb Drill A Success, District Leaders Say," *New York Times*, October 2, 1952: 31.

27. "203,000 'Die' in Mock Atom Raid on N.Y.," *Star Tribune* (Minneapolis, MN), December 14, 1952: 4; "New York Silenced by Air Raid Drill," *The Kingston Daily Freeman* (Kingston, NY), December 13, 1952: 5.

28. "Civil Defense Chiefs to Meet," *Arizona Republic* (Phoenix, AZ), September 5, 1952: 3; "Owen Again Heads CDA Directors," *Arizona Republic* (Phoenix, AZ), October 17, 1952: 3.

29. "Columbus Man Heads Group," *Norwalk Reflector Herald* (Norwalk, OH), November 11, 1952: 1; "New Civil Defense Group Formed," *Delphos Daily-Herald* (Delphos, OH), November 21, 1952: 1.

30. "Air Raids on U.S. 'Probable,' Civil Defense Leaders Hear," *The Baltimore Sun*, November 21, 1952: 10.

31. *Ibid.*

32. "Convention Hears Blast at Civil Defense Apathy," *Los Angeles Times*, September 24, 1952: 23.

33. "Warns People of Apathy to Civil Defense Work," *The Herald-Palladium* (Saint Joseph, MI), October 10, 1952: 13.

34. "Caldwell Out as CD Chief; Blasts Apathy," *The Atlanta Constitution* (Atlanta, GA), October 15, 1952: 2.

35. "Leadership Needed to End Civil Defense Apathy," *The Philadelphia Inquirer*, October 2, 1952: 12.

36. "Apathy as Usual," *The Journal News* (White Plains, NY), December 17, 1952: 4.

37. Wayne Blanchard. "American Civil Defense 1945–1984: The Evolution of Programs and Policies." Retrieved from https://www.orau.org/ptp/pdf/cdhistory.pdf.

38. *Ibid.*

39. "Atom Rockets Declared Ready for Combat Use," *New York Times*, December 21, 1952: 25.

40. "Capital Sets Royal Welcome," *Nevada State Journal* (Reno, NV), November 18, 1952: 1.

41. "Ike Says Faith in God Can Beat Reds," *Lansing State Journal* (Lansing, MI), December 22, 1952: 2.

42. Harry Truman, 1953 State of the Union retrieved from http://www.let.rug.nl/usa/presidents/harry-s-truman/state-of-the-union-1953.php.

43. Dwight Eisenhower, 1953 Inauguration Address. Retrieved from http://www.presidency.ucsb.edu/ws/index.php?pid=9600.

44. Malcolm Johnson, "Civil Defense in U.S. 'Tragic,'" *Lubbock Avalanche-Journal* (Lubbock, TX), December 6, 1953: 3.

45. "Civil Defense Apathy Laid to U.S. Leaders," *The Tampa Tribune* (Tampa, FL), October 9, 1953: 33.

46. "Mayors Ask More Federal Funds for Civil Defense," *Shamokin News-Dispatch* (Shamokin, PA), December 15, 1953: 1.

47. Quoted in Paul Boyer, *By the Bomb's Early Light* (New York: Pantheon Books, 1985); 282.

48. Guy Oakes and Andrew Grossman, "Managing Nuclear Terror: The Genesis of American Civil Defense Strategy," *International Journal of Politics, Culture, and Society*, vol. 5, 3 (1992), 383.

49. *Ibid.*

50. "Inadequacies of Civil Defence All to Evident in America," *The Ottawa Citizen* (Ottawa, Ontario, Canada), February 25, 1955: 27.

51. Dorothy Thompson, "Apathy Invites Grim Nuclear Reality," *Dayton Daily News* (Dayton, Ohio), July 29, 1956: 18.

52. Harry Truman, Statement on Civil Defense. Retrieved from https://www.trumanlibrary.org/publicpapers/index.php?pid=606.

53. *Federal Civil Defense Administration 1952 Annual Report*: 49.

54. "Alert America Campaign: Progress Report." October 15, 1951. PHST, Official File, Box 1671, Folder 1591-C.

Bibliography

Alert America! (Washington, D.C.: FCDA and Valley Forge Foundation, 1951).

Blanchard, B. Wayne. "American Civil Defense 1945–1984: The Evolution of Programs and Policies." Retrieved from https://www.orau.org/ptp/pdf/cdhistory.pdf.

Boyer, Paul. *By the Bomb's Early Light* (New York: Pantheon Books, 1985).

Brady, James. *The Coldest War* (New York: Orion Books, 1990).

Burtch, Andrew. *Give Me Shelter* (Toronto: UBC Press, 2012).

Churchill, Winston. "'Iron Curtain' Speech." March 5, 1946. Retrieved from https://www.thoughtco.com/winston-churchills-iron-curtain-speech-1779492.

"Civil Defense, 1956." Retrieved from http://library.cqpress.com/cqresearcher/document.php?id=cqresrre1956070300#H2_2.

Davis, Tracy C. *Stages of Emergency: Cold War Nuclear Civil Defense* (Durham, NC: Duke University Press, 2007).

Eisenhower, Dwight. 1953 Inaugural Address. Retrieved from http://www.presidency.ucsb.edu/ws/index.php?pid=9600.

Emmons, Caroline S., Editor. *Cold War and McCarthy Era: People and Perspectives* (Santa Barbara, CA: ABC-CLIO, 2010).

Engelhardt, Tom. *The End of Victory Culture* (New York: Basic Books, 1995).

Federal Civil Defense Act of 1950. Retrieved from https://www.hsdl.org/?abstract&did=456688.

Federal Civil Defense Administration. *1951 Annual Report* (Washington, D.C.: Government Printing Office, 1951).

_____. *1952 Annual Report* (Washington, D.C.: Government Printing Office, 1952).

Fehr, Kregg Michael. "Sheltering Society: Civil Defense in the United States, 1945–1963." Dissertation retrieved from http://hdl.handle.net/2346/16965.

Frank, Richard D. *Downfall: The End of the Imperial Japanese Empire* (New York: Random House, 1999).

Garrison, Dee. *Bracing for Armageddon* (New York: Oxford University Press, 2006).

Gelbond, Florence. "The Impact of the Atomic Bomb on Education." *The Social Studies* 65 (March 1974): 109–114.

Graeber, William. *The Age of Doubt* (Boston: Twayne, 1991).

Grossman, Andrew D. *Neither Dead Nor Read* (New York: Routledge, 2001).

Halverstam, David. *The Coldest Winter: American and the Korean War* (New York: Hyperion, 2007).

_____. *The Fifties* (New York: Villard Books, 1993).

Hand, Harold. "Living in the Atomic Age: A Resource Unit for Teachers in Secondary School." *University of Illinois Bulletin* 23 (December 3, 1946).

"How America Adopted Radio: Demographic Differences in Set Ownership Reported in the 1930–1950 U.S. Censuses." *Journal of Broadcasting & Electronic Media* 48, 2 (June 2004): 179–195.

Isaacs, Jeremy, and Taylor Downing, *Cold War: For Forty-Five Years the World Held Its Breath* (London: Abacus, 1998).

Krugler, David F. *This Is Only a Test* (New York: Palgrave Macmillan, 2006).

May, Elaine Tyler. *Homeward Bound* (New York: Basic Books, 1988).

Meacham, Jon. *The Soul of America* (New York: Random House, 2018).

Moving Image Section—Motion Picture, Broadcasting and Recorded Sound Division. Retrieved from https://memory.loc.gov/ammem/awhhtml/awmi10/television.html.

"Newspaper Fact Sheet." Pew Research Center. Retrieved from http://www.journalism.org/fact-sheet/newspapers/.

Oakes, Guy, and Andrew Grossman. "Managing Nuclear Terror: The Genesis of American Civil Defense Strategy," *International Journal of Politics, Culture, and Society*, vol. 5, 3 (1992): 361–403.

Rhodes, Richard. *Dark Sun: The Making of the Hydrogen Bomb* (New York: Simon & Schuster, 1995).

_____. *The Making of the Atomic Bomb* (New York: Simon & Schuster, 1986).

Scheibach, Michael. *Atomic Narratives and American Youth: Coming of Age with the* Atom, *1945–1955* (Jefferson, NC: McFarland, 2003).

_____. *Atomics in the Classroom: Teaching the Bomb in the Early Postwar Era* (Jefferson, NC: McFarland, 2015).

_____. *Protecting the Home Front: Women in Civil Defense in the Early Cold War* (Jefferson, NC: McFarland, 2017).

This Is Civil Defense (Washington, D.C.: Government Printing Office, 1951).

Tillman, Barrett. *Whirlwind: The Air War Against Japan 1942–1945* (New York: Simon & Schuster, 2010).

Truman, Harry. Annual Message to the Congress on the State of the Union. January 9, 1952. Retrieved from http://www.presidency.ucsb.edu/ws/?pid=14418.

_____. Executive Order 10186. Retrieved from http://www.presidency.ucsb.edu/ws/index.php?pid=78352.

_____. Joint Statement Following Discussions with Prime Minister Churchill. January 9, 1952. Retrieved from http://www.presidency.ucsb.edu/ws/index.php?pid=14429.

_____. 1952 State of the Union Address. Retrieved from http://www.presidency.ucsb.edu/ws/index.php?pid=14418.

_____. 1953 State of the Union Address. Retrieved from http://www.let.rug.nl/usa/presidents/harry-s-truman/state-of-the-union-1953.php.

_____. Proclamation 2914—Proclaiming the Existence of a National Emergency. Retrieved from http://www.presidency.ucsb.edu/ws/?pid=13684.

_____. Radio and Television Address to the American People on the Situation in Korea, July 19, 1950. Retrieved from http://www.presidency.ucsb.edu/ws/?pid=13561.

_____. Statement by the President on the Need for Operation Skywatch. December 7, 1952. Retrieved from https://www.trumanlibrary.org/publicpapers/index.php?pid=2105&st=civil+defense&stl=.

_____. Statement on Civil Defense. Retrieve from https://www.trumanlibrary.org/publicpapers/index.php?pid=606.

_____. Truman Doctrine Address Before Joint Session of Congress. March 12, 1947. Retrieved from http://avalon.law.yale.edu/20th_century/trudoc.asp.

_____. *Years of Trial and Hope: 1946–1952* (Garden City, NY: Doubleday, 1956).

Van Der Grinten, Willem J. "Not Only Science Teachers." *The Clearing House*, 24, 8 (April 1950): 487.

Weisbrode, Kenneth. *The Year of Indecision, 1946* (New York: Viking, 2016).

Whyte, William. *The Organization Man* (New York: Simon & Schuster, 1956).

Winkler, Allan M. *Life Under a Cloud* (New York: Oxford University Press, 1993).

"Woman's Club." *Helper Journal* (Helper, UT). November 27, 1952.

Zarlengo, Kristina. "Civilian Threat, the Suburban Citadel, and the Atomic Age Woman." *Signs* 24/4 (Summer 1999): 925–958.

Index

193